Hyundai Motor Company
RETRACE Collection

PONY

HYUNDAI MOTOR COMPANY

REFERENCE			ISSUE JUN 2024
DRAWN	**CHECKED**	**APPROVED**	**DO NOT SCALE**

MATERIAL	PRINTING	PART NO.	ISSUE QTY 1000
FABRIC	PANTONE WG 3 C	360 PAGES	**EDITION** 001
HEAD&TAILBAND	PANTONE WG 9 C	4 CHAPTERS	
PAPER	CMYK	HARD COVER	

FINISH FOIL STAMPING / VARNISHING	SIZE 240×320

THEME

PONY

PART NAME

RETRACE COLLECTION

HD

목차
Contents

하나의 길이 또 다른 길을 열다
Where one road ends, another begins

오늘날 인류는 대변혁의 시기를 맞이하고 있습니다. 지구온난화로 기후 위기가 가시화되면서 탄소중립은 인류의 생존 과제로 부상했습니다. 또한 전 세계적 화두로 떠오른 인공지능과 로보틱스의 등장으로 우리는 보다 근원적인 질문인 '인간의 존재 이유'와 '지향점'에 대해 깊이 성찰하고 자문(自問)하게 됩니다. 그리고 오래된 역사 속에서 변치 않는 한 가지, 즉 역사의 중심에는 늘 사람이 있었고, 인류가 조화롭게 공존하기 위해 혁신은 궁극적으로 사람을 향해야 한다는 사실을 상기합니다.

대한민국 산업화를 이끈 현대자동차그룹 창업주 정주영 선대회장은 전후 폐허가 된 국토에 길을 만들어 도시와 도시를 연결했습니다. 그리고 그 길 위를 달리는 자동차를 만들어 사람들의 풍요로운 삶에 기여하고자 했습니다. 자동차 산업을 통해 잘사는 나라를 만들고자 했던 창업주의 인본주의 정신과 자주성을 토대로 대한민국 최초의 양산형 독자 모델 포니가 출시될 수 있었습니다. 포니는 자동차 산업 불모지였던 대한민국을 훗날 자동차 산업 선진국으로 발돋움할 수 있게 한 자양분이 되었습니다. 또한 포니는 지금의 현대자동차를 있게 한 원형(原型)으로서 정체성 확립의 근간인 동시에 지속 가능한 미래를 위한 창의적 영감의 원천이기도 합니다.

길에 대한 역사를 써온 현대자동차는 미래 모빌리티 기업으로서 '인류를 향한 진보'를 향해 미래의 길을 새롭게 개척해 나가고 있습니다. 「RETRACE Collection - PONY」는 창업주의 인본주의 정신과 포니가 남긴 유산이 오늘날 현대자동차에 어떻게 계승되고 있는지 지난 반세기 동안의 행보를 반추하는 또 다른 여정의 시작입니다. 이 책을 통해 첫 독자 모델을 만든다는 사명감을 가지고 헌신한 수많은 사람의 노력이 오늘날 현대자동차의 기틀을 세웠음을, 그리고 인본주의는 새로운 도전을 지속해 온 현대자동차가 계승 발전해 나가야 할 정신적 유산임을 다시금 확인하고자 합니다. 더불어 이 책이 1970~1980년대를 살아간 한국인에게 우리 가족의 첫 차인 포니와 함께한 추억을 떠올릴 수 있는 따뜻한 시간을 선사할 수 있기를 기대합니다.

Humanity is currently facing a time of great transformation. Climate change has made carbon neutrality a survival challenge for humankind, while the emergence of artificial intelligence and robotics as a global topic forces us to deeply question and ponder upon existential issues like the purpose and direction of human existence. Despite the changing times, one thing has remained constant throughout history: People have always been at the center of progress, and innovation led to harmonious coexistence when it served people. By building roads that connect cities and manufacturing vehicles to run on them, Hyundai Motor Group's Founding Chairman Ju-yung Chung played a crucial role in the industrialization of Korea and contributed to the prosperity of its people. In pursuit of creating a better country through the automotive industry, Hyundai's founding spirit of humanity and autonomy led to the birth of Pony in 1975 as the nation's first mass-produced independent model and a timeless icon of automotive design ever since.

In retrospect, Pony was the embryo that catapulted Hyundai onto the world stage. Through the changing tides of fashion and technology, it remains to this day a vital source of inspiration and creativity pointing towards a sustainable future. Looking ahead, Hyundai is busy pioneering new paths towards "Progress for Humanity" as a smart mobility services provider. The 「RETRACE Collection - PONY」 enables us to trace back Hyundai's journey over the past half-century, as well as how the legacy of Pony and its founder's philosophy of humanity are being relived ingeniously five decades later. Through this book, we aim to acknowledge two things. First is the unwavering dedication of countless individuals who laid the foundation for Hyundai as a daring enterprise, fueled by a sense of mission to architect its first original model. Second is that humanism is a spiritual legacy that Hyundai has steadfastly embodied and materialized in the process of overcoming new challenges. Moreover, through this book, we hope to revitalize those warm memories of the 1970s and 80s of Korea and its people, in which Pony energized their myriad dreams and connections for a better tomorrow.

정의선
현대자동차그룹 회장

Euisun Chung
Executive Chair, Hyundai Motor Group

확고한 신념으로
가보지 않은
길을 가다

An untrodden
path opened
by unwavering
confidence

대한민국의 근대화는 길을 재건하는 것으로 시작되었다. 창업주 정주영 선대회장은 전후 황폐화한 대한민국 국토에 도로를 건설했고, 도로 위를 달리는 자동차를 만들었다. 국민의 풍요로운 삶으로 이어질, 그 누구도 가보지 않았던 길을 열었다.

The modernization of Korea began with rebuilding the roads devastated by the Korean War. Hyundai's Founding Chairman Ju-yung Chung not only built roads but also produced cars that would run on them. He opened up new paths that no one had ever seen, leading to a prosperous life for the people.

현대자동차 창업주 정주영 선대회장은 1915년 강원도 통천군 송전면 아산리에서 가난한 농민의 아들로 태어났다. 아산리는 대한민국이 분단되기 전에는 서울(당시 경성) 청량리역에서 늦은 밤 기차를 타면 중간 역에서 환승을 해 새벽에나 도착할 수 있는 동해안의 오지였다. 당시 한국은 식민지 시대로 접어들던 때라 대부분 사람이 극심한 가난과 억압으로 힘들게 살았다.

정주영 선대회장은 고향에서 가족과 농사일로 유년기를 보냈지만, 일찍부터 신문을 읽는 등 세상의 변화에 관심이 많고 독립심이 강했던 터라 더 나은 삶을 찾아 몇 차례 가출을 시도한 끝에 혈혈단신 도시로 나와 노동자로서 삶을 개척하게 된다. 인천항 부두 노동자로서 하역 일을 하기도 하고, 서울의 신축 학교 현장에서 막노동을 하는 등 힘겹게 생활하던 그가 비교적 안정된 일자리를 갖게 된 것은 서울에 있는 '복흥상회'라는 쌀가게에 취직하면서부터다. '더 하려야 할 게 없는 마지막의 마지막까지 최선을 다하는'¹ 성실함으로 주인의 신임을 얻은 그는 쌀가게를 물려받게 되었다. 젊은 정주영은 '경일상회'라는 간판을 내걸고 쌀가게 주인이 되었고, 생애 최초로 시작한 자기 사업은 번창했다. 중일전쟁(1937)이 일어나면서 일제가 시행한 쌀 배급제에 의해 조선의 쌀가게가 모두 문을 닫으면서 그의 가게도 문을 닫았지만, 그 사이 정주영은 얼마간 자산을 모았고, 사업 수완도 키울 수 있었다. 이 자산과 경험을 바탕으로 20대의 젊은 나이에 시작한 회사가 '아도서비스'(1940)라는 자동차 수리 공장이었다.

경성공업사에 다니는 엔진 기술자 이을학, 공장 직원 김명현과 함께 시작한 아도서비스는 규모는 작았지만 빠르게 성장했다. 당시 조선은 포장된 길이 거의 없었고, 수도인 서울에서조차 개인 승용차는 손에 꼽을 만큼 척박한 교통 환경이었지만, 청년 정주영은 세상의 변화를 감지하는 예민함

Ju-yung Chung, the founder of Hyundai Motor Company, was born into a poor farming family in the Korean countryside (Asan-ri, Songjeon-myeon, Tongcheon-gun, Gangwon) in 1915. His hometown was a village near Korea's eastern coast. Before Korea was divided, it took almost half a day to get there by train from Cheongnyangni Station in Korea's capital Seoul (then known as 'Gyeongseong'). People would take a late-night train, transfer in the middle, and then arrive at Asan-ri at dawn the next day. At the time, with Korea having just fallen under Japanese colonial rule, most people suffered from extreme poverty and oppression.

As a young boy, Chung had a great interest in the changes occurring in the outside world, even though he was very busy helping his family farm. A day never passed without him reading the newspaper — he possessed a very independent mind. After several attempts to run away from home in search of a better life, he eventually reached the city alone and started to find his way in the world. He spent time loading cargo at Incheon Port and carrying bricks at a school construction site in Seoul. But it was when he started working at Bokhung Rice Store that he finally found a relatively stable job. He gave his best, and his diligence earned him the trust of the owner¹, who eventually gave him ownership of the store. Chung embarked on his first business venture by hanging up the sign 'Kyoungil Rice Store', which flourished remarkably.

However, during the Sino-Japanese War (1937) many Korean rice stores, including Chung's, were forced to close because Japan began rationing rice supply. Despite this, Chung

을 지니고 있었다. 현 상황에 안주하기보다는 더 나은 사업 기회를 찾아 움직이는 그의 진취적 성격이 당시에는 흔치 않았던 자동차 사업에 눈을 뜨게 했다. 이는 자동차 수리업이 훗날 현대자동차 같은 대기업의 기반이 되리라고 상상하지 못한 출발이었다.

이 시기는 정주영에게 자동차를 직접 수리해 보는 것은 물론 선진 문물인 자동차 부품과 기계의 기본적 기능 및 원리를 이해할 수 있는 소중한 기회였다. 그는 이때 쌓은 경험이 두고두고 유용한 자동차 공부가 되었다고 회고하곤 했다. 또 아도서비스의 운영 방식은 훗날 그가 자동차 사업을 크게 일으킨 후 회사를 운영하는 데에도 중요한 발판이 되었다. 기존 수리 공장이 수리 기간을 길게 잡아 이윤을 늘리는 식으로 운영하던 데 비해, 아도서비스는 서울의 어떤 자동차 수리 공장보다 신속하게 작업을 완료하는 역발상으로 접근했다. 이는 자동차 수리를 의뢰하는 사람들에게 큰 호응을 얻어 회사가 성장하는 데 기여했다. 아도서비스는 밀려드는 일감에 손이 모자랄 정도로 크게 번창했다. 그러나 청년 정주영이 혼신의 힘을 다해 키워가던 아도서비스는 일본 제국주의자들이 일으킨 태평양전쟁(1941)으로 인해 기업정리령(1942)이 내려지면서 종로의 '일진공작소'와 강제 합병되는 시련을 맞았다.

청년기에 자동차라는 선진 기계에 일찌감치 눈을 뜬 정주영의 도전이 다시 시작된 것은 해방 직후 자동차 수리 공장 '현대자동차공업사'(1946)를 설립하면서다. 일찍부터 자동차 수리업을 하면서 자동차가 현대 문명의 이기(利器)라는 사실을 명확히 인지한 그가 '보다 발전된 미래를 살아보자'는 취지에서 직접 작명한 '현대(現代)'라는 상호도 이때부터 사용되었다. 당장 경제적·사회적 현실은 궁핍했지만 보다 나은 삶이 가능하다는 긍정성과 의지, 미래를 내다보는 너른 시야가 깃든 희망찬 상호명이었다. 초창기에 현대자동차공업사

— still in his 20s — utilized this opportunity to open an auto repair shop called Ado Service (1940) with the business skills and money he accumulated.

Chung opened the repair shop with two business partners, an engine technician (Eul-hak Lee), and a handyman (Myeong-hyun Kim). The shop was not large, but it quickly grew. At the time, most roads in Korea were unpaved and there were only a few personal cars in the nation's capital. However, young Chung had a sharp ability to sense changes in the world. Far from being complacent, his enterprising personality motivated him to find a business opportunity and awakened him fully to the promise of the automotive business. This was an industry where few people saw potential at the time. Who could possibly have imagined that this experience would ultimately give birth to Hyundai Motor Company, one of the world-class car producers?

Chung's shop provided him with a valuable opportunity to learn how auto parts and machines worked — these were considered cutting edge technologies at the time. Looking back, he would say that those experiences proved invaluable in understanding cars, and he would rely on them for many years thereafter. In addition, the managerial techniques he used running Ado Service became the basis for his corporate management style. The convention at the time was maximizing repair times to increase profits, but Ado Service took the opposite approach: repairing cars faster than any other competitors in Seoul. This earned Chung a great reputation with his customers, further powering the shop's

젊은 시절의 정주영
Ju-yung Chung in his youth

창업 당시 현대자동차가 입주한 현대건설 무교동 사옥
Hyundai Engineering & Construction's
Mugyo-dong headquarters, where Hyundai
Motor Company moved in at the time of
establishment

는 미군 병기창에서 의뢰받은 단순 수리 일을 하다가, 이후에
는 자동차를 용도에 맞게 개조하는 일을 주로 했다. 1.5톤짜
리 트럭의 중간을 이어 붙여 2.5톤 트럭을 만들거나, 휘발유
가 귀했기에 휘발유 차를 목탄 차나 카바이드 차로 개조하는
일이었다. 교통량이 급격히 늘어나면서 현대자동차공업사도
번창해 나갔다.

이후 현대자동차공업사는 국가 재건에 초점을 맞춘 당
시 정부 시책에 맞게 회사 체제와 규모를 정비해야 할 필요성

growth and enabling it to prosper. In fact, it became so popular that the shop soon became shorthanded.

Chung poured all his strength into the business, but it faced an unexpected crisis after Japanese military adventurism provoked the Pacific War (1941). The Japanese government enacted the so-called 'Small and Medium Enterprise Liquidation Order' (1942), forcing his repair shop to merge with 'Iljin Workshop' in Jongro.

His ambitious spirit reignited when he established Hyundai Motor Service Center (auto repair shop) in 1946, straight after Korea's liberation from Japan. From early on, working in auto repair, Chung saw cars as a benefit of modern civilization. This inspired him to choose the name Hyundai, meaning "modern times" — hoping for for a better future. Despite the economic and social hardships at the time, the name reflected optimism, determination, and a clear vision for enriching people's lives.

Hyundai Motor Service Center initially provided simple car repair services for the U.S. military armory and then expanded its service range to car modification. It would connect two 1.5t trucks to make a 2.5t truck, and convert gasoline cars into wood gas cars since gasoline was scarce. Traffic volumes increased sharply and the business boomed.

Following government policies focused on national reconstruction, Chung felt a need to reorganize the structure and size of Hyundai Motor Industry Co. Based on this thought, he merged the company with 'Hyundai Civil Work', creating 'Hyundai Engineering & Construction' (Hyundai E&C) in 1950. In 1967, 'Hyundai Mo-

을 느낀 정주영 선대회장의 판단에 따라 '현대토건사'와 합병해 '현대건설'(1950)로 거듭났다. 그러고는 마침내 그룹다운 모습을 갖춘 현대의 체제 정비 전략 속에 '현대자동차'(1967)가 새롭게 탄생했다.

tor Company' finally emerged as a result of a broader company restructuring strategy aimed at creating a single 'Hyundai Motor Group'.

나라의 길을 닦은 현대

Hyundai paving the nation's roads

해방 이후 현대자동차의 성장 과정에서 눈에 띄는 점은 현대건설의 도로 건설 경험이 현대자동차의 시작과 깊은 연관성이 있다는 사실이다. 이러한 산업사적 특이성은 당시 현대건설이 처한 한국의 정치적·경제적 상황에서 비롯되었다. 자동차 산업은 막대한 초기 자본, 높은 기술력, 인적 자원, 충분한 소비자 구매력과 시장 규모를 모두 갖춰야 하는 고도 산업이다. 세계 자동차 산업사에 등장하는 모든 자동차 브랜드는 예외 없이 이와 같은 요소를 갖춘 나라에서 탄생했다. 현대자동차가 설립된 1960년대 전후 세계 자동차 시장을 분점하고 있던 유럽, 미국, 일본은 모두 그러한 조건을 충족한 공업 선진국이었다. 유럽은 근대 산업자본주의를 이끌었을 뿐 아니라 다수의 식민지를 거느렸던 경험에서 풍족한 자원과 소비 시장을 갖고 있었다. 제2차 세계대전 이후 세계 중심국으로 확실히 부상한 미국은 광대한 국토 면적을 기반으로 한 자원 부국이었으며, 세계 최대 규모의 자동차 국내 시장과 타의 추종을 불허하는 막강한 자본력 및 기술력을 보유한 초강대국이었다. 일본은 세계대전 패전국의 오명과 굴레 속에 있었으나 이미 20세기 초에 잠수함과 항공모함, 전투기를 제조할 수 있는 기술력을 보유한 공업 국가였다.

이에 비해 당시 한국은 20세기 초 일본의 식민지가 되면서 근대 국가로 정상적인 성장이 지연되었고, 분단과 한국전쟁으로 독립국가로서의 성장 동력마저 상실한 상태였다. 1953년 한국의 국내총생산은 13억 달러, 1인당 국민소득은 67달러에 불과했다. 제1차 경제개발 5개년계획으로 국가 재건의 시동을 걸고 있었던 1970년도에조차 한국의 국내총생산은 81억 달러, 1인당 국민소득은 254달러에 머무르고 있었다.[2] 1960년 미국의 국내총생산이 5,433억 달러, 일본이 443억1,000만 달러[3]이고, 미국의 1인당 국민소득이 3,007 달러, 일본이 475달러[4]인 것과 비교할 때 당시 한국은 경제력

After Korea's liberation in 1945, Hyundai E&C's experience in road construction played an important role in the beginning of Hyundai Motor Company. This special path in the firm's history stemmed from the political and economic circumstances Korea faced and to which Hyundai E&C was bound.

The automotive industry is highly capital intensive — it requires significant initial investment and human resources, technological capabilities, and a sufficiently large market with consumer purchasing power. Without exception, every car manufacturer in the history of the global automotive industry was born in countries that met such preconditions. When Hyundai Motor Company was established in the 1960s, the global automotive industry was dominated by Europe, the United States, and Japan, all of which were industrially advanced with large domestic markets.

Europe was equipped with abundant resources and a large consumer market, due to its experinece in leading modern industrial capitalism as well as its colonial endeavors. In addition, the United States solidified its position as a world leader after World War II. As a resource-rich country with a vast territory, it possessed the world's largest domestic car market with unmatched capital and technological capabilities. Despite bearing the stigma of defeat in World War II, Japan was already an industrial nation by the early 20th century — capable of producing submarines, aircraft carriers, and even fighter jets.

In contrast, Korea had not been able to grow into a modern economy because of Japanese colonial rule. The colonial era began in the early

이 매우 약한 가난한 나라였다.

　현대건설은 이런 시대적 맥락에서 남다른 의미를 지닌다. 미군정에서 수주한 경험을 기반으로 점차 국가 재건 사업 참여를 확대해 나갔으며, 이러한 현대건설의 출범은 본격적인 자본 축적의 계기가 되었다. 이로부터 20여 년이 훨씬 지난 후 대량 양산형 독자 모델 자동차 출시와 자동차 종합 공장은 이 시기에 축적한 현대건설의 자본, 사업 경험, 창조적 역량, 국가 공동체 재건을 위한 의지가 있었기에 가능했다. 특히 주목할 점은 이 일이 한국의 국가 재건, 도시화 과정과 긴밀히 맞물려 있다는 점에서 큰 공공적 가치를 지닌다는 사실이다.

　현대건설의 초기 사업은 도로 및 교량 복구 같은 '길' 건설에 집중되었다. 정주영 선대회장은 자본과 기술, 경험 부족 등 여러 어려움 속에도 도로 건설에 적극적으로 뛰어들었다. 이는 회사를 확장하기 위한 자연스러운 과정이기도 했지만, 우리나라 기업이 재건 사업을 담당함으로써 자본과 기술 등 여러 측면에서 경제적 자주성을 확보해 나가자는 국가 비전과 사회적 책임감도 크게 작용했다. 국가적 차원의 경제 발전과 기업의 성장이 분리될 수 없는 개발도상국에 '건설'은 핵심 산업이었다. 이는 현대건설이 국민 기업으로 성장하는 과정이기도 했다. 회사가 막대한 손해를 보면서도 전후 복구 차원에서 완수할 수밖에 없었던 고령교 복구 공사(1953~1955), 전후 최대 복구 사업이었던 한강 인도교 복구 공사(1957~1958), 건국 이래 최대 공사였던 인천 제1독(dock) 복구 공사(1959), 한국 역사상 최초의 해외 수주 공사인 태국 파타니~나라티왓 고속도로 공사(1965), 대한민국 최대 토목 공사였던 경부고속도로 건설(1968~1970), 제3한강교 건설(1969) 등이 모두 현대건설에 의해 이루어졌다. 국가적 차원의 파급력과 상징성이 매우 컸던 이 공사들은 대부분 교통 및 운송과 관련한 사회 인프라 구축 사업으로, 파

20th century, and as a result, South Korea's potential engines of growth lay dormant even after liberation from Japan due to the Korean War and the division of the peninsula into North and South. South Korea's GDP was barely $1.3 billion, with its per capita income $67 in 1953. Even in 1970, when the South Korean government sought to ignite growth during the first phase of its five-year economic development plan, South Korea's GDP was $8.1 billion, equating to a per capita income of $254.[2] In comparison, the U.S. GDP was $543.3 billion and per capita income was $3,007, while Japanese GDP was $44.31 billion[3] and per capita income was $475[4] in 1960. In a nutshell, South Korea was a very poor country back then, having been devastated by war.

　'Hyundai Engineering & Construction' meant something distinct in the context of time. Taking advantage of the experience gained from working with the United States Military, the company gradually expanded its participation in national regeneration projects. This became an opportunity for Hyundai E&C to accumulate substantial capital. The launch of a mass-produced independent model and the construction of a comprehensive automobile plant, which would only be possible more than two decades later, was feasible due to the accumulated capital, business experience, creative competence, and willpower of Hyundai E&C to regenerate the national community. Here, it should be noted that these elements were of public importance as they were closely linked with the national reconstruction and urbanization process.

　Early projects by Hyundai E&C mainly focused on the construction of 'routes', such as

주한 미군 공사와 계약을 체결 중인 정주영 선대회장
Ju-yung Chung signing a contract with the
United States Forces in Korea

괴된 국토를 온전한 모양으로 정상화하는 데 크게 기여했을
뿐 아니라 한국의 경제적 도약에 필요한 인적·기술적 잠재성
을 대내외적으로 알린 상징적 공사였다.

그중에서도 제2차 경제개발 5개년계획의 핵심 사업인
경부고속도로 건설은 산업사를 넘어 한국 현대사에 상징성
을 지닌 '길'을 건설했다는 점에서, 또 추후 현대자동차의 정
체성 형성과 관련해서도 의미심장한 사업이었다. 당시 세계
토목 공사 역사상 최단기간, 최저 비용 공사의 신화를 쓴 이
공사에서 현대건설은 총 428km 건설 구간 중 5분의 2를 시

the restoration of roads and bridges, despite facing several significant difficulties including a lack of capital, technology, and experience. Admittedly, it was part of the natural route that Founding Chairman Ju-yung Chung took in order to generate profits and expand the business, but there was more to it than that. He was aware of the national vision and social responsibility that Korean companies had to secure economic autonomy in many areas including capital and technology through direct participation in national regeneration projects. In a developing country, economic development at the national level and private firm growth are inseparable, hence 'construction' was the core industry.

Through this process, Hyundai E&C grew into a company that worked for the benefit of the nation, doing projects including the Koryoung Bridge (1953-1955), which the company had to complete to help restore the country despite massive financial losses; the Han River Footbridge (1957-1958), the largest restoration project since the Korean War; Incheon Dock No. 1 (1959), the largest construction project since the foundation of the nation; the Pattani-Narathiwat Highway project in Thailand (1965), its first overseas contracted project; the Gyeongbu Expressway (1968-1970), the largest civil engineering project in Korean history; and the 3rd Han River Bridge (1969). Most of these were social transportation infrastructure projects that generated huge spillover effects and held symbolic significance nationally. They not only contributed to normalizing life in a country devastated by war, but also demonstrated the human and technological potential that South

공했으며, 정주영 선대회장은 공사 전체 기획에 참여해 노동자들과 함께 현장에서 근무하며 직접 진두지휘했다.

당시 한국에서는 누구도 총 428km에 이르는 장거리 고속도로를 건설해 본 적이 없었다. 또 기술력과 장비, 자본 모두 매우 부족한 상황이었다. 그러나 국가 재건 계획에 박차를 가하고 있던 박정희 정부는 고속도로 개통을 최우선 과제로 삼고, 경부고속도로의 신속한 완공을 독촉했다. 정부와 기업이 긴밀한 관계를 유지하며 국가 인프라를 구축하고 있던 상황에서, 주도적으로 이 사업에 참여하고 있던 현대건설 정주영 선대회장은 정부의 자문 역할과 사업 수행자 역할을 동시에 수행했다.

현대건설은 공사 기간을 단축하기 위해 가격은 더 비싸지만 응고 시간은 훨씬 빠른 시멘트를 사용하는 결단을 내리는 등 갖은 노력과 창의적 방법으로 난관을 극복해 나갔다. 이때 정주영 선대회장은 노동자들과 대화하며 작업장에서 잠을 자는 날이 많았다. 평소 자신을 노동자라고 여긴 그는 한국 노동자들의 뛰어난 기술력을 신뢰했고, 그들과 함께라면 이 일을 성공시킬 수 있다는 확신과 연대감 속에서 사업을 진행해 나갔다. 그가 시간이 한참 지난 후에도 회고록 등 여러 자리에서 이 사업에 헌신한 건설 노동자들에게 특별한 감사의 마음을 반복해서 표현한 것은 이 연대감의 증거다.

경부고속도로 개통으로 15시간 걸리던 통행 시간은 약 5시간으로 단축되었고,[5] 철도 위주였던 수송 구조는 도로 위주로 재편되었다. 비로소 국가 교통 체계가 도로 중심으로 바뀐 것이다. 신속성이 장점인 도로 수송으로 교통 체계가 전환됨으로써 물류가 대량화되었고, 유통 부문에 대변혁이 일어났다. 고속도로를 따라 산업 단지가 들어서고 노동 인구가 유입되면서 도시화가 급속하게 이루어졌다. 또 고속도로를 따라 다른 도로가 이어지고, 전 국토가 일일생활권이 되면서 한국이 진정한 의미의 도시국가로 탄생하는 계기가 되었다. 지

Korea needed to harness in order to make significant economic progress.

Among other initiatives, the construction of the Gyeongbu Expressway, a key project in the second phase of the five-year economic development plan, was symbolically and historically significant for Korea, transcending industrial history. It also held profound meaning for the formation of Hyundai Motor Company's identity. In this project, which became known for completing in record time and at the lowest cost in the history of global civil engineering, Hyundai E&C handled two-fifths of the total construction work. Chung directly oversaw the planning and personally led efforts on-site.

At the time, domestic companies had no experience in constructing such a long-distance (428km) highway. Hyundai E&C also lacked both technological capabilities and capital. However, the Park Chung-hee government at the time, which was pushing for national reconstruction, prioritized the construction of the Gyeongbu (Seoul-Busan) Expressway and urged its rapid completion. In a situation where the government and businesses maintained close relations to build national infrastructure, Hyundai E&C's Ju-yung Chung played a leading role in the project, serving both as a government advisor and project executor.

In the process of construction, Hyundai E&C faced several difficulties but tackled them with wit, effort, and creative methods. To shorten the construction period, Hyundai E&C made the bold decision to use a more expensive but faster-setting cement, among other creative solutions to overcome challenges. During this

전후 국가 재건 사업으로 추진된 고령교 복구 공사
The restoration of Goryeong-gyo Bridge as part of the post-war reconstruction efforts by the Korean state

역과 지역 간 이동 시간이 대폭 단축됨에 따라 여행과 인적 교류가 활성화되면서 삶의 풍경은 크게 다양해졌다. 경부고속도로를 포함한 도로 인프라 확장이 자동차 산업의 성장에 결정적 역할을 했다는 것은 두말할 나위가 없다.

현대건설의 성장 과정은 대한민국의 현대화 여정에서 '길' 건설이 지닌 의미와 리더십을 갖춘 기업가의 특별한 역할을 보여준다. 인류 문명사가 '길'을 디자인하고 길을 개척해 온 역사였다는 것은 잘 알려진 사실이다. 일례로 로마제국은 도로 건설을 통해 문명을 디자인하고 도시를 유지했을 뿐아니라, 이를 주변 국가 운영과 교역 기술로 활용했다. 문명전환의 거대한 흐름을 읽지 못한 18세기 조선에서 당대의 문

time, Chung frequently discussed with workers and slept on the job site. Considering himself a worker, Chung trusted the skills of Korean workers and was confident that together they could successfully complete the project. This sense of belief and solidarity led him to repeatedly express his special gratitude towards the construction workers involved in the project, even long after its completion, as evidenced in his memoirs and various speeches.

The opening of the Gyeongbu Expressway reduced travel time between Seoul to Busan from 15 hours to about 5 hours[5], leading to a shift from a rail-centered to a road-centered transport system. The move to a more efficient road transport system led to an increase in logistics volume and eventually transformed the distribution sector. Industrial complexes emerged along the highway, and an influx of the labor population accelerated urbanization. Connections to other roads along the expressway and the creation of a nationwide daily living sphere led to Korea's emergence as a true 'city state'. With significantly reduced travel times between regions, travel and human exchange flourished, greatly diversifying life experiences. It goes without saying that the expansion of road infrastructure, including the Gyeongbu Expressway, played a critical role in the development of the automotive industry.

The growth of Hyundai E&C demonstrates the significance of road construction in South Korea's modernization journey and highlights the role of entrepreneurial leadership. It is well-known that human civilization has evolved through the design and development of roads.

인이자 '미래학자'였던 연암 박지원이 크게 개탄한 것도 교역과 이동을 편리하게 해줄 운송 수단 부재와 길, 도로의 미발달 상태였다. 이런 점에서 식민지와 전쟁을 겪으며 20세기에 들어서도 여전히 진척되지 못한 대한민국 도로의 현대화를 이끈 정주영 선대회장의 사업 여정은 각별하다 할 수 있다. 20세기의 위대한 경영학자이자 기업 철학자 피터 드러커 교수가 정주영 선대회장에게 호의를 느끼고 만남(1977)을 가진 데에는 여러 가지 이유가 있었을 테지만, 그중에서도 현대가 공공 영역과 긴밀한 관계를 맺으며 성장했다는 사실은 특별한 의미로 다가왔을 것이다. 현대자동차공업사에서 시작된 '현대'라는 사명의 사회적 의미는 이처럼 현대건설이 수행한 도로 건설 역사에서 먼저 찾아볼 수 있다.

For instance, the Roman Empire not only designed its civilization through road construction but also used it for governance and trade with neighboring states. In the 18th century, "Yeonam" (pen name) Ji-won Park, a scholar and 'futurist' of his time in Korea, that was known as Joseon, lamented the lack of convenient transportation and underdeveloped road infrastructure. In this context, one can see that Chung indeed played a unique role in modernizing South Korea's roads, which had seen little progress due to colonialism and war in the 20th century. Prof. Peter Drucker, a renowned business scholar and corporate philosopher of the 20th century, had several reasons for admiring and meeting with Chung in 1977, one of which was Hyundai's close relationship with the public sector. The social mission proclaimed in the company name 'Hyundai', which began with 'Hyundai Motor Industry Co.', began with Hyundai E&C's role in building modern routes across the Korean peninsula.

1970년대 경부고속도로
The Gyeongbu Expressway and
surrounding scenery in the early 1970s

대한민국의 경제성장을 견인한 경부고속도로 건설 현장
The construction of the Gyeongbu Expressway,
which helped in fueling Korea's economic growth

Chapter 1

대한민국의 경제성장을 견인한 경부고속도로 건설 현장
The construction of the Gyeongbu Expressway,
which helped to fuel Korea's economic growth

현대자동차라는 시대정신과 기업가 휴머니즘의 길

Hyundai Motor Company: the spirit of the times and the humanitarian path of its founder

"한 나라를 인체에 비유한다면 그 국토에 퍼져 있는 도로는 인체의 혈관과 같은 것이고, 자동차는 그 혈관을 돌아다니는 피와 같은 것이라고 생각합니다. 몸에 피가 원활하게 흐를 때 인체가 성장하고 활력을 갖게 되듯 도로가 만들어지고 그 위를 자동차가 원활하게 다닐 때 그 나라의 경제가 생동력을 가지고 발전할 수 있게 됩니다."[6]

정주영 선대회장이 남긴 이 말은 한 나라에서 잘 만들어진 도로의 중요성과 자동차의 관계에 관한 그의 생각을 단적으로 보여준다. 현대건설이 1950년대부터 1960년대에 수행한 국가 도로 건설은 단순히 길을 만드는 과정이 아니었다. 도로와 자동차의 연관성을 더욱 깊이 인식하게 되었고, 길과 자동차에 관한 기술적 이해도도 훨씬 높아지면서 자동차 산업을 부흥해야한다는 의지와 확신이 더욱 확고해지는 과정이자 공부였다.

정주영 선대회장은 자동차 산업을 대한민국이 선진 공업 국가로 거듭나기 위한 가장 중요한 산업으로 생각했다. 그는 "자동차는 그 나라 산업 기술의 척도이며 '달리는 국기'다. 우리 자동차가 수출되는 곳에서는 어디서나 자동차를 자력으로 생산, 수출할 수 있는 나라라는 이미지 덕분에 다른 상품도 덩달아 높이 평가된다"라고 말했다. 그는 자동차 산업을 통해 식민지와 내전의 폐허에서 허우적대던 가난한 나라의 기상과 잠재성을 세계에 알리고 싶어 했다. 국가의 이익보다 기업의 이익을 우선시하는 기업은 대성할 수 없으며, 기업가는 기업가의 방식대로 애국·애족하는 사람이라는 것은 그가 가장 중요하게 여기는 기업 철학이었다. 자동차 산업은 자본 집약적인 동시에 기술 집약적인 산업이었으며, 또한 우수한 노동 인력이 존재하지 않으면 성공하기 어려운 산업이었기에 그는 자동차 산업이야말로 자신의 기업 철학을 실현할 수 있는 현장으로 보았다. 대량 양산형 독자 모델을 개발하려

"If we compare a country to the human body, the roads that spread across the land are like blood vessels, and cars are like blood circulating within them. Just as a body grows and becomes vibrant when blood flows smoothly, a country's economy can thrive and develop when roads are built and cars move freely on them."[6]

This quote highlights Founding Chairman Chung's views on the importance of well-constructed roads in a country as well as the relationship between roads and automobiles. The national road construction undertaken by Hyundai E&C from the 1950s to the 1960s was not just about building physical roads. It deepened the understanding of the connection between roads and cars, increased technical knowledge about them, and reinforced the determination and confidence to revitalize the automotive industry.

Chung believed the automotive industry was vital for South Korea to become a leading industrial nation. He said, "Cars are a measure of a country's industrial technology and serve as a 'moving national flag'. Wherever our cars are exported, they elevate the image of our country as capable of producing and exporting cars on its own, boosting the reputation of other products as well." He wanted to showcase the spirit and potential of a nation recovering from colonialism and civil war through the automotive industry. Chung argued that a company cannot succeed if it prioritizes corporate over national interests, emphasizing that entrepreneurs should patriotically support both their country and people.

The automotive industry, being capital and

건설 현장에서 노동자들과 함께하며 산업화의 '길'을 닦은 정주영 선대회장
Ju-yung Chung laid the foundation for industrialization with the workers at a construction site.

는 현대자동차의 도전을 만류하던 주한 미국 대사 리처드 스나이더에게 "도로를 만들면서 번 모든 돈을 자동차 산업에 투자했다가 실패해도 결코 후회하지 않을 것이다. 왜냐하면 그것이 밑거름이 되어 훗날 한국 자동차 산업의 디딤돌이 된다면 보람이 될 것이기 때문이다"라고 한 말은 '길'의 승부사 정주영 선대회장의 신념을 보여주는 일화로 추후 유명한 이야기가 되었다.

그가 보기에 수만 개의 부품을 조립해 완성하는 자동차는 철강, 정밀기계 등 여러 분야에 걸쳐 엄청난 산업적 파급력을 지닐 뿐 아니라 기술적 자부심과 함께 대규모 고용 창출이 이루어질 것이 분명했다. 기업 측면에서나 노동자 및 시장 측면에서 기술이 열어갈 잠재력이 자동차 산업에 응축되어 있기에 현대자동차가 대한민국 국민의 풍요로운 삶에 기여하는 기업이 되기를 원했다.

그러므로 현대자동차는 근대 산업화의 길을 닦은 현대가 또 다른 방식으로 특별한 '길 위'의 출발점에 서게 되었음을 예고하는 것이었다. 비전(vision)이 아직 존재하지 않는 것을 미리 보는 것이고, 리더십(leadership)이 그 비전을 실현하는 능력까지 포함한다면 창업주 정주영 선대회장은 비전을 만들고 실현하는 디자이너이자 실천가였다. 이 비전과 리더십의 바탕에는 사람, 특히 한국인의 우수한 능력과 성실함

technology-intensive, required skilled labor, making it an ideal platform for Chung to apply his business philosophy. He famously told the former U.S. Ambassador to South Korea, Richard L. Sneider, who had advised against Hyundai's attempt to develop its mass production models, "I would never regret investing all the money earned from road construction into the automotive industry, even if it fails. If it lays the groundwork for the future of the automotive industry, it will be worthwhile." This anecdote reflects Chung's conviction and it has become a well-known story illustrating his entrepreneurial spirit.

In his view, assembling thousands of parts to create a car not only has a significant industrial impact across various sectors like steel and precision machinery but also ensures the creation of a large number of jobs, accompanied by technical pride. He wanted Hyundai Motor Company to contribute to enriching people's lives because he believed that all the potential of the future was encapsulated in the automotive industry, in its impact on firms, labor, markets, and even technology.

Thus, Hyundai Motor Company marked a new beginning on the special 'road' of modern

"우리 현대는 이 나라 발전의 진취적인 선도 역할과 경제 건설의 중추 역할을 사명으로 하는 유능한 인재들의 집단이다."

"We are a group of gifted individuals united by the call to lead our country, to build our national economy, and to serve as the backbone of our economic prosperity."

정주영 선대회장 **Founding Chairman Ju-yung Chung**

에 대한 믿음이 있었다. 이 믿음은 현대자동차 기업 정신의 핵심이 되었다. 이윤을 추구하기 위해 움직이는 일반 기업과 달리 현대자동차는 한국 현대사의 굴곡과 뜨거운 숨결, 사람에 대한 믿음 위에서 시작되었다. 개발도상국에서는 상상조차 할 수 없었던 대량 양산형 독자 모델 자동차 '포니'가 시판된 것은 현대자동차가 설립된 지 10년이 채 지나지 않았을 때다. 길을 닦고, 이제 그 길 위를 포니가 '현대'라는 꿈을 안고 달리게 된 것이다.

industrialization, heralding a future where vision illustrates what does not yet exist, and leadership embodies the ability to realize that vision. Chung was both a visionary and a true leader, grounded in a belief in people — especially the exceptional talent and diligence of Koreans. This belief stood firmly at the center of Hyundai's corporate spirit. Unlike typical companies driven by profit, Hyundai started with a dedication to Korea's dynamic history and a deep faith in its people. The launch of the mass-produced, independent model 'Pony' less than a decade after Hyundai's establishment was something unimaginable in developing countries. It paved the way for 'Pony' to run with the dream of 'Hyundai' — or modern times.

현대건설이 수행한 고속도로 건설 공사
경인고속도로(위), 영동고속도로(아래)
Expressway construction being conducted by
Hyundai Engineering & Construction
Gyeongin Expressway (above)
Yeongdong Expressway (below)

2

새로운 길을
개척하다

Pioneering
a new path

새로운 길을
개척하다

자동차 산업 불모지에서 고유 모델 개발과
생산은 기존에 없던 새로운 길을 닦아야 하는
험난한 선택지였다. 그러나 현대자동차는
사람의 잠재력을 믿고 독자적인 길로
나아갔다. 자주적 결단과 수많은 사람의
헌신을 통해 대한민국 첫 대량 양산형 고유
모델 포니가 출시될 수 있었다.

Developing and producing an
original model in the early stages of
Korea's automotive industry was a
choice that required finding
new paths. Nevertheless, Hyundai
believed in human potential and
chose to go its own way. Through
Hyundai's firm determination and
the dedication of countless people,
Pony, Korea's first domestically
produced model, successfully
made its debut.

가보지 않은 길을 선택하다 To the road untraveled

국내외에서 현대건설의 신화를 만들어가던 정주영 선대회장이 마침내 자동차 산업에 진출하려 한다는 계획이 알려지자 당시 사내 안팎에서는 우려의 시선이 많았다. 이미 신진자동차와 기아산업이 협소한 국내 자동차 시장에서 경쟁하고 있었고, 고도의 기술이 요구되는 자동차 산업에 경험이 부족한 현대가 후발 업체로서 성공할 수 있을지 미지수였기 때문이다.

현대가 초기에 포드(Ford)와의 전략적 제휴에 힘을 쏟은 것도 이런 이유에서였다. 선진 기술 업종으로 분류되던 자동차 산업에 진출하기 위해서는 당시 정부 정책상 외국 선진 기업과 기술 제휴가 필수적이었다. 정주영 선대회장은 외국 기업과 제휴할 수밖에 없다면 세계 최고 수준의 기업과 해야 한다고 생각했다. 당시 포드는 GM(General Motors)과 더불어 세계 자동차 시장의 양대 산맥이었다. 그는 규모는 더 크지만 기존 회사를 매입하거나 경영에 직접 참여하는 방식으로 해외 사업을 하는 GM보다는, 상대적으로 협력 회사에 자율성을 부여하는 포드와 손잡는 것이 현대 입장에서 더 좋을 것이라고 보았다. 처음에는 외국 회사의 기술을 배워나가지만, 장기적으로는 국산차를 만들어 해외에 수출하겠다는 의지를 가지고 있었기에 포드를 파트너로 삼는 것이 독자 경영에 더 유리하다고 판단했기 때문이다.

이 무렵 아시아 지역으로 사업 확장을 모색하고 있던 포드는 1967년 초 한국 시장 진출 타당성을 조사하기 위해 내한했다. 당시 현대는 포드의 접촉 대상이 아니었는데, 이는 포드가 현대를 자동차와 관련 없는 건설 회사로 보았기 때문이다. 이 소식을 접한 정주영 선대회장은 미국에 나가 있던 동생 정세영을 통해 현대가 자동차 산업에 관심이 있음을 포드 본사에 전달함으로써 제휴 협상이 본격적으로 시작되었다. 결론적으로 현대건설이 쌓은 높은 신용도와 추진력, 그리고 정주영 선대회장이 자동차 수리 공장을 운영하면서 쌓은 해박

Founding Chairman Ju-yung Chung finally revealed his ambition to enter the automotive industry after his legendary success with Hyundai E&C at home and abroad. Concerns were soon raised both in and outside the company. Shinjin Motors and Kia Industries were already competing in the small and emerging domestic automobile market at the time. So there were many doubts about whether Hyundai, lacking experience, could succeed as a latecomer in the automotive business that requires advanced technology.

In these early days, government policy required technological partnerships with advanced foreign companies to enter the automotive industry. This is because the automotive industry was classified as an "advanced technology industry" at that time. Chung acknowledged that Hyundai should collaborate with a top-notch global company if an alliance were to be inevitable. As such, it may have been more realistic for Hyundai to pursue a strategic alliance with Ford Motor Company (Ford), one of the two largest powerhouses in the global automobile market along with General Motors (GM). Chung assumed that it would be better for Hyundai to cooperate with Ford, which granted autonomy to partners, rather than GM, which was larger but did overseas business by purchasing existing companies or through direct control. Chung regarded that acquiring autonomy for the company's management was of high importance since Hyundai had a will to make domestic cars and export them overseas after learning technology from foreign companies.

Around this time, Ford, seeking to expand

한 자동차 관련 지식과 열의에 힘입어 현대가 포드의 제휴 대상으로 최종 선정되었다. 이어 자동차를 수출 전략 산업으로 육성하겠다는 계획이 담긴 '사업 계획서'와 '자동차 생산 공장 허가서'를 정부에 제출, 정부가 자동차 회사 설립을 승인함으로써 1967년 12월 29일 현대자동차가 설립되었다. 현대자동차 창립은 국내 자동차 시장이 독과점 체제에서 벗어나 비로소 새로운 경쟁 체제에 돌입했을 뿐 아니라, 자동차에 대한 정주영 선대회장의 오래된 꿈이 실현되는 시작점을 의미했다.

business into the Asian region, sent a team to Korea in early 1967 to explore the feasibility of entering the Korean market. Ford viewed Hyundai as a construction company unrelated to automobiles and decided not to move further. Hearing this news, Chung conveyed Hyundai's intention to enter the automobile business to the head office of Ford through his younger brother Se-yung Chung, who was away in the United States. Thanks to this, the two companies began to formally negotiate a partnership. Ultimately, Hyundai E&C was chosen as Ford's partner due to its high credit rating, proactive attitude, and Chung's extensive knowledge and passion for automobiles, which he acquired while operating an auto repair shop. Subsequently, a business plan to foster the automotive sector as a strategic export industry and a license application for an automobile manufacturing factory were submitted to and approved by the Korean government. As a result, Hyundai Motor Company was born on December 29, 1967. Its founding marked the beginning of the materialization of Chung's long-held dream for cars, as well as the domestic automobile market breaking free from monopoly and finally entering into a new competitive stage.

정주영 선대회장은 자동차 산업이 국민의 생활 수준 향상에 이바지할 것으로 믿었다.
"여러분은 텔레비전이나 냉장고 한 대씩은 다 사게 될 겁니다. 지금은 어렵겠지만
열심히만 하면 여러분도 잘살게 됩니다"라며 그의 신념을 공장 직원들에게 이야기하곤
했다. 당시 대한민국은 텔레비전을 보유한 가정이 극히 드문 가난한 나라였지만,
현대차가 전 세계에 수출되던 1980년대 중반 텔레비전은 가정의 일상재가 되었다.
Ju-yung Chung believed the automotive industry could help elevate
people's quality of life. "You'll be able to buy your very own television
or refrigerator. Things are hard right now, but if you work hard, you
will live well." These are the words that he would often share with
plant workers. At the time, Korea was a poor country where few
owned a television. However, televisions became common in Korean
households in the mid-1980s, when Hyundai cars were being
exported worldwide.

창립 후 얼마 지나지 않은 1968년 2월, 현대는 포드와 자동차 조립 기술 협정을 체결한다. 당시 선진 업체인 포드와의 협정 체결 과정은 녹록지 않았는데, 현대자동차는 자사에 불리한 조항을 강요하는 포드의 요구를 감내하는 과정을 통해 독자 경영권의 중요성을 인식하게 되었다. 협정 체결 후 현대자동차는 바로 대규모 자동차 조립 공장 건설 작업에 착수했다. 그러나 자동차 공장을 처음 건설해 보는 신생 회사에게 이는 쉽지 않은 작업이었다. 공장 부지로 선택한 울산은 당시 공업 지역으로 선포되어 향후 사회간접자본 혜택을 받을 수 있고, 바다와 인접해 생산 설비 하역과 수출입이 용이한 곳이었다. 그러나 현실은 전통적 촌락이 있던 농경지로 근거리에 시멘트 공장이 부재했고, 공업용수도 부족했으며, 비포장도로가 많아 자재 운반도 쉽지 않았다. 설상가상으로 폭우로 공장 부지 일부가 침수되는 사태가 발생하기도 했다. 현대자동차는 어려운 환경 속에서 공장 건설과 더불어 생산 및 판매를 위한 준비를 동시에 진행해 나가야 했다. 이를 위해 직능별로 직원을 파견해 호주 포드사에서 생산기술 연수, 미국 대도시의 포드 대리점에서 판매 연수, 일본 포드사에서 애프터서비스 연수를 받도록 했다.

또 현대자동차는 어떤 차종을 주력 모델로 생산할 것인지 심사숙고한 끝에 영국 포드사의 '코티나'를 첫 조립 생산 차종으로 결정했다. 화려한 미국형 포드와 달리 영국 포드사의 코티나는 실용적이고 견고해 비포장률이 높았던 당시 도로 실정을 감안했을 때 적절한 모델로 평가되었다. 현대자동차는 조립 생산자로서 부품을 전량 수입해 국내에서 조립 생산하는 방안 대신, 국산차를 제작한다는 장기적 목표 아래 사업 초기부터 부품 국산화율을 높이기 위한 노력을 병행했다.

그리고 공장 건설을 시작한 지 6개월여 만인 1968년 11월, 현대자동차의 첫 승용 모델 코티나 1호 차가 생산되었

In February 1968, not long after Hyundai Motor Company's establishment, the Hyundai-Ford Motor Company Assembly Technology Agreement was signed. However it was not easy to strike a deal with a leading company. Hyundai had come to recognize the significance of autonomous management rights while enduring Ford's unfavorable demands. After signing the agreement, Hyundai began constructing a large-scale automobile assembly factory. It took considerable work for the inexperienced company to build a car plant for the first time. Ulsan was chosen as the factory's site soon after it was declared an industrial zone that would benefit from social overhead capital in the future. In addition, since Ulsan was adjacent to the sea, it was suitable for unloading production facilities and trading. However, there was no cement factory within the immediate vicinity as the site had been farmland with traditional villages. Moreover, industrial water was barely accessible, and transporting materials was yet another headache as most roads had been unpaved. To make things worse, a part of the factory site was flooded due to heavy rain. Despite such challenges, Hyundai had to move forward with building a factory as well as preparing for production and sales simultaneously. Employees were sent for training to learn different skills including production technology training at Ford in Australia, sales training at Ford dealerships in large cities in the United States, and after-sales service training at Ford in Japan.

Hyundai deliberated on which model to produce as its flagship model and concluded on the Cortina by Ford of England as its first produc-

코티나 1호 차 제작 광경
Production of the first Cortina

다. 당초 포드 관계자들은 한국의 자동차 공업 수준이 낮아 단기간에 자동차를 생산하기는 어려울 것으로 판단했다. 그러나 실제로 목표한 기한 내에 승용차 생산이 이루어지자 현대자동차의 추진력에 감탄하지 않을 수 없었다. 포드 창립 이래 직접 보유하거나 제휴한 전 세계 118개 공장 중 6개월 만에 공장을 건설하고 자동차를 생산한 사례는 없었기 때문이다. 특히 착수 3개월 만에 자동차 부품의 21%를 국산 제품으로 조달한 경우는 처음이었다. 이는 현대자동차의 추진력을 보여주는 동시에 한국에 대한 포드 관계자들의 인식을 바꾸는 계기가 되었다.

tion model. Unlike the exquisite cars by Ford in the United States, the Cortina was practical and robust, therefore deemed an appropriate model considering Korea's road conditions as many were still unpaved. Instead of importing all parts from abroad, Hyundai made extra efforts to increase the localization rate of Ford parts from the outset of their business with the long-term goal of making domestic cars.

In November 1968, just six months after the construction of the factory began, Hyundai's first model, the Cortina, rolled off the production line. Ford officials had initially thought it would be too far-fetched to make cars so quickly due to Korea's lack of experience in the automotive industry. However, when the passenger car was produced within the planned period, the U.S. motor company was blown away by Hyundai's driving force. Since Ford's founding, out of 118 factories directly owned or affiliated worldwide, there had never been a single successful case in which a factory was built and started producing automobiles in just six months. In particular, it was the first time that 21% of the auto parts were procured domestically within three months of a project's start. This event demonstrated that Hyundai was a highly-driven business and served as an opportunity to change Ford officials' perception of Korea.

가보지 않은 길을 선택하다   To the road untraveled   현대자동차의 첫 번째 승용차이자 조립 생산 모델인 코티나
Cortina, the first model to be assembled
by Hyundai

도로 포장률이 높은 선진국을 기준으로 개발된 코티나는 비포장도로가 많은 한국에서
고장이 잦아 '섰다 하면 코티나'라는 조롱을 듣게 됐다. 이 문제에 대해 포드는
'비포장도로에서 차를 운행하지 말 것'이라는 소극적인 해결책을 제시했다. 이 사건을
통해 현대자동차는 조립 생산자의 한계를 체감하고 국내 실정에 맞는 차를 개발하기
위해 독자 기술 확보가 얼마나 중요한지를 깨닫게 된다.

Because the Cortina was developed for advanced markets with paved
roads, it suffered frequent malfunctions on Korea's unpaved roads.
This led to people derisively saying, "Every car stopped is a Cortina."
Ford suggested a solution: "Don't drive on unpaved roads."
From this incident, Hyundai realized the limitations of being an
assembly-only manufacturer: To develop a car that suits the conditions
in Korea, the company would have to acquire proprietary technology.

현대자동차는 코티나의 내구성 문제를 해결하기 위해 생산 전 샘플 차량을 도입, 울산
방어진 인근의 비포장도로에서 가혹한 주행 테스트를 실시했다. 이를 통해 차체에
일어나는 문제를 보강해 출시한 뉴코티나는 큰 인기를 끌었다.

To ensure the durability of the upcoming Cortina model, Hyundai
introduced pre-production sample vehicles for the Cortina to undergo a
rigorous road test on unpaved roads near Bangeojin, Ulsan.
As a result, the new Cortina, which made improvements to the chassis
derived from this testing process, was launched with great acclaim.

코티나를 정비 중인 현대자동차 서울사업소의 정비공들
Mechanics at Hyundai service center in Seoul
working to maintain the Cortina

1968년 코티나 한 차종만 생산하던 현대자동차는 1969년 '국-750' 트럭 생산을 비롯해 고급 승용차 '포드 20M'과 버스 'R-192' 생산도 시작함으로써 승용차-화물차-승합차 라인업을 갖춘 종합 자동차 회사로 거듭나게 되었다. 종합 자동차 회사로 성장한 현대자동차는 경영 체제 전반을 정비하고, 조립 단계에서 벗어나 제조 단계로 진입하기 위한 목표를 수립했다. 여기에는 국산화율 제고에 핵심 역할을 할 엔진 공장 건설도 포함되어 있었는데, 때마침 정부가 공표한 1969년 '자동차 완전 국산화 정책'에도 부응하는 계획이었다. 이즈음 정부는 국산화 정책의 일환으로 1970년 엔진 주물 공장 건설 일원화 방침을 세우고 최적의 요건을 충족시키는 회사 한 곳만 엔진 주물 공장 설립을 허용하겠다고 밝혔다. 해당 요건에는 기술, 외자, 시장성 확보를 위해 합작 투자를 우선시한다는 내용도 포함되어 있었다. 마침 한국을 발판 삼아 동아시아 시장 확대를 꾀하던 포드는 현대자동차와 이해관계가 맞물려 엔진 공장 합작을 위한 협상을 시작했다.

Hyundai produced only one model, the Cortina, in 1968. But the company started producing luxury passenger cars like the Ford Taurus 20M and other vehicles such as the R-192 buses and the D-750 trucks in 1969, gradually evolving into a comprehensive automobile company with a lineup of various vehicle types. Hyundai, which had grown into a comprehensive automobile company, had established a goal to revamp its management system and move on from the assembly stage to the manufacturing stage. This next-stage plan included the construction of an engine factory that would play a key role in raising the localization rate in line with the 'Complete Automobile Localization Policy' announced by the government in 1969. Around this time, as part of its localization policy, the government established a policy to unify the construction of engine foundries in 1970. They announced that only one company that meets the optimal requirements, including prioritizing

```
                    OVER-ALL AGREEMENT


      Agreement dated November 30, 1970 among and between Ford
Motor Company, a Delaware corporation with its principal place
of business at Dearborn, Michigan, U.S.A. (hereinafter called
"Ford"), Chung-Ju Yung, Chung-Se Yung, Kim-Young Ju, Chang-Jung
Ja and Hyundai Construction Co., Ltd, of Seoul, Korea (herein-
after called "Construction"), who in the aggregate directly or
indirectly own substantially all of the outstanding capital
stock of Hyundai Motor Company, and Hyundai Motor Company, a
Korean corporation with offices in Seoul and an automotive
assembly plant at Ulsan, Korea (hereinafter called "Motor"). All
of the above named parties, except Ford, will be referred to
hereinafter in the aggregate as the "Korea Group" and indi-
vidually as a "member of the Korea Group".


                   W I T N E S S E T H :


      Whereas, Ford is engaged in the business of developing,
manufacturing and selling automotive vehicles and components:
and

      Whereas, the Korea Group controls various enterprises in
Korea, including Construction and Motor; and

      Whereas, Motor owns and operates an automotive assembly
plant at Ulsan, Korea and automotive retail sales and service
establishments located at various places in Korea;  and

      Whereas, Construction owns certain land including a por-
tion of the land on which Motor's assembly plant is located; and

      Whereas, Motor's activities presently are confined to the
assembly, distribution and servicing of products of Ford and its
affiliated companies;  and


                     마- 1 -
```

1970년 11월에 체결한 포드와 합작 투자 계약서
Joint venture agreement with Ford signed in November 1970

엔진 주물 공장으로 시작된 협상은 포드의 제안으로 제조 및 판매 기능까지 아우르는 새로운 합작사 설립에 대한 논의로 이어졌다. 협상이 시작되자 경영권과 수출에 대한 양사 간 견해 차이로 난항이 거듭되었으나, 수차례에 걸친 협의를 통해 50 대 50 비율로 양사가 함께 회사를 운영하는 것으로 겨우 합의를 보았다. 그러나 그즈음 변화한 국제 정세로 인해 토요타가 신진자동차와의 제휴를 철회하고 한국에서 철수하는 일이 발생하고 만다. 사태를 관망하던 포드는 기존에 합의했던 사항들조차 자사에 유리한 방향으로 변경하고자 했다. 현대자동차는 새로운 합작사에서 만든 국산차와 국산 부품을 포드의 해외 영업망을 이용해 수출하겠다는 생각을 가지고 있었던 반면, 포드는 한국을 단순 부품 생산 기지로 여기는 관

joint ventures to secure technology, foreign capital, and marketability, would be allowed to build an engine foundry. Coincidentally, Ford, seeking to expand its presence into East Asia using Korea as a stepping-stone, started negotiations on a joint venture with Hyundai with aligned interests.

These negotiations then led to discussions on establishing a new joint venture with manufacturing and sales operations at the suggestion of Ford. Once these negotiations began, difficulties arose due to different views on management rights and exports. After rounds of intense bargaining, the two companies finally agreed to operate the joint venture in a 50:50 ratio. However, an unexpected event surprised the market under international dynamics: Toyota decided to withdraw its alliance with Shinjin Motors and exit the Korean market. Ford, observing this, tried to amend previously agreed terms in their favor. Above all, while Hyundai had the idea of exporting automobiles made in the new joint venture using Ford's overseas sales network, Ford still considered Korea as merely a parts production base. As such, the irreconcilable gap between the two companies on exports continued to persist. Ford chose to maintain a lukewarm attitude by delaying capital investment to establish a joint venture. Therefore, Hyundai's options for paths forward were narrowed down to two: 1) accept the unfavorable terms offered by Ford and sign a joint venture agreement or 2) break up with Ford and seek an independent path. Considering how underdeveloped the Korean automotive industry was at the time, it seemed inconceivable and almost reckless to take an

점을 고수했다. 이렇듯 수출에 대해 양사 간 좁힐 수 없는 입장 차이가 계속되었고, 포드가 합작사 설립을 위한 자본금 투입을 차일피일 미루며 미온적 태도를 지속하는 상황에서 현대자동차가 나아갈 길은 크게 두 가지로 좁혀졌다. 포드가 제시하는 불리한 조건을 수용하고 합작 계약을 체결하거나, 포드와 결별하고 독자 노선을 모색하는 것이었다. 불모지와 같았던 당시 한국 자동차 산업 수준을 고려할 때 독자 노선을 택한다는 것은 감히 상상하기 어려운 일이었다. 그러나 정주영 선대회장은 "우리는 우리의 길을 가겠다"라며 포드와의 합작 결렬을 선언했다. 독자적으로 고유 모델을 개발하겠다는, 그 누구도 가보지 않은 길을 선택한 것이다. 현대자동차가 고유 모델을 개발하고 기술 자립을 통해 외국 기업의 기술력에 의존하지 않고 당당히 자사의 차를 만드는 회사로 성장할 수 있었던 것은 이와 같은 정주영 선대회장의 자주적 결단에서 시작되었다고 할 수 있다. 만일 종속 관계에 가까운 포드의 조립 생산자로 남았다면, 단기적으로 안정적 매출 확보는 가능했겠지만 오랜 기간 한국은 선진국의 차량 및 부품 생산 기지로 남았을 것이다.

따라서 포드와의 협상 결렬은 현대자동차에 위기라기보다는 오히려 기회였다고 할 수 있다. 독자 모델 개발 의지가 더욱 굳건해졌고 그 필요성을 충분히 인식하는 계기가 되었기 때문이다. 더욱이 자동차 산업은 규모의 경제를 달성해야만 생존이 가능한데, 이는 협소한 국내 시장을 넘어 해외로 수출을 해야 하고, 수출을 하기 위해서는 대량생산이 가능한 독자 모델을 개발해야 함을 의미했다. 하지만 이 계획 공표로 현대자동차는 자동차 사업에 처음 뛰어들었던 때보다도 더 거센 반발에 부닥치게 된다. 자본금보다 수십 배나 많은 대규모 투자가 필수적이었는데, 이를 위해서는 천문학적 액수의 차관을 들여와야 하는 재무 리스크가 존재했기 때문이다. 또 당

independent route. However, Chung said, "We will go our own way," and announced the dissolution of the joint venture. He chose a path no one else had taken to independently develop his company's own models. Through Chung's brave self-determination, Hyundai was able to build its own model and grow to proudly manufacture its own cars by developing independent technology without relying on foreign companies' technological prowess. If Hyundai had remained an assembler of Ford, which was nearly a subordinate relationship, it could have generated stable sales in the short term. However, Korea would have remained only as a vehicles and parts production base of developed countries for a significantly longer period of time.

In retrospect, for Hyundai, the breakdown of negotiations with Ford may have served as a precious opportunity rather than a crisis. This served as an opportunity for Hyundai to solidify its commitment to developing its own models and clearly recognized the urgency from this point on. Furthermore, a firm can be viable in the automotive industry only by achieving economies of scale, suggesting the company had to look beyond the narrow domestic market and export to foreign countries. Thus inevitably, the company had to develop and mass-produce its own models for export. Nonetheless, when Hyundai announced its intent to operate independently, it faced opposition even fiercer than when it first entered the automotive business. A large-scale investment, significantly larger than the firm's paid-up capital, was essential, bearing a financial risk requiring an astronomical loan. In addition, considering the domestic automotive

시 불모지에 가까운 국내 자동차 산업 수준을 고려할 때 자동차 제조는 실현 불가능하다는 비관론이 대두되는 등 고유 모델 개발은 차원이 다른 모험적 결단을 필요로 했다. 당시 국내에는 독자 모델 개발을 어디서부터 어떻게 추진해야 할지 방법을 일러줄 이조차 없었다. 현대건설이 수행한 도로 건설 과정이 그러했듯이, 자동차 독자 모델 개발 역시 새롭게 내야만 하는 길이었다. 아니, 어쩌면 그보다도 더 험난하고 뛰어난 창조성이 필요한 일이었다. 이 길을 내기 위해서는 가보지 않은 이들의 경험적 한계뿐 아니라 이 도전을 지켜보는 이들의 부정적 시선까지도 극복해야 했기 때문이다.

industry had barely begun, pessimism arose about the feasibility of automobile manufacturing. Developing an original model was a decision taking this venture to an entirely different level, and no one in Korea was able to guide the company on where or how to begin building its own model. Similar to the road construction done by Hyundai E&C, the path towards developing an independent model was uncertain, or perhaps even more arduous, and required extraordinary creativity. To embark on this journey, it was necessary to overcome the limitations stemming from inexperience in addition to the adverse public opinion surrounding this challenge.

현대자동차가 포드와 체결한 '엔진 주물 및 기계 공장
건설을 위한 외국인 투자 및 기술 도입 계약'의 정부 인가
(1970년 12월)
Government approval for the "Foreign
Investment and Technology Introduction
Contract to Construct Engine Molding and
Machinery Plant" signed between Hyundai
and Ford (December 1970)

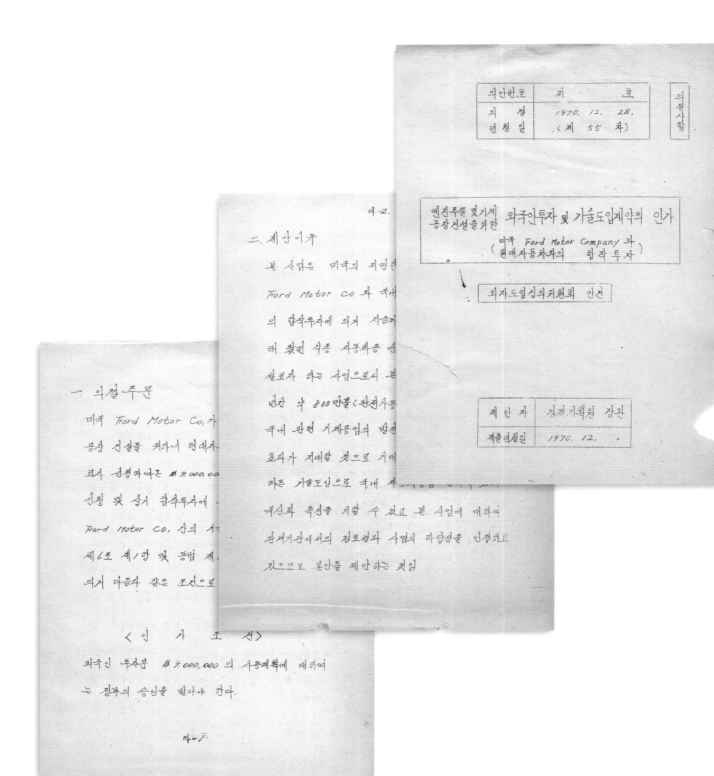

대한민국 최초 대량생산 독자 모델 개발로 향하는 길

The birth of Korea's first mass-produced independent model

독자 모델 개발 및 양산을 위한 첫걸음은 1973년 4월 현대자동차 기획실 주관으로 향후 9년간의 자동차 수요와 1,200cc 승용차의 원가를 추정하는 것으로 시작됐다. 기획실에서 추정한 결과 국내 시장의 자동차 수요는 1976년 4만 6,000대에서 1978년 10만5,000대, 1981년 28만5,000대로 급증할 것으로 예상됐다. 원가 추정 결과도 고무적이었다. 1,200cc급 승용차의 감가상각비를 감안하면 수출가를 1,785달러까지 낮출 수 있어 국제 경쟁력이 충분히 있는 것으로 나타났다.

현대자동차는 이러한 추정 결과를 토대로 본격적인 고유 모델 개발 및 양산 전략 수립에 돌입했다. 전략 방향은 네 가지로 압축됐다. 첫째, 외국의 설계 전문 회사와 용역 계약을 체결해 차체 설계를 의뢰하고, 둘째, 완성차 제작 시 전문 분야별로 외국인 전문가를 초빙해 자문을 받으며, 셋째, 차체 스탬핑용 금형 중 고도의 기술을 요하는 부분은 1차에 한해 외국 전문 기업의 기술 지원을 받아 개발하며, 넷째, 스탬핑 및 금형 제작 기술은 우리 기술자를 해외에 파견해 습득하기로 한 것이다. 요약하자면, 필요한 부분은 선택적으로 해외 업체와 전문가의 도움을 받되, 관련 기술을 단기간에 효과적으로 내재화해 한국 실정에 맞게 현실화한다는 전략이었다.

The first step toward developing and mass-producing an independent model began in April 1973, under the supervision of the Hyundai Planning Department, by estimating automobile demand for the next nine years as well as the production cost of a 1,200cc passenger car. The demand for automobiles in the domestic market was expected to rapidly jump from 46,000 units in 1976 to 105,000 in 1978 and further to 285,000 in 1981. In addition, the result of the cost estimation was encouraging. Considering the reduction in depreciation cost for 1,200cc passenger cars, the company could secure sufficient international competitiveness by lowering the export price to US $1,785.

Based on these estimations, Hyundai established a strategy for developing its model and mass production which was compressed into four principles: (1) sign a service contract with a foreign design company with a request for a body design; (2) invite foreign experts from each specialized field for consultation during the manufacturing of complete vehicles (3) seek technical support from foreign manufacturers during the primary development stage for the body stamping molds that require advanced technology and (4) acquire stamping dies and press manufacturing skills through training by sending technicians abroad. Simply put, the strategy was to seek selective support from foreign companies and experts for crucial areas while effectively and quickly internalizing other technologies to fit the conditions in Korea.

현대자동차는 독자 모델 개발과 양산에 도움을 줄 해외 업체를 물색하기 시작했다. 유럽과 일본을 숱하게 오가며 유력 업체에 의사를 적극 타진한 결과 마침내 1973년 9월 이탈디자인(Italdesign)과 차체 설계 용역 계약을 맺었고, 미쓰비시(Mitsubishi)와 가솔린엔진 및 변속기, 후차축 등 플랫폼 제조 기술 협조 계약을 체결했다. 이듬해인 1974년 3월에는 완성차 공장을 짓기 위해 해외 전문가 조지 턴불(George Turnbull)을 영입했고, 7월에는 미쓰비시와 엔진, 주조·단조 시설 설치 등 공장 설계와 양산 라인 구축에 필요한 기술 협조 계약을 체결함으로써 독자 모델을 개발하기 위한 일련의 해외 협력 라인업을 완성했다.

Under this strategy, Hyundai began to look for foreign companies to help develop and mass-produce its own model. In September 1973 after traveling back and forth to Europe and Japan, a body design contract was signed with Italdesign and a contract for platform manufacturing technology cooperation, such as gasoline engines, transmissions, and rear axles, was signed with Mitsubishi. In March the following year, an overseas expert, George Turnbull, was hired to build a complete vehicle manufacturing plant. In July of the same year, a technical cooperation agreement was signed with Mitsubishi for factory design and mass production line construction, such as engine and casting as well as forging facility installation, completing a series of overseas cooperation lineups to develop Hyundai's independent model.

전도유망한 젊은 디자이너 조르제토 주지아로와의 만남

고유 모델을 만들려면 타사와 차별되는 독창적 디자인을 확보해야 한다. 현대자동차도 고유 모델을 개발하기로 결심한 후 가장 먼저 고민한 것이 디자인이었다. 하지만 조립 생산 단계에 머물러 있던 당시 국내에는 차를 디자인할 수 있는 인력이 전무했기에 현대자동차는 차체 디자인을 맡아줄 해외 업체를 백방으로 수소문했다. 그 결과 이탈리아의 자동차 공방 카로체리아(carrozzeria)와 접촉하게 되었는데, 공방은 원래 마차를 제조하던 곳이었으나 자동차 시대가 열리면서 자동차 차체를 디자인 및 제작하는 용역업체로 발전했다. 현대자동차는 13개 업체에 서한을 보내 고유 모델 디자인 개발 협업 의사를 타진했고, 회신이 온 업체 중 자사 조건에 부합하는 카로체리아 여섯 곳을 직접 방문해 협의를 진행한 끝에 미켈로티와 이탈디자인이 후보군으로 좁혀졌다. 이탈디자인에는 30대 중반의 젊은 디자이너 조르제토 주지아로(Giorgetto Giugiaro)가 있었는데, 그는 폭스바겐의 파사트(Passat)와 골프(Golf), 알파로메오(Alfaromeo)의 줄리아(Giulia) 등을 디자인한 실력자로 자동차업계에서 큰 주목을 받고 있었다. 유서 깊은 명문 미켈로티는 디자인 비용으로 70만 달러를 제안했고, 새롭게 부상하는 이탈디자인은 120만 달러를 요구했다. 둘 중 한 곳을 선택하기는 쉽지 않았다. 공장을 짓기 위해 차관을 들여와야 할 형편인 현대자동차에 차액 50만 달러는 매우 큰 돈이었기 때문이다. 그러나 현대자동차는 심사숙고한 끝에 이탈디자인과 손을 잡았다. 젊은 디자이너의 창의적 아이디어와 열정, 미래의 가능성을 높이 산 과감한 선택이었다.

"솔직히 처음 디자인 의뢰를 받았을 때만 해도 의구심이 컸습니다. 현대자동차에 대해 아는 게 거의 없었고, 이전에 한

Meeting with Giorgetto Giugiaro, a promising young designer

A unique original design is essential when developing an independent model, thus it was top priority on the action list. However, at the time of the knock-down production stage, neither Hyundai nor Korea had human resources capable of designing cars. Therefore, Hyundai checked all possible routes to search for overseas companies to commission for styling and design. Letters were sent to 13 companies inquiring about their intention to collaborate on developing new model designs. Among the companies that responded, Hyundai visited six Carrozzerias that met its conditions to discuss. A Carrozzeria is an automobile workshop in Italy which initially manufactured wagons but evolved into a service company that designed and manufactured car bodies as the automobile era opened. As a result, the candidates were narrowed down to Michelotti and Italdesign. Giorgetto Giugiaro from Italdesign was a young designer in his mid-thirties. As a competent designer who designed the Passat and Golf (Volkswagen) and the Giulia (Alfa Romeo), he drew significant attention in the automotive industry. The prestigious Michelotti offered a price of US $700,000 for design costs, while the emerging Italdesign asked for US $1.2 million. As Hyundai had to borrow money to build its factory, choosing between the two was challenging because the difference of US $500,000 at the time was huge. After careful consideration, Hyundai partnered with Italdesign. A bold choice was made as Hyundai valued the young designer's creative ideas, passion, and potential.

대한민국 최초 대량생산 독자 모델 개발로 향하는 길

The birth of Korea's first mass-produced
independent model

1973년 7월 현대자동차가 카로체리아 열세 곳에 보낸 차체
설계 용역 의뢰 서한
A letter from Hyundai to thirteen carrozzerias
to commission car design services (July 1973)

HYUNDAI MOTOR COMPANY

PHONE
27-5111/9
27-6111/9

ASSEMBLER & OVERSEAS DEALER OF
FORD PRODUCTS

CABLE ADDRESS:
"HYUNDAIMOTOR SEOUL"
TELEX NO: 2391x

9th July 1973

Dear Sirs,

We learned your respectable firm name from Italian Chamber
of Commerce in London, and I am writing this letter in the hope
to receive information from your firm.

We, Hyundai Motor Company, are the leading automobile assembler and manufacturer as a member of Hyundai group which comprises
Hyundai Construction Co as a parent company, a cement manufacturing company, a super tanker shipyard with a 700,000 ton dry dock
and presently constructing 260,000 dwt tankers, and other companies manufacturing various products. The holding company, Hyundai
Construction Co. is one of the largest general contractors in
Korea enjoying good reputation both in domestic and abroad.

In the wake of the present Korean economic growth, our government has assigned us to build our own passenger car model with a
view to developing it to export articles in the possible near
future instead of present confinement to our assembling Ford cars
or third party's cars.
Therefore, we are now greatly obliged to explore our own car model
to begin to build as soon as possible. We are well aware that the
passenger car design is not so easy for us to start from the very
beginning. Our own first car to begin with will be 1100 cc to
1300cc range.

If you have any good car design in that range for our purpose
at the moment, we would like to discuss with you for that design,
and it would be grateful if you could inform us the approximate
cost of the design.

If arrangements are found mutually satisfactory, we would
like to discuss the matter with you both at our office in London
or at your office in Italy.

When you send the letter, would you please send main copy
to:

      H.D. Shin
      Hyundai Motor Company
      55-4 Seosomoon-dong
      Seodaemoon-ku
      Seoul, Korea

and copy to: S.C. Lee
      Hyundai Construction Co., Ltd.
      Zimmer House, 1st Floor
      178 Brompton Road
      London SW3
      United Kingdom
      Telephone 01-584-4237

Anticipating your reply, we thank you in advance for your
kind attention, I remain,

Yours faithfully,

H. D. Shin
Director
Hyundai Motor Company

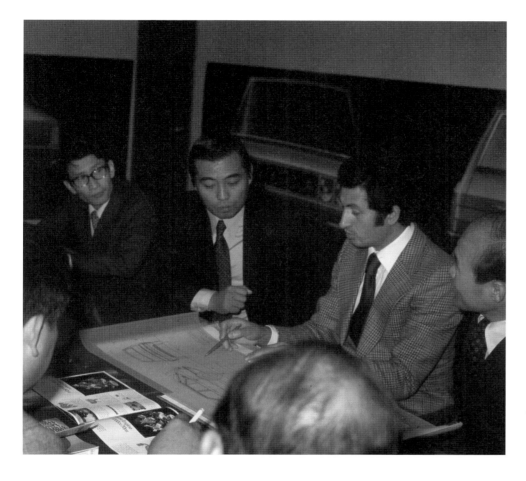

이탈디자인 조르제토 주지아로와 현대자동차 관계자들이
함께한 포니 디자인 회의
Design meeting for Pony, held with Giorgetto
Giugiaro and Hyundai officials

국 기업과 인연을 맺은 적도 없었으니까요. 게다가 포드의 코
티나를 조립 생산하고 있다고 해도 고유 모델 양산은 차원이
다른 일이었죠. 하지만 현대자동차 울산 공장과 울산 조선소
현장을 직접 둘러본 후 확신을 갖게 됐어요. 고유 모델 개발
과 완성차 공장 건설에 대한 현대자동차의 의지는 굳건했고,
특히 울산 연안의 선박 건조 현장은 놀라움 그 자체였습니다.
3년도 채 안 되는 기간에 대형 유조선을 건조할 수 있을 만
큼 빠르게 성장했다는 설명에 강렬한 인상을 받았습니다."
(조르제토 주지아로)

1973년 9월 이탈디자인과 차체 설계 용역 계약을 체결한 지
한 달여 만에 주지아로가 네 종류의 스타일 스케치를 보내왔
다. 그해 10월 정주영 선대회장, 정세영 당시 사장 등 관계자
가 참석한 가운데 최종 디자인을 선정했고, 이후 선정된 디
자인을 바탕으로 기본 도면과 품평 모델 제작에 들어갔다. 약
4개월 후인 1974년 2월 이탈디자인에서 모델 품평회를 열
고 일부 수정을 거쳐 당시 최신 트렌드였던 전면이 길고 후면
이 짧은 롱노즈 패스트백(long-nose fast-back) 스타일의
'꽁지 빠진 닭' 모양 디자인이 확정되었다. 이 디자인은 감각

"To be honest, I had doubts when I first received the design request. I knew very little about Hyundai Group and never had a relationship with a Korean company. In addition, even if they made Ford Cortina, mass production of an original model was at a different level. However, I was convinced after touring the Hyundai Motor Ulsan plant and the Ulsan shipyard. Their commitment to developing their own models and building a complete vehicle manufacturing plant was genuine, and the shipbuilding site off the coast of Ulsan came to me as a surprise. I was impressed by the explanation that the company had grown so quickly enough to build large tankers in less than three years." (Giorgetto Giugiaro)

About a month after signing the body design contract with Italdesign in September 1973, Giugiaro sent four sketches, and one was selected by Founding Chairman Chung, then-President Se-yung Chung, and other officials. Afterward, basic drawings and evaluation models of the chosen design were produced. About four months later, in February 1974, Italdesign held a design presentation. After some modifications, the long-nose fast-back (long front and short end) style following the latest trends at that time was confirmed. This design was stylish yet practical, and its straight-line styling made it easier to mass-produce by lowering the difficulty of the press die. At the end of February 1974, work for engineering design began. In March, the construction of a prototype began and on October 30, the Pony and Pony Coupe prototypes were finally exhibited at the Turin Motor Show. After selecting these two models' designs, it

대한민국 최초 대량생산 독자 모델 개발로 향하는 길

The birth of Korea's first mass-produced
independent model

대한민국 최초 대량생산 독자 모델 개발로 향하는 길

The birth of Korea's first mass-produced
independent model

이탈디자인에서 진행된 포니 모델 품평회(1974년 2월)
The Pony design presentation held at Italdesign
(February 1974)

당시 3-박스형 세단에 익숙했던 한국인에게 유럽의 최신 트렌드가 반영된 포니의
2-박스형 롱노즈 패스트백 차형은 신선하게 다가왔다. 이에 현대자동차에서는
포니의 디자인을 '꽁지 빠진 닭' 같다고 평가했다.

Koreans were used to the three-box sedans, so it was a surprise
when Pony brought Europe's latest trends in its two-box fastback
construction to Korea. Hyundai said that Pony's design resembled a
rooster without a tail.

적이고 실용적이면서도 직선 기조의 스타일링으로 프레스 금형의 난도를 낮춰 보다 쉽게 양산할 수 있다는 점을 고려해 개발되었다. 1974년 2월 말에는 설계 업무가 시작되었고, 3월부터는 시험 차인 프로토타입을 제작했으며, 10월 30일 마침내 '포니'와 '포니 쿠페'가 토리노 모터쇼에 출품되었다. 두 모델의 디자인을 선정한 후 프로토타입을 제작해 모터쇼에 출품하기까지 약 1년이라는 매우 짧은 시간이 소요되었는데, 이는 한국인 특유의 끈기와 성실성, 그리고 이탈리아인의 투철한 장인 정신과 자신감이 어우러져 이룬 결과였다.

took only about one year to develop and present a prototype for the motor show, thanks to the combination of the persistence and diligence of the Koreans and the craftsmanship and confidence of the Italians.

SCHEDULE B

PROGRAM TIMING:
Activities

TIME

1. Arrival of white body and BU Car from Hyundai

By 10. Oct. 1973

2. Master Drawing for presentation Model

10/29 - 11/30, 1973

3. Completion of Presentation model

11/30,73 - 1/31, 74

4. Prototype construction n.1

3/15 - 6/30, 74 (shipped to Hyundai)

5. Prototype construction n.2

9/20 - 11/30, 74

6. Prototype construction n.3

9/20 - 11/30, 74

7. Prototype construction (Coupé)

6/1 - 10/30, 74 (for Turin Motor Show and shipped to Hyunda

이탈디자인과 체결한 차체 설계 용역 계약서 중 일정 관련 조항
Provisions related to the schedule in the body and chassis work contract signed with Italdesign

약 1년이라는 대단히 짧은 기간에 모델 디자인부터 프로토타입을 제작해 토리노 모터쇼에 출품하기까지 방대한 업무가 진행되었다.
Within the short time period of a year, extensive work was carried out for the submission for the Turin Motor Show ranging from model design to prototype creation.

포니 디자인 후보 - 렌더링
A Pony design candidate - renderings

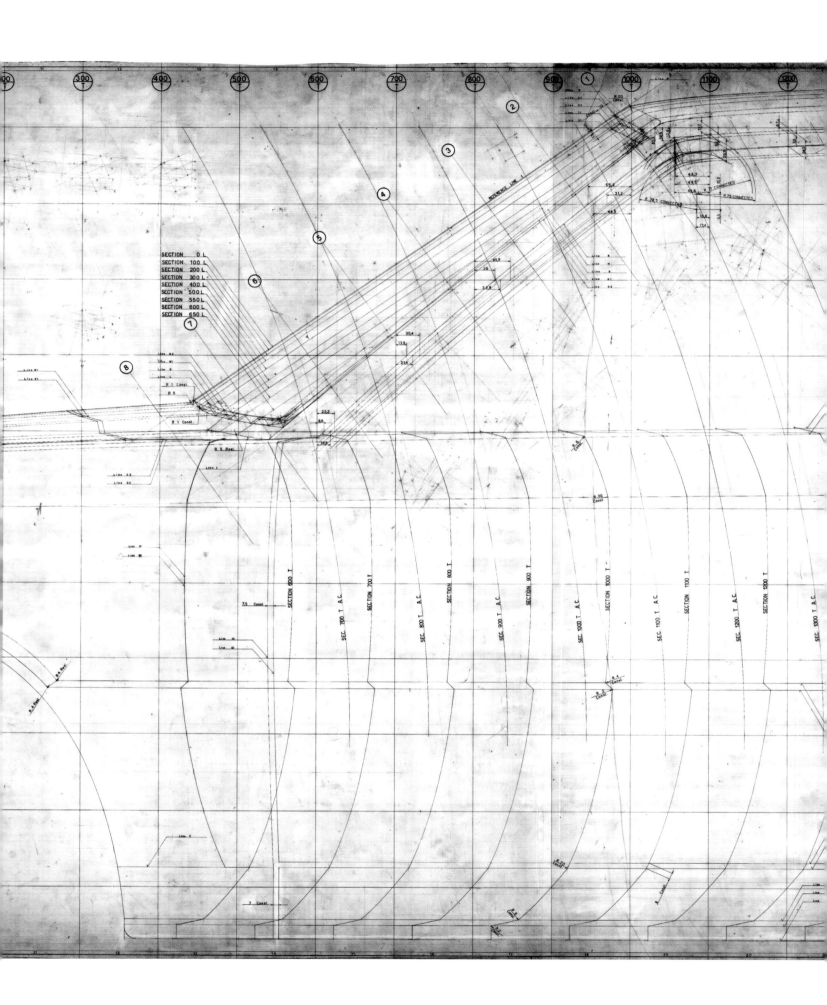

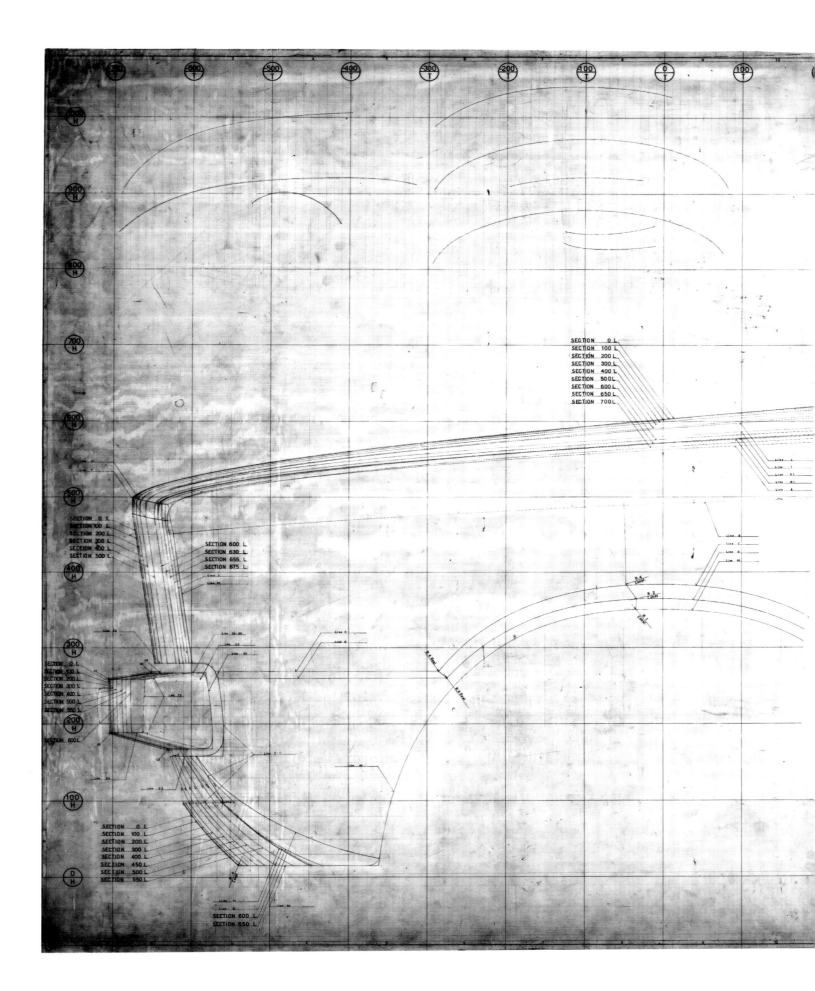

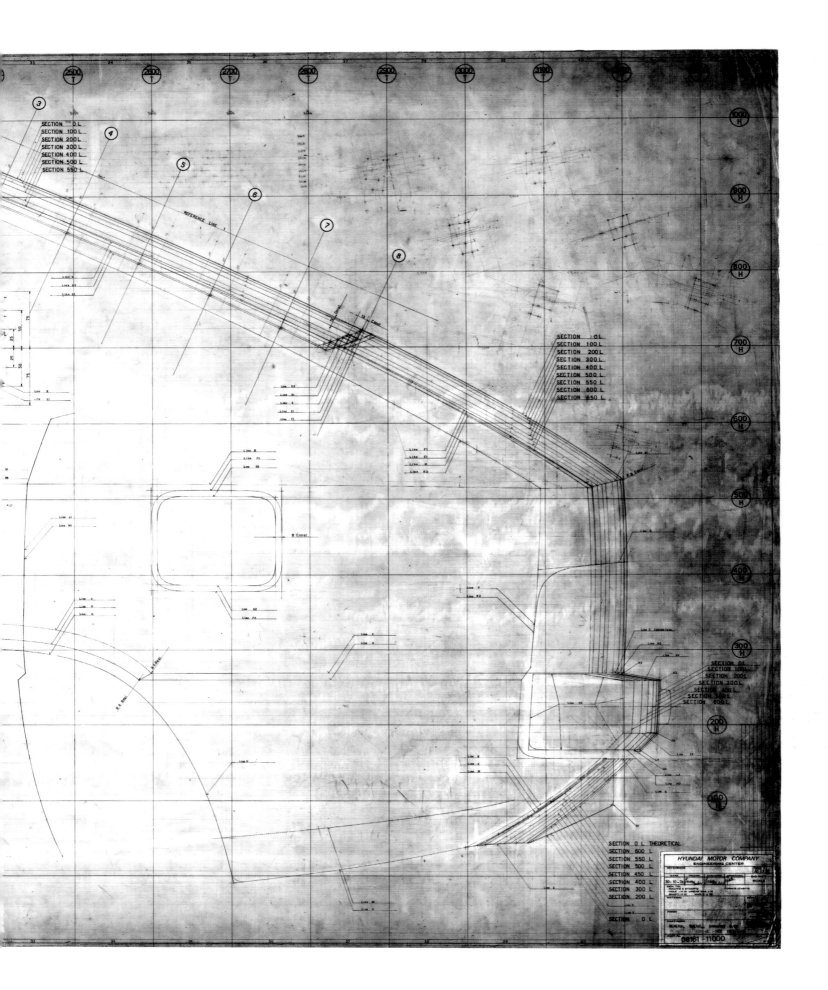

HYUNDAI MOTOR COMPANY
ENGINEERING CENTER

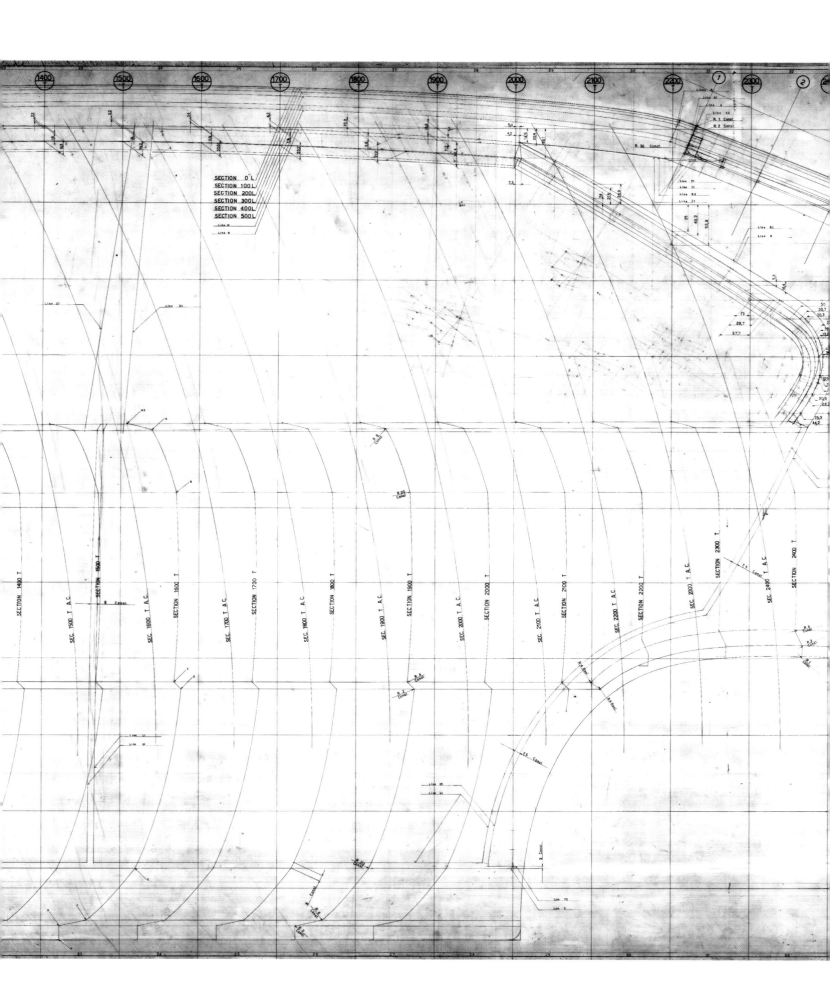

포니 디자인 후보 - 렌더링(전면 및 후면)
A Pony design candidate - renderings (front and back)

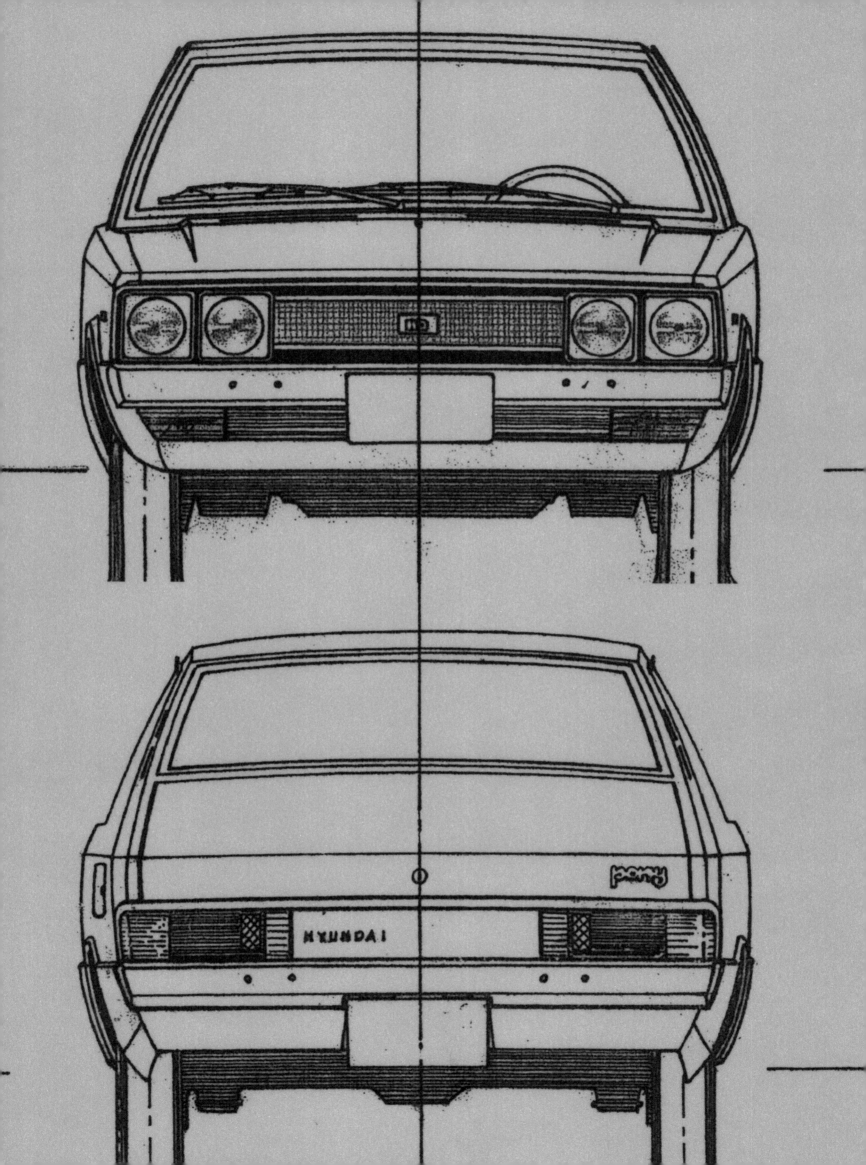

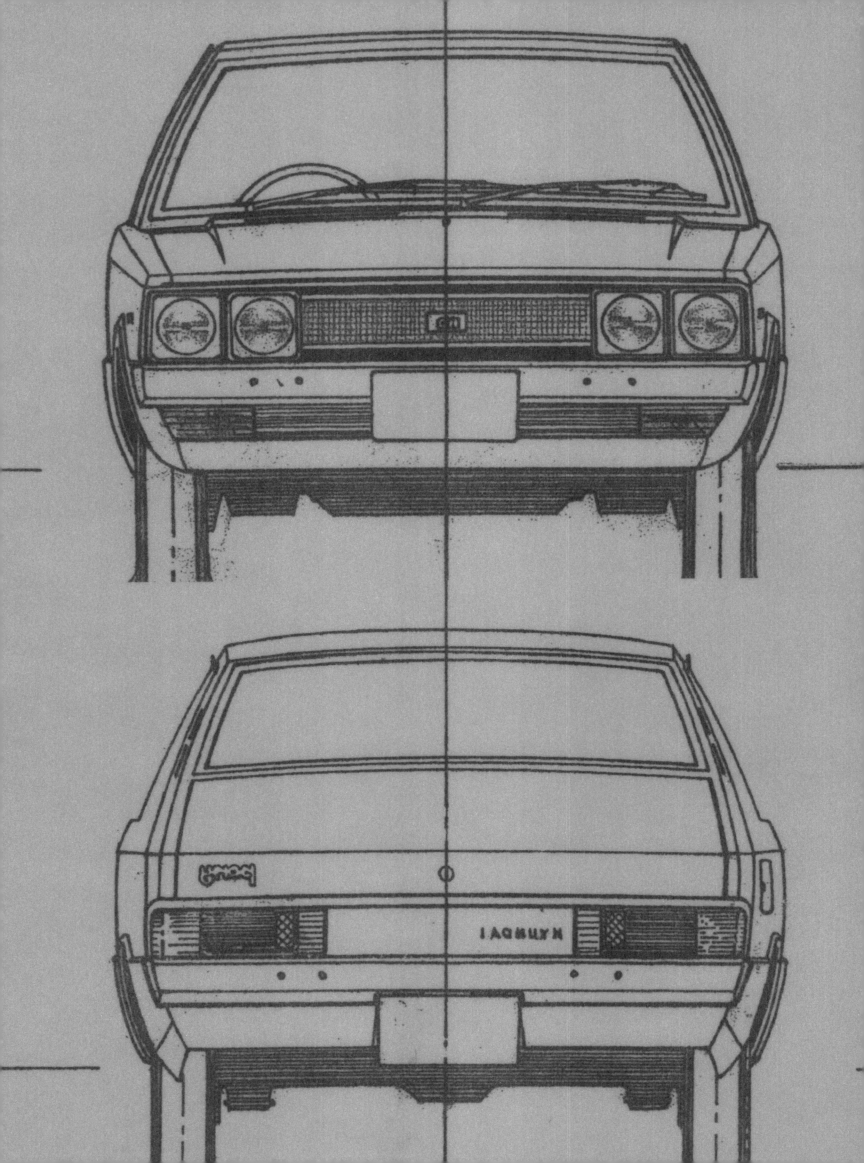

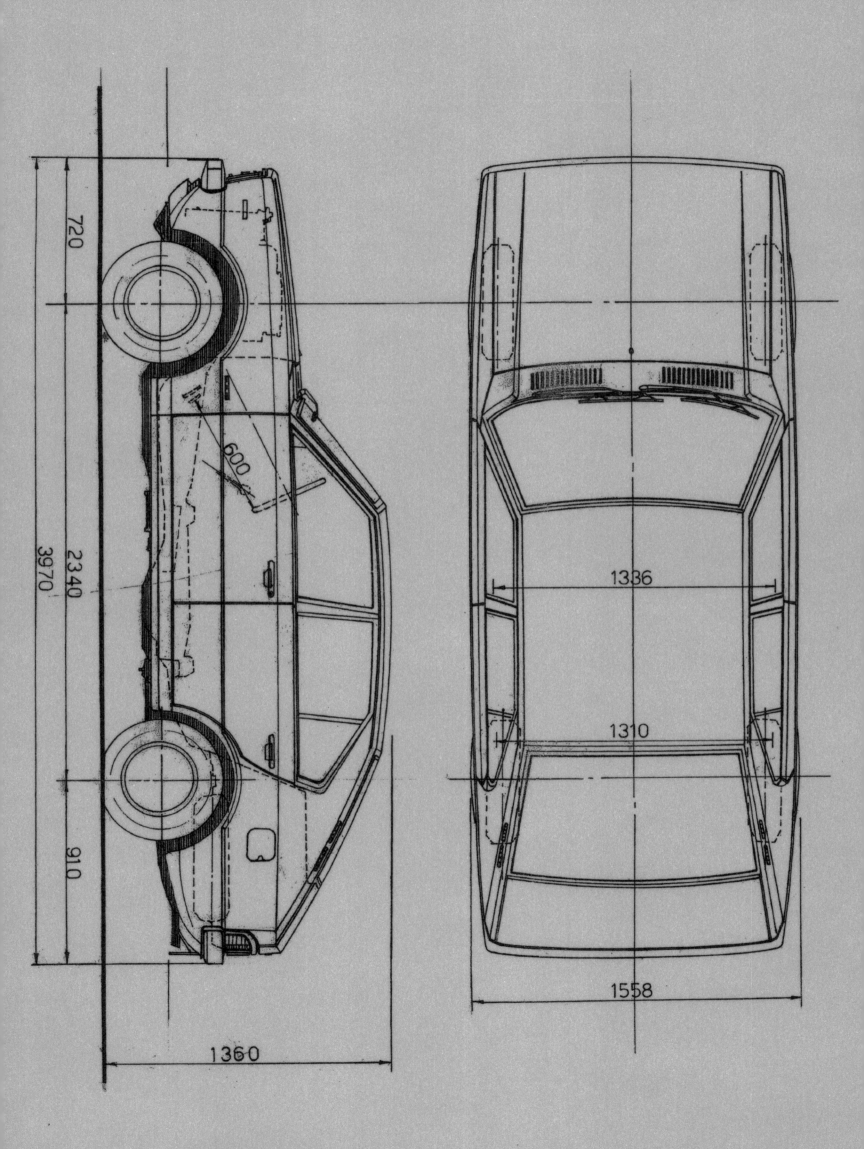

720

600

2340

3970

910

1360

1336

1310

1558

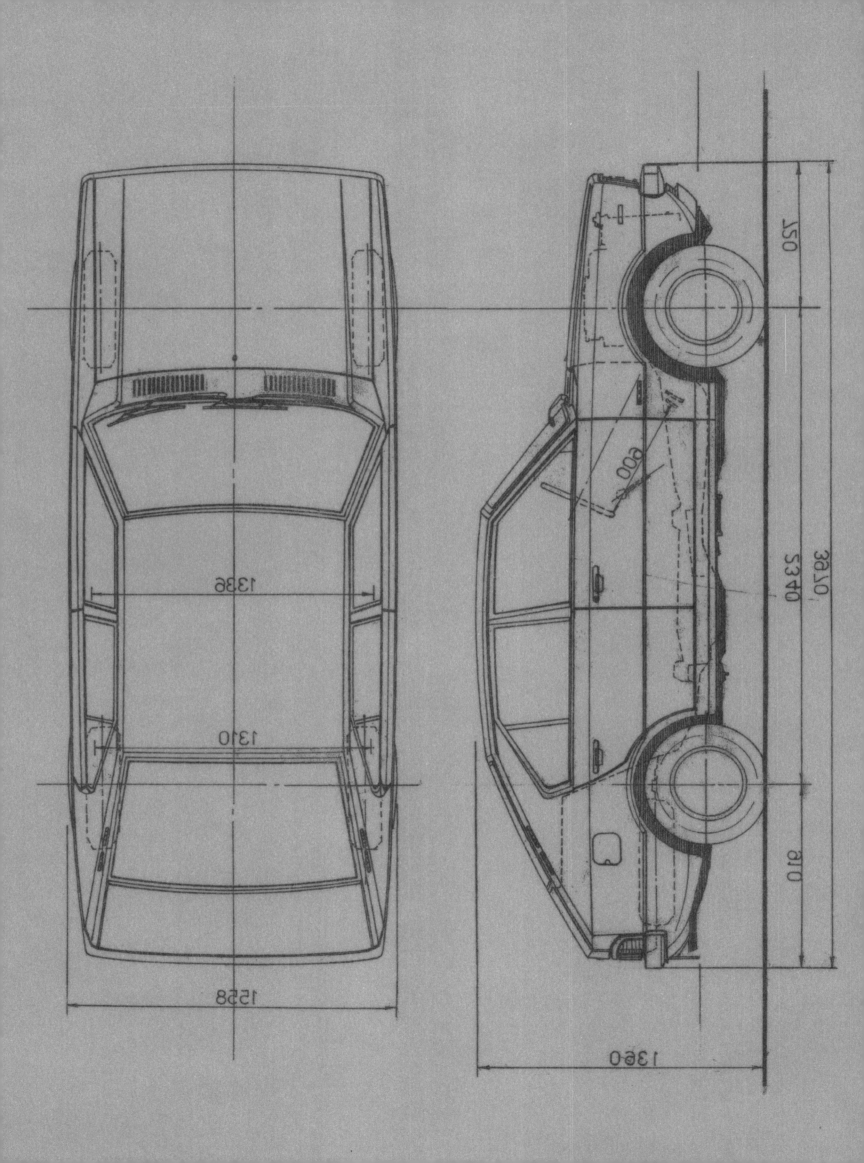

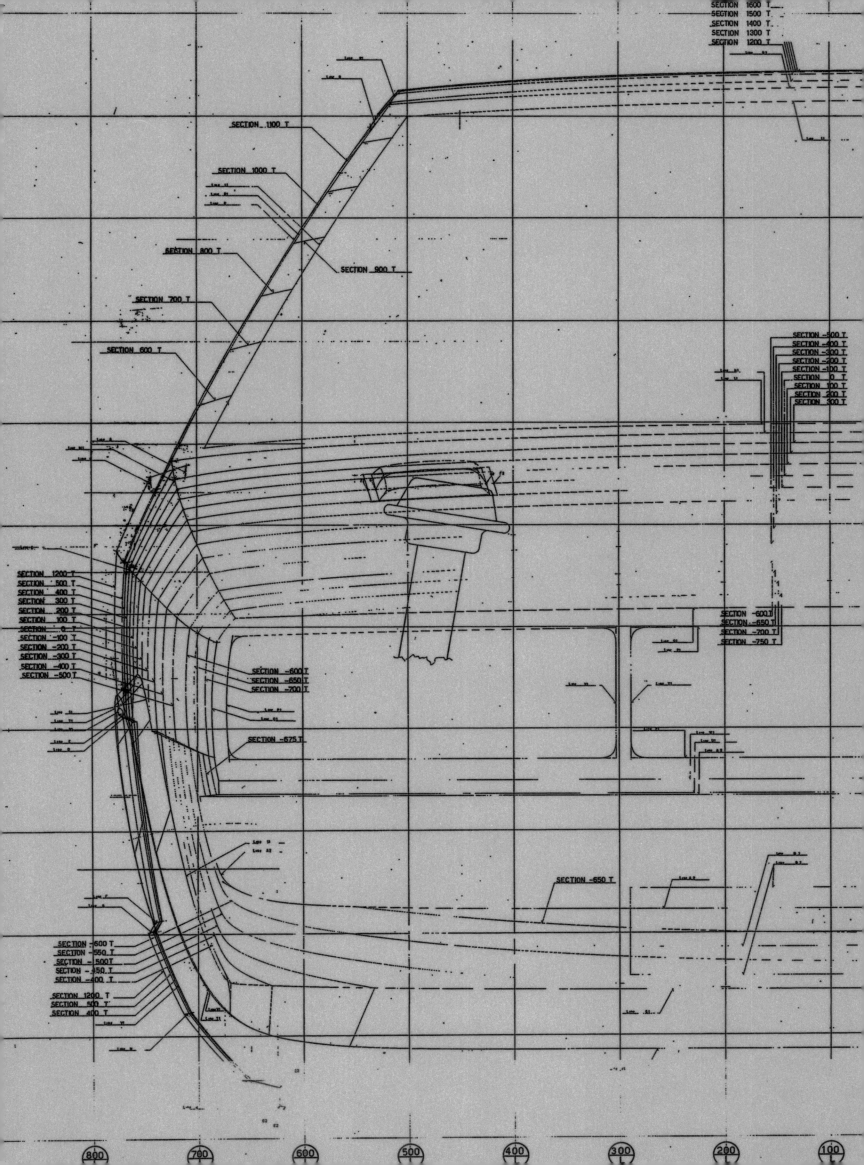

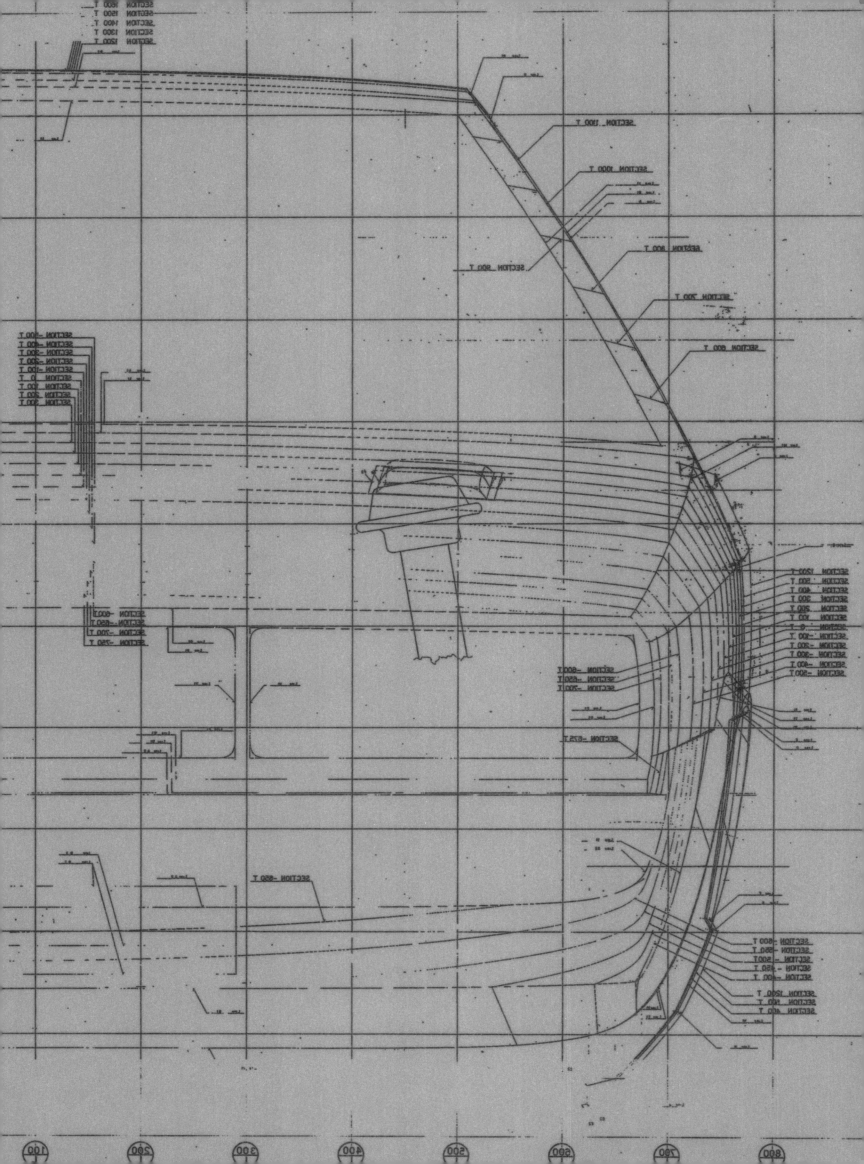

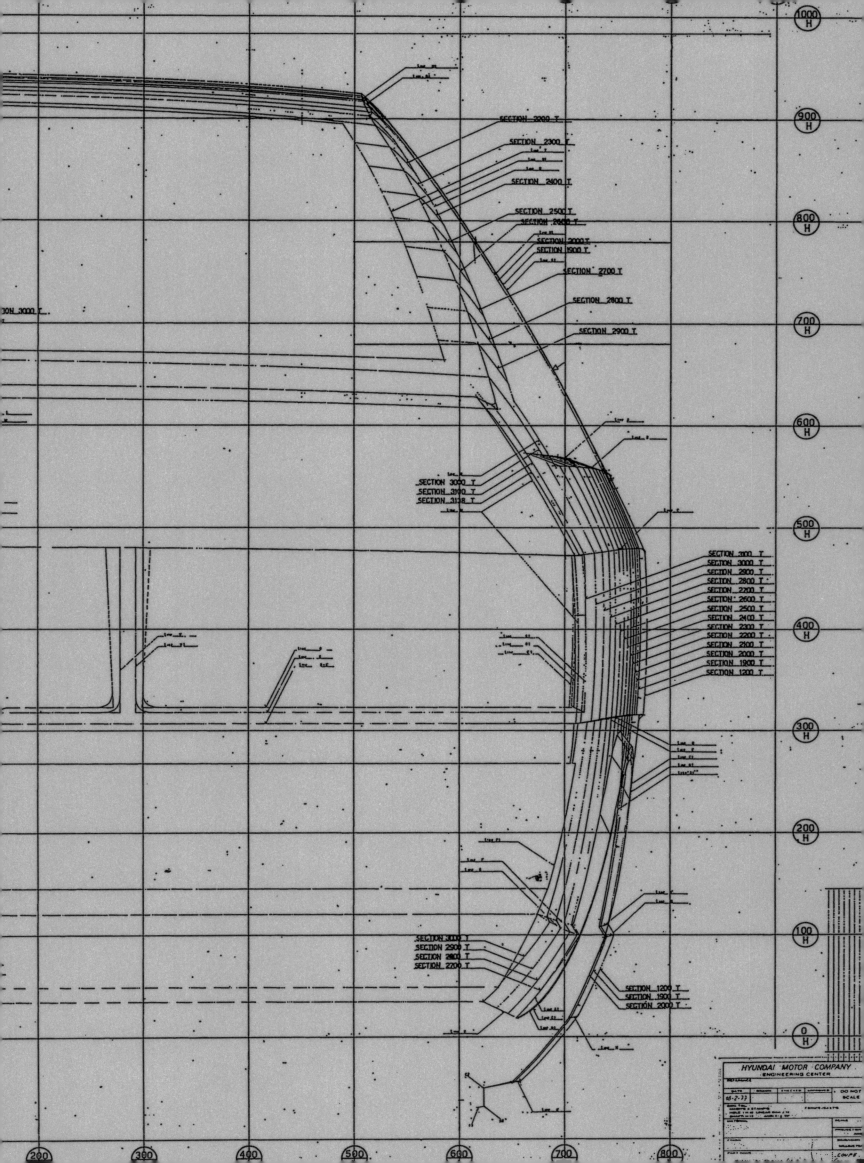

SECTION 2200 T
SECTION 2300 T
SECTION 2400 T
SECTION 2500 T
SECTION 2600 T
SECTION 2000 T
SECTION 1900 T
SECTION 2700 T
SECTION 2800 T
SECTION 2900 T

SECTION 3000 T
SECTION 3100 T
SECTION 3138 T

SECTION 3000 T
SECTION 3000 T
SECTION 2900 T
SECTION 2800 T
SECTION 2700 T
SECTION 2600 T
SECTION 2500 T
SECTION 2400 T
SECTION 2300 T
SECTION 2200 T
SECTION 2100 T
SECTION 2000 T
SECTION 1900 T
SECTION 1200 T

SECTION 3000 T
SECTION 2900 T
SECTION 2800 T
SECTION 2200 T

SECTION 1200 T
SECTION 1900 T
SECTION 2000 T

HYUNDAI MOTOR COMPANY
ENGINEERING CENTER

DO NOT
SCALE

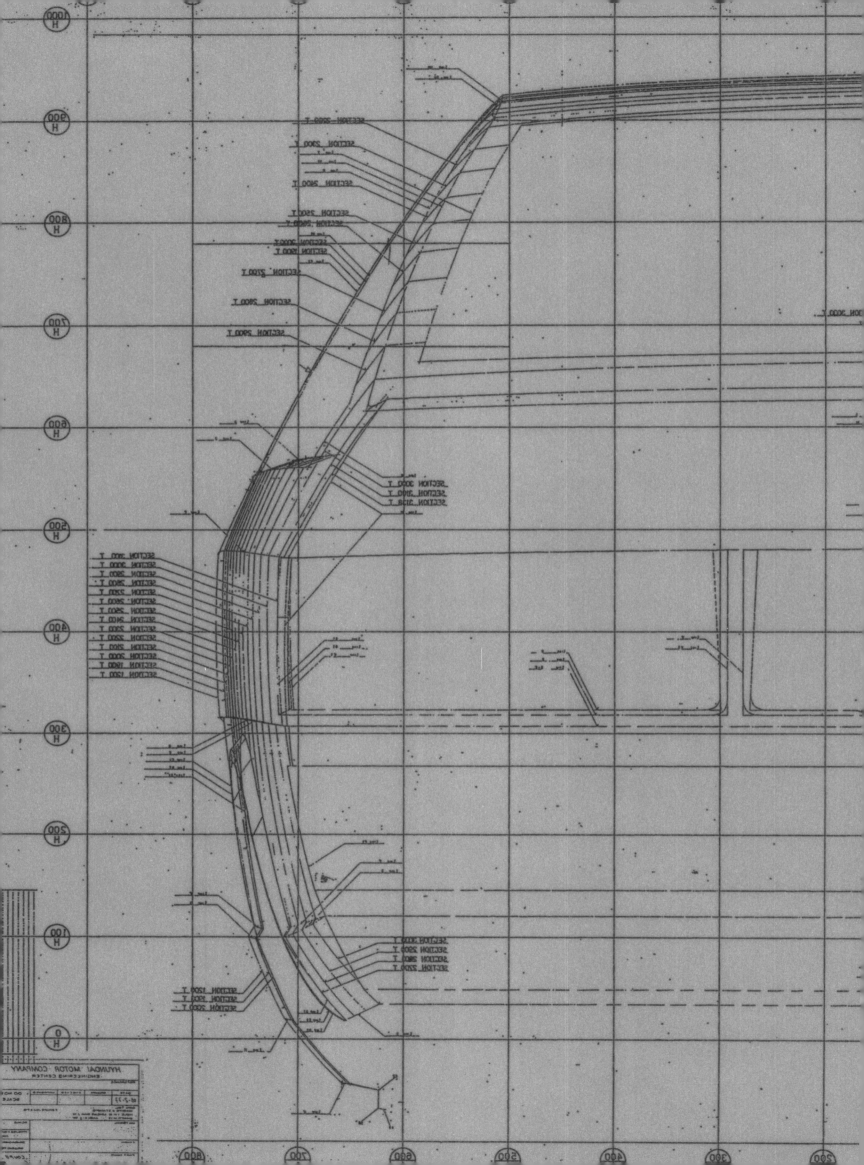

포니 쿠페 디자인 후보 - 렌더링
A Pony Coupe design candidate -
renderings

포니 쿠페 렌더링
The Pony Coupe rendering

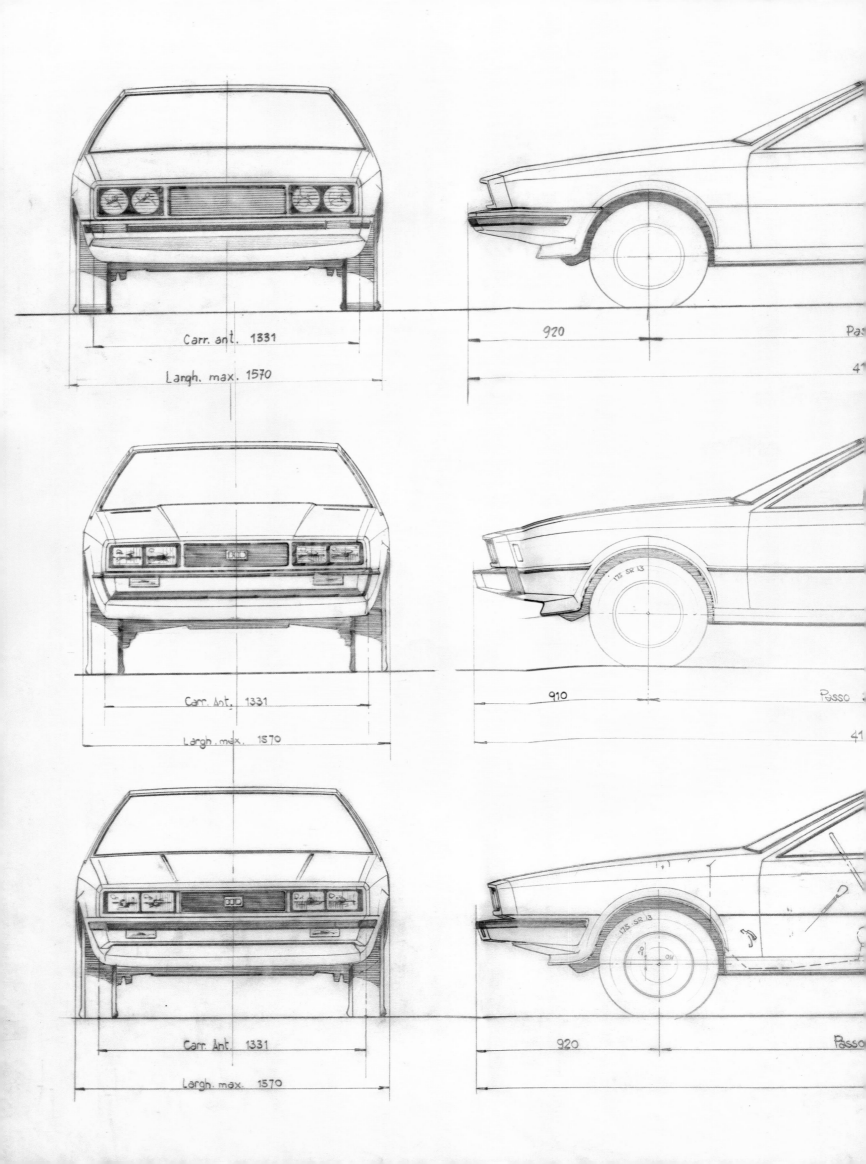

Carr. ant. 1331

Largh. max. 1570

920

Pas

41

Carr. Ant. 1331

Largh. max. 1570

910

Passo

41

Carr. Ant. 1331

Largh. max. 1570

920

Passo

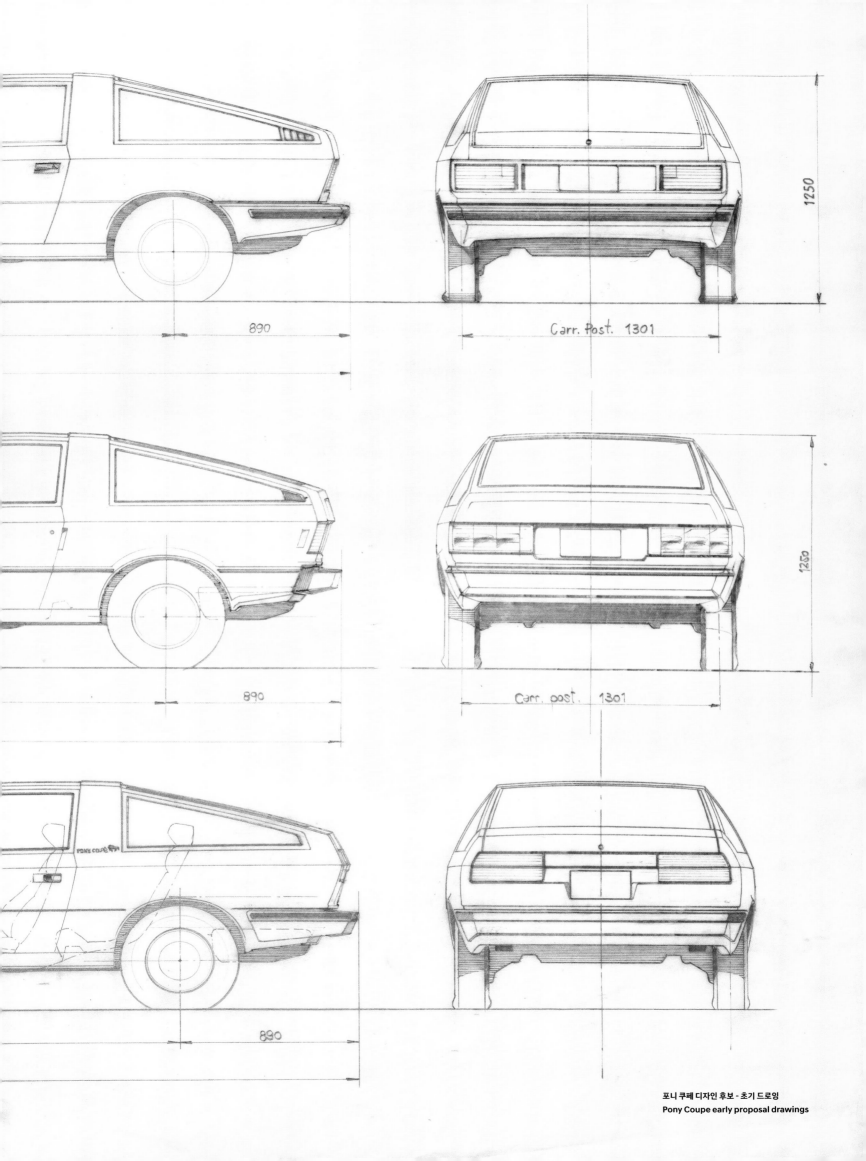

890

Carr. Post. 1301

1250

890

Carr. post. 1301

1250

890

포니 쿠페 디자인 후보 - 초기 드로잉
Pony Coupe early proposal drawings

현대자동차가 주도한 다국적 드림팀 결성

차체 설계 용역 계약과 플랫폼 기술 협조 계약은 거의 동시다
발적으로 추진됐다. 특히 엔진, 변속기, 서스펜션 등 자동차
기술의 핵심인 플랫폼의 경우 미국, 유럽, 일본 등 거의 모든
자동차 기업에 기술 협력 가능성을 타진했으나 뚜렷한 성과
가 없었다. 하지만 어떻게든 새로운 길을 개척하겠다는 현대
자동차의 의지와 긍정적 자세가 그다음 활로를 만들어냈다.

현대자동차는 정주영 선대회장이 조선소 건설 과정
에서 미쓰비시의 구보 도미오(久保富夫) 회장과 인연을 다
진 적이 있는 바, 마지막으로 미쓰비시를 찾아가 플랫폼 기
술 협조를 요청했다. 그러나 미쓰비시는 추후 경쟁자로 성장
할 가능성이 있는 현대와의 기술 제휴를 망설이며 확답을 회
피했다. 이런 상황에서 1973년 7월 현대자동차가 디젤엔진
을 생산하는 영국의 매시 퍼거슨 퍼킨스(Massey Ferguson
Perkins)사와 체결한 기술 계약은 당시 가장 유력한 협상 파
트너였던 미쓰비시를 자극하기에 충분했다. 퍼킨스사와 현
대자동차가 계약을 맺자 미쓰비시가 적극적인 자세로 협상
에 임하기 시작한 것이다. 현대자동차의 추진력으로 미루어
짐작하건대 독자 모델 개발은 반드시 이루어질 것이 분명하
니, 다른 회사에 기회를 주기보다 차라리 먼저 계약을 맺는 것
이 이익이라고 판단한 것이다.

당시 미쓰비시 자동차 교토 제작소 책임자였던 아라이
세이유(荒井齊勇) 소장은 현대자동차가 엔진을 제조할 역
량을 갖추고 있는지 살핀 후 기술 제휴 여부를 최종 판단하겠
다는 계획으로 한국을 방문했다. 현대자동차 울산 공장 현장
을 둘러본 아라이 소장은 처음에는 공장의 빈약한 수준에 실
망했다고 한다. 하지만 경주를 관광하며 다양한 유물을 유심
히 살펴보고는 '이런 작품을 만든 민족이라면 엔진도 충분히
만들 수 있겠다'고 생각을 바꾸고 현대자동차와의 기술 제휴

A multinational dream team led by Hyundai Motor Company

The body design contract and platform technology cooperation contract were advanced
almost simultaneously. Hyundai had especially
explored the possibility of technical cooperation with nearly all automotive companies in
the United States, Europe, and Japan to gain
platforms (especially for engines, transmissions,
and suspensions), the core of automobile parts.
But there was no apparent result. However,
Hyundai's positive attitude and its will to pio-
neer a new path had somehow created one.

During the shipyard construction process,
Chung was acquainted with Chairman Kubo of
Mitsubishi. So Hyundai visited Mitsubishi and
asked for cooperation regarding platform technology as a last resort. However, Mitsubishi hes-
itated to form a technical alliance with Hyundai,
which had the potential to grow into a competitor in the future, and avoided giving a definite
answer. In this situation, the technical contract
signed by Hyundai in July 1973 with Massey
Ferguson Perkins of England, which produced
diesel engines, was enough to provoke Mitsubishi, the most influential negotiating partner
at the time. After Perkins and Hyundai entered
into a contract, Mitsubishi started negotiating
enthusiastically. Judging from Hyundai's progress, the development of its independent model
would undoubtedly be carried out in any means,
so Mitsubishi made the decision that collabo-
rating with Hyundai would be better than giving
opportunities to other companies.

Director Arai, then in charge of Mitsubishi
Motors Kyoto Works, visited Korea with the in-

技 術 協 助 契 約

本契約은 日本国 東京에 本社를 두고 日本国 法律下에 組織된 法人體 '미쓰비시' 自動車株式会社 (以下 '미쓰비시' 라고 称하며 이는 以後의 承継者 와 指名人을 包含한다)와 大韓民国 서울에 本社를 갖고 大韓民国 法律下에 組織된 法人體인 現代自動車株式会社 (以下 '現代' 라고 称하며 이는 以後의 承継者와 指名人을 包含한다) 사이로 1973年 9月 20日字로 締結된 契約임

證

이에 現代는 以下 定義된 認可製品들을 韓国에서 組立, 製造할 権利와 販 売할 権利를 獲得하기를 願하며 그리고 이와 関聯한 技術協助 및 技術資料 를 獲得하기를 願하는 바이며 미쓰비시는 現代에게 그러한 権利를 賦与하고 그러한 技術에 対한 技術協助와 技術資料를 提供하고 現代가 이를 提供받도 록 周旋할 立場에 있으며, 이에 当事者는 下記와 같이 合意한다.

1. 定義

本契約의 文脈上 單数가 複数의 意味를 包含하기도 하며 이와 反対로 複数가 單数의 意味를 包含하기도 한다. 그리고 下記의 表現들은 下記와 같은 意味를 各各 나타낸다.

1.1 '認可製品'이라 함은 技術的인 変更事項을 包含하여 附表 A에 明示 된 미쓰비시 가소린 엔진, 트랜스밋숀 및 리야엑슬을 意味한다.

1.2 '部分品'이라 함은 本契約条件과 一致하여 韓国内에서 現代에 依 해 或은 現代를 代身하여 製造 및 組立되는 認可製品에 使用되는 部品, 組 立品 및 小組立品을 意味한다. 但, 認可製品을 為한 代替部品은 除外한다.

1.3 'A/S部品'이라 함은 認可製品을 為한 代替部品으로써 使用되는 部分品을 意味한다.

IV - 89

附

技 術 訓

職 責
工 程 技 士
工 務 技 士
工 具 設計技士
工具研磨 - 工 具
補修担当 - 工 具
自動制御装置技術者
生 産 技 士
機械加工班長
機械加工担当工具
組 立 班 長
品質管理技士
加 工 検査員
試験検査員

附

本契約 3.8条에

提供되

미쓰비시에 依하여 現代에 提供되
및 1.3의 部分品 또는 部品 56
基準으로 生産하기 為한 加工 및
된 品目을 1日 10時間, 年 300日
施設의 建設을 包含한다.

1973년 9월 20일 자로 체결된 미쓰비시와의
가솔린 엔진 기술 협조 계약서
A technological cooperation agreement for
a gasoline engine, signed with Mitsubishi on
September 20, 1973

에 긍정적 의사를 표명했다. 이렇게 1973년 9월 현대자동차와 미쓰비시 간 가솔린 엔진, 변속기 및 후차축 제조 기술 도입 계약이 극적으로 성사됐다. 이 계약으로 현대자동차가 미쓰비시에 지불해야 할 로열티는 상당했지만, 미쓰비시 랜서의 플랫폼에 조르제토 주지아로가 디자인한 보디를 씌운 대한민국 최초의 대량 양산형 독자 모델 '포니'의 탄생에 한 발 더 다가설 수 있게 되었다.

이제 남은 과제는 실제 양산 시스템 구축을 담당할 적임자를 찾는 것이었다. 공교롭게도 그즈음 정세영 당시 사장은 엔지니어 출신으로 영국 최대 자동차 그룹 BLMC(British Leyland Motor Corporation) 부사장이었던 조지 턴불이 경쟁자와의 파워 게임에 밀려 사임했다는 소식을 접하고 영입을 제안한다. 그러나 영국 자동차업계의 거물이 잘 알려지지 않은 개발도상국 신생 자동차 회사의 영입 제안에 흔쾌히 응할 리가 없었다. 지속적인 설득 끝에 그를 한국으로 초청한 현대자동차는 울산 조선소 건설 현장과 울산 공장을 보여주며 "현대자동차는 아직 아무도 손대지 않은 원석과 같다"라는 말로 성장 잠재력을 강조했다. 이 같은 노력의 결실로

tention of making a final decision regarding a technical alliance after checking whether Hyundai had the capabilities to manufacture engines. Touring Hyundai's Ulsan factory site, he said he was initially disappointed with the poor quality of the factory. However, after carefully looking at various historical artifacts while touring Gyeongju, he changed his mind, saying, "if the people in Korea could create such a work of art, they could surely make engines as well," expressing a positive intention for a technical partnership with Hyundai. Thereafter, in September 1973, Hyundai and Mitsubishi dramatically concluded and signed a contract to introduce manufacturing technologies for gasoline engines, transmissions, and rear axles. This contract required Hyundai to pay Mitsubishi substantial royalties. However, Hyundai moved one step closer to the birth of the Pony, Korea's first mass-produced independent model with a body designed by Giorgetto Giugiaro on the Mitsubishi Lancer platform.

The remaining task was to find the right person to oversee building the actual mass production system. Coincidentally, around that time, then-President Se-yung Chung proposed the recruitment of George Turnbull, a former engineer and Vice President of British Leyland Motor Corporation (BLMC), after hearing that he had resigned following a power struggle with a competitor. However, it took a lot of work for the British car giant to accept an offer from an unknown developing country's company. Hyundai invited him to Korea after persistent persuasion and showed him the Ulsan shipyard construction site as well as the Ulsan factory, emphasizing its growth potential with the

포니 차체 설계 현안을 기재한 문서(1974년 7월)
Documents regarding Pony's body
engineering queries (July 1974)

19.   Rear Fender & D-Post

These two panels may be made as separate parts instead of
being a single panel. This is considered desirable to
reduce the complications of tool design, however if it is
possible to make the two pieces economically it is also
important that the welding condition where the two panels
meet is carefully studied to ensure neat welding.

As you will see from the foregoing there are many detail
changes which are already in hand at I.D. having been accepted
by them as sensible and practicable. There are however
matters which are still under discussion with the I.D.
designers and which are being progressed and handled by
Mr. J. W. Jeong and his team. These will need continual
review and follow-up and I would like to discuss with you
the most effective and practical way that we can confirm
the action being taken by Mr. Jeong and also give him
assistance and instruction as necessary from time to time.

When we establish a full drawing office system at Ulsan for
the Body Engineering Department under Mr. Barnett these
changes can be handled directly between Ulsan and I.D.
provided they do not affect changes in the cost of the
timing of the overall program. Only in cases where timing,
cost or visual appearance is affected should headquarters
be consulted.

Perhaps you would like to think over this question and
let me have your proposals as to how we should deal with
these changes now and in the future.

G. H. Turnbull

GHT/dbk

1974년 3월 조지 턴불이 현대자동차 부사장으로 취임함으로써 포니 프로젝트에 합류하게 된다. 이렇게 이탈리아, 일본, 영국 등 각국의 자동차업계를 대표하는 전문가와 현대자동차가 만나는 다국적 드림팀이 결성되면서 포니 프로젝트가 본격적으로 가동될 수 있게 된 것이다.

words, "Hyundai Motor Company is like a gem-stone that no one has yet touched." As a result of these efforts, in March 1974, George Turnbull took office as Vice President of Hyundai and joined the Pony project. With the formation of a multinational dream team between Hyundai and experts from Italy, Japan, and the United Kingdom, the Pony project was able to move forward in full swing.

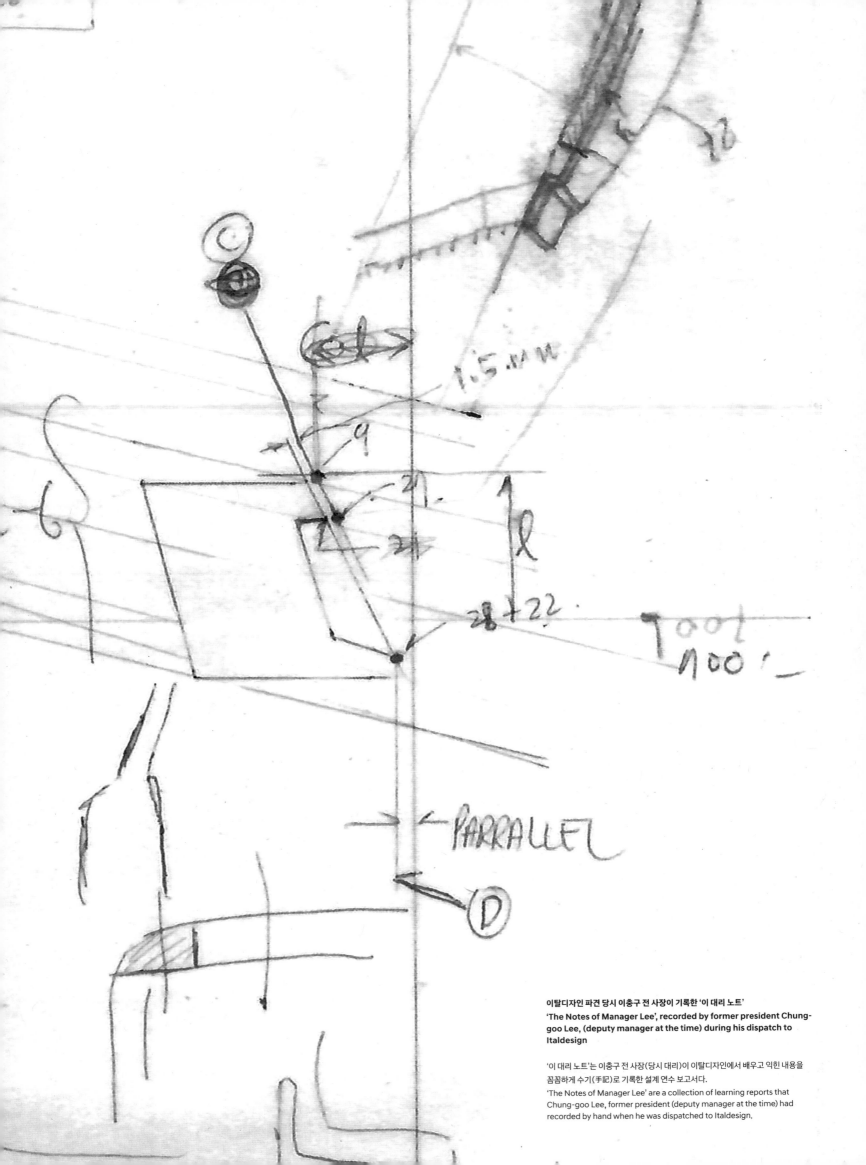

이탈디자인 파견 당시 이충구 전 사장이 기록한 '이 대리 노트'
'The Notes of Manager Lee', recorded by former president Chung-goo Lee, (deputy manager at the time) during his dispatch to Italdesign

'이 대리 노트'는 이충구 전 사장(당시 대리)이 이탈디자인에서 배우고 익힌 내용을 꼼꼼하게 수기(手記)로 기록한 설계 연수 보고서다.
'The Notes of Manager Lee' are a collection of learning reports that Chung-goo Lee, former president (deputy manager at the time) had recorded by hand when he was dispatched to Italdesign.

17. DOOR INNER PANEL 作圖

2. 1) DOOR INNER PANEL 의 ⓐ L화트 결정 (DOOR OUTERPNL ~ INNE
   PANEL 의 톡격함) 요소.
   ① DOOR REGULATOR 작동 레졍 STUDY
   ② DOOR REINF. STRUCTURE DIM. STUDY
   ③ DOOR LOCK SYSTEM STUDY
   ④ DOOR HINGE STUDY

   ⓑ*FRT DOOR 경우 DOOR INNER PNL은 L화트가 전부目-하려
   L668 선을 지난다.

18. DOOR HEADER PANEL 線 作圖 — FRT VIEW에

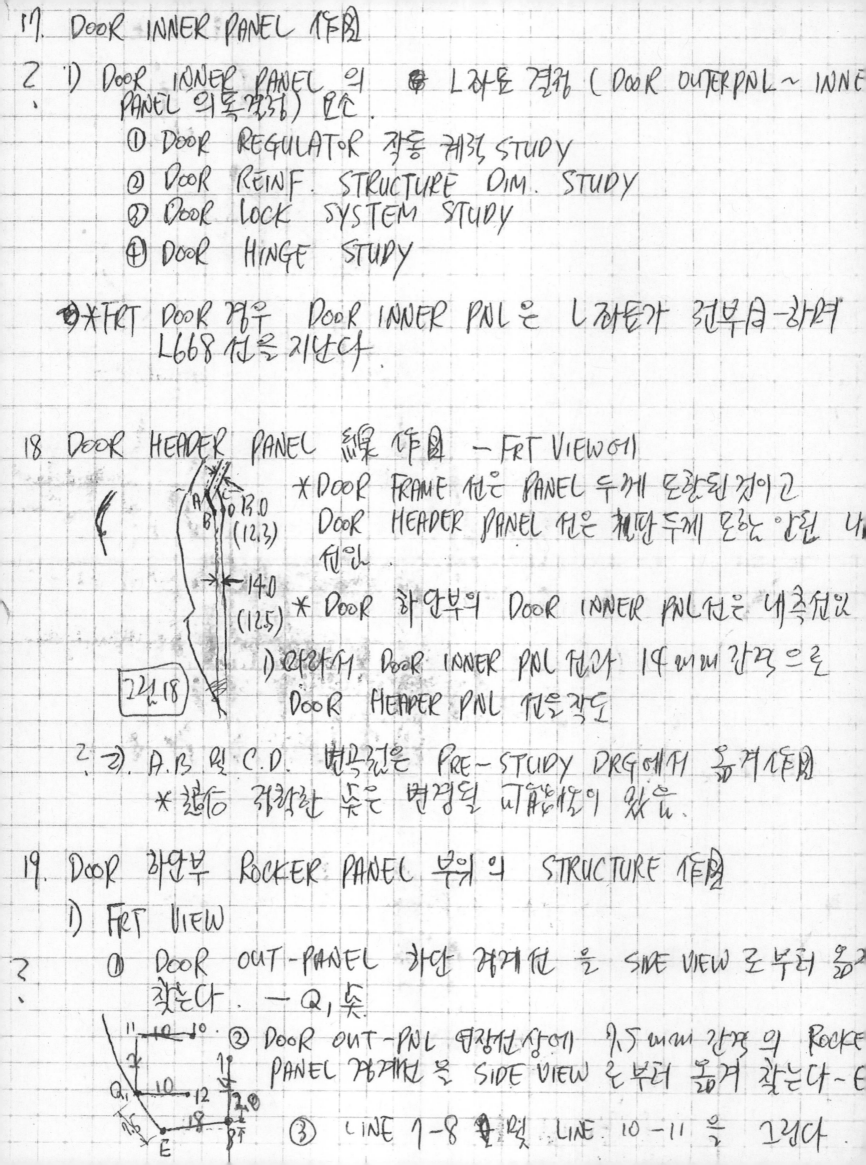

*DOOR FRAME 선은 PANEL 두께 도랑된것이고
 DOOR HEADER PANEL 선은 체딴두게 또랑 안린 나
 선이다.

* DOOR 하안부의 DOOR INNER PNL선은 내측선있

1) 여라서 DOOR INNER PNL 선과 14 미미 간격으로
   DOOR HEADER PNL 선은작도

2. 2). A.B 및 C.D. 변곡겂은 PRE-STUDY DRG에서 옮겨作圖
   * 최ㅎ 거랑한 ㅎ는 변경될 吋合ㅎ이 였음.

19. DOOR 하안부 ROCKER PANEL 부위의 STRUCTURE 作圖

   1) FRT VIEW

   ① DOOR OUT-PANEL 하단 겨계선 을 SIDE VIEW로부러 옮
     작는다. — Q, 옽

   ② DOOR OUT-PNL 연장선 상에 9.5 미미 간경의 ROCKE
     PANEL 겨계선 을 SIDE VIEW 로부러 옮겨 작는다 — E

   ③ LINE 7-8 및 LINE 10-11 을 그렸다

④ [illegible]
6과 7을 잇는다

⑤ 점 9를 찾는다

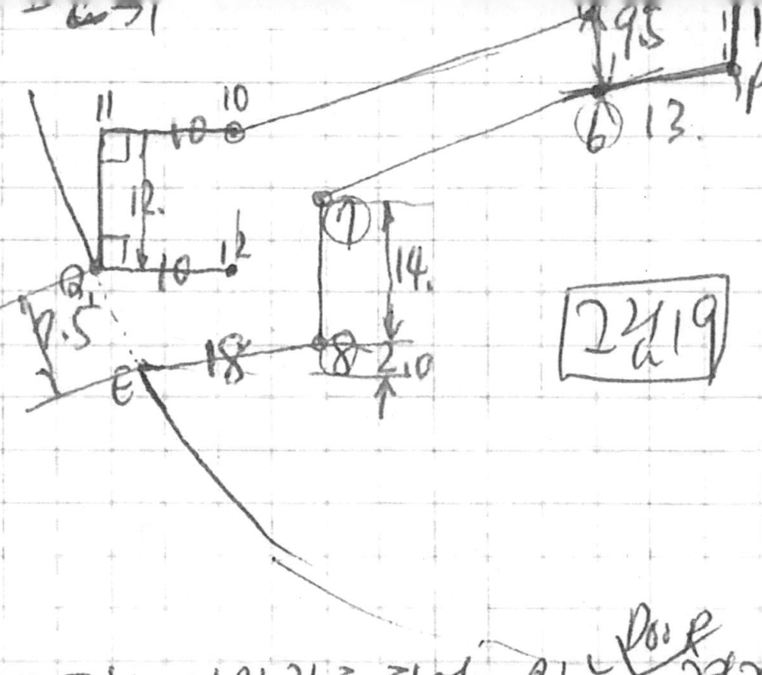

그림19

2) SIDE VIEW 작

* 직선으로 그린다.

① LINE Q1-12 및 LINE E는 이미 작도 되어 있는 Door 경계선임

② LINE 6, 7, 8, P 및 P1 을 H좌표를 FRT VIEW에서 옮긴뒤 직선으로 그림

③ LINE 9, LINE 10-11을 H좌표는 FRT VIEW에서 옮긴뒤 직선으로 그림

④ SIDE VIEW에 그려져 있는 DOOR SEC (FRT VIEW) LINE 700T --- 1500T 에 DOOR INNER PANEL LINE 및 하단부 STRUCTURE 를 전부 그려 넣는다 (DIMENSION 同-하게 FRT VIEW에서 COMPASS로 옮겨서.

3) Top VIEW

① LINE Q1 및 E1 선은 작도되어 있음

② LINE 10-12, 8 및 9를 옮겨그린다

4) FRT VIEW, SIDE VIEW 및 Top VIEW에 LINE 명칭및 숫의 명칭을 기입해 넣는다 (INKING)

1. B-PILLAR 의 GLASS CHANNEL SECTION 및 SIDE VIEW 作図

* DOOR FRAME이 끝나는 점 (530H) 및 GLASS CHANNEL 하단부의 임의점 (250H) 의 SECTION을 그린뒤 직선으로 각 SECTION의 점끼리 잇는다.

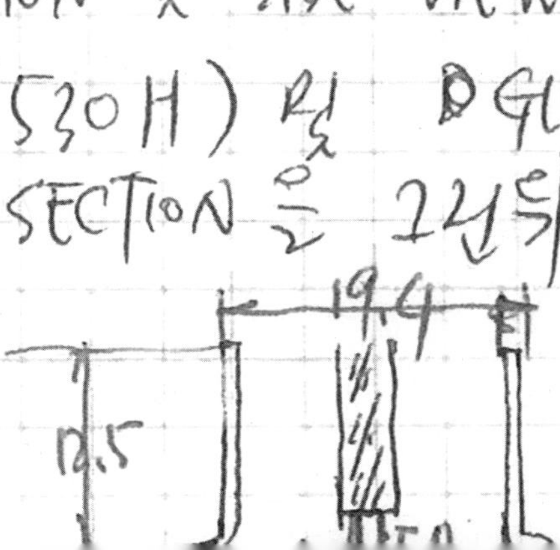

SOLUTION

23. A PILLAR STRUCTURE SIDE VIEW 作圖

1) 그림24 로부터 P₁선을 그린다. (582.5T선상).

2) "   P선을 그린다. (P₁선과 12.5mm간격)

* P선은 HINGE부위는 HINGE 축중심과 일치한다

3) 상단부 변곡값작도.

① P₁선 의 RADIUS를 60mm 로 그린다.

② P₁선 변곡 RADIUS의 중심점에서 ↑12.5R 을 그린다

4) 하단부 (A'PILLAR 와 ROCKER PNL) 라의 변곡작도

作圖   ① P₁선 RADIUS 60mm로 作圖 중심점9

② P선   "   12.5mm로 값은중심점 9 에서작도

③ 원6. 선④를 중심 b덕 c를

중심으로 하여 작도.

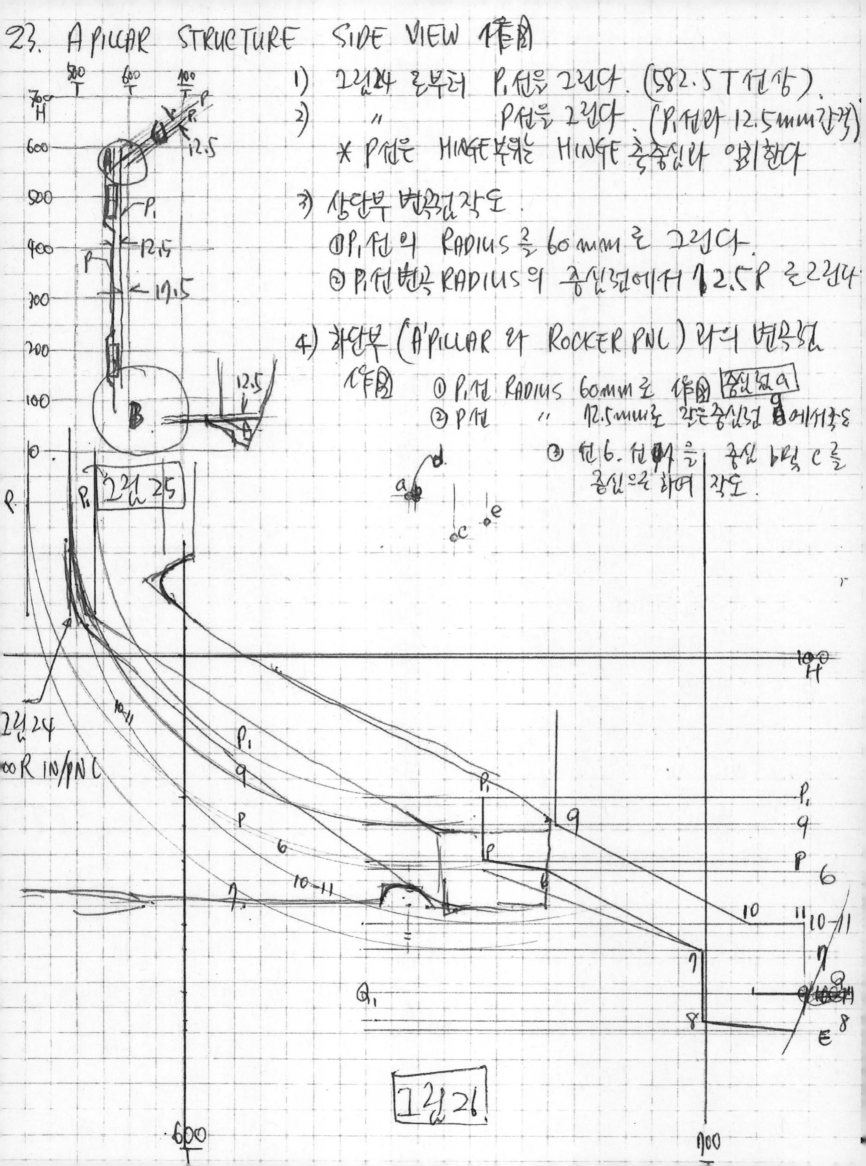

그림24

∞R IN/PNL

그림25

그림26

④ DOOR INNER PNL 선을 그림 24로부터 SIDE VIEW에 옮긴다
⑤ 선9, 선10~11은 중심점 d 및 e를 중심으로하여 작도.

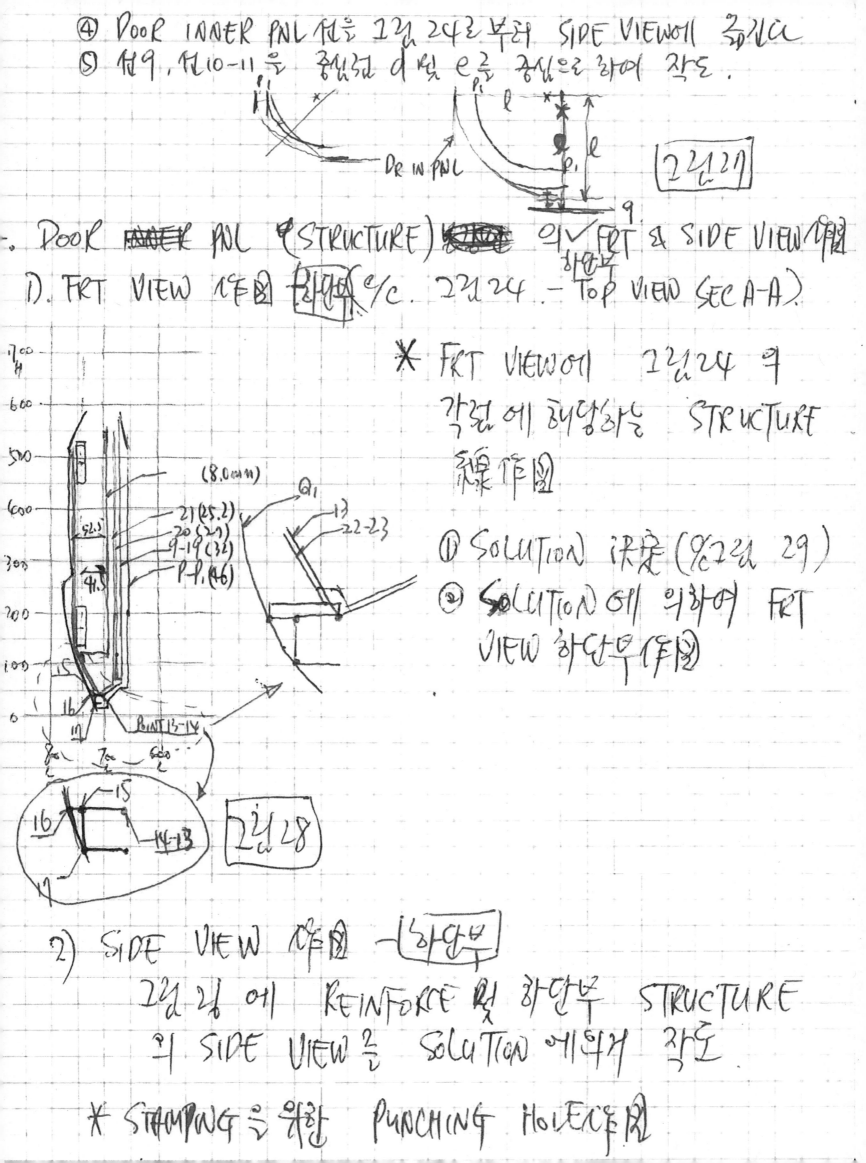

2림27

- . DOOR ~~PANEL~~ PNL (STRUCTURE) ~~의 작도~~ 의√FRT & SIDE VIEW작도
1). FRT VIEW 작도 하단부 %C. 그림24 - TOP VIEW SEC A-A).

※ FRT VIEW에 그림24 의
각선에 해당하는 STRUCTURE
線作圖

① SOLUTION 決定 (%그림 29)
② SOLUTION에 의하여 FRT
   VIEW 하단부(作圖)

2) SIDE VIEW 作圖 — 하단부
   그림 27 에 REINFORCE 멀 하단부 STRUCTURE
   의 SIDE VIEW를 SOLUTION 에의거 작도

※ STAMPING을 위한 PUNCHING HOLE작圖

3) HINGE 의 {폭이 60mm
{총길이 직경 15mm (FIAT 128 19mm) } 로 예상.

22. FRT DOOR UNR HINGE 하단부의 TOP VIEW SEC 작성 (H ?
※ 22의 14 의 'B' AREA 에   800 L

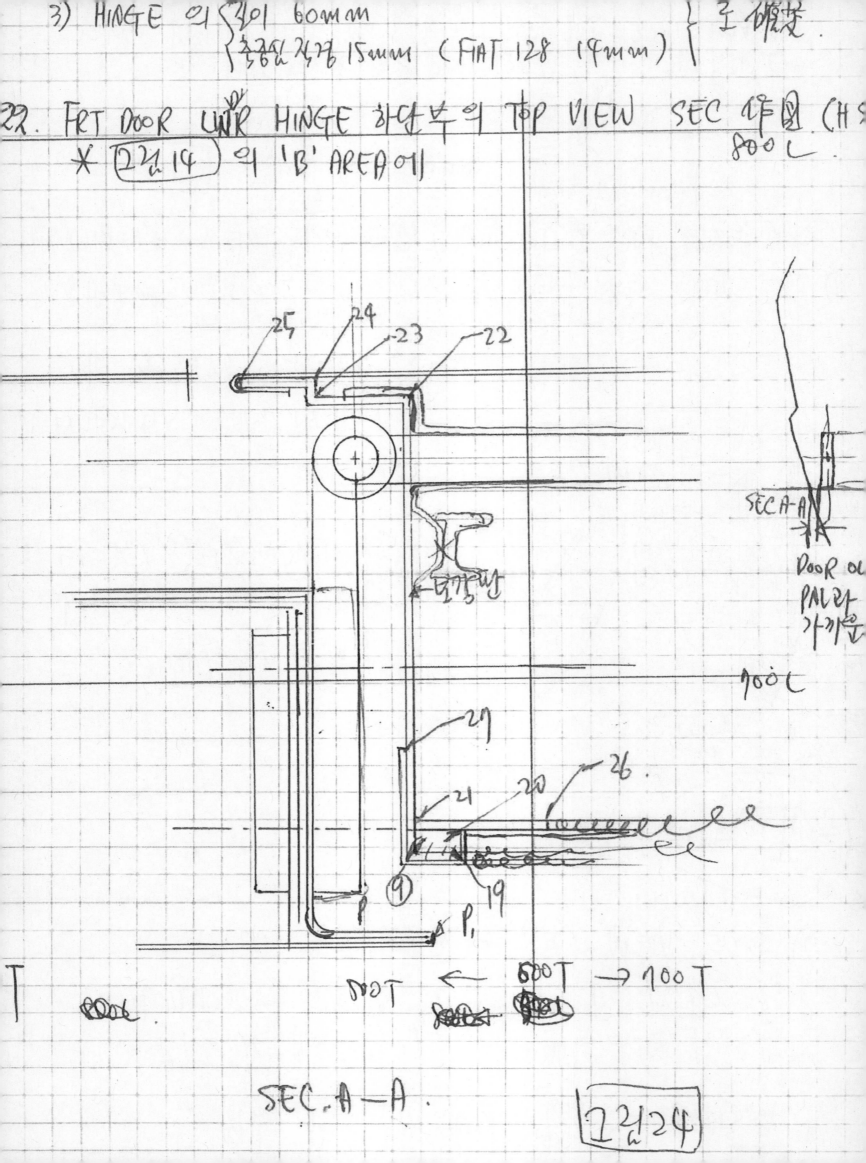

25   24   23   22

면강판

SEC.A-A

DOOR 의
PANEL
가까운

700 L

27
21   20   26.
9   19

P₁

800T ← 600T → 700T

DOOR.   {   }

SEC. A—A.

22의24

① B-PILLAR 에서 위와 또한 경계선 LINE-S 의 "방향으로 실선으로 그린다

② 60H 에서 20mm 간격으로 보조선을 그린디 'A' PILLAR 및 DOOR FRAME 작도법과 동일한 방법으로 2차 AUX-VIEW 에 의해 實像을 그린다.

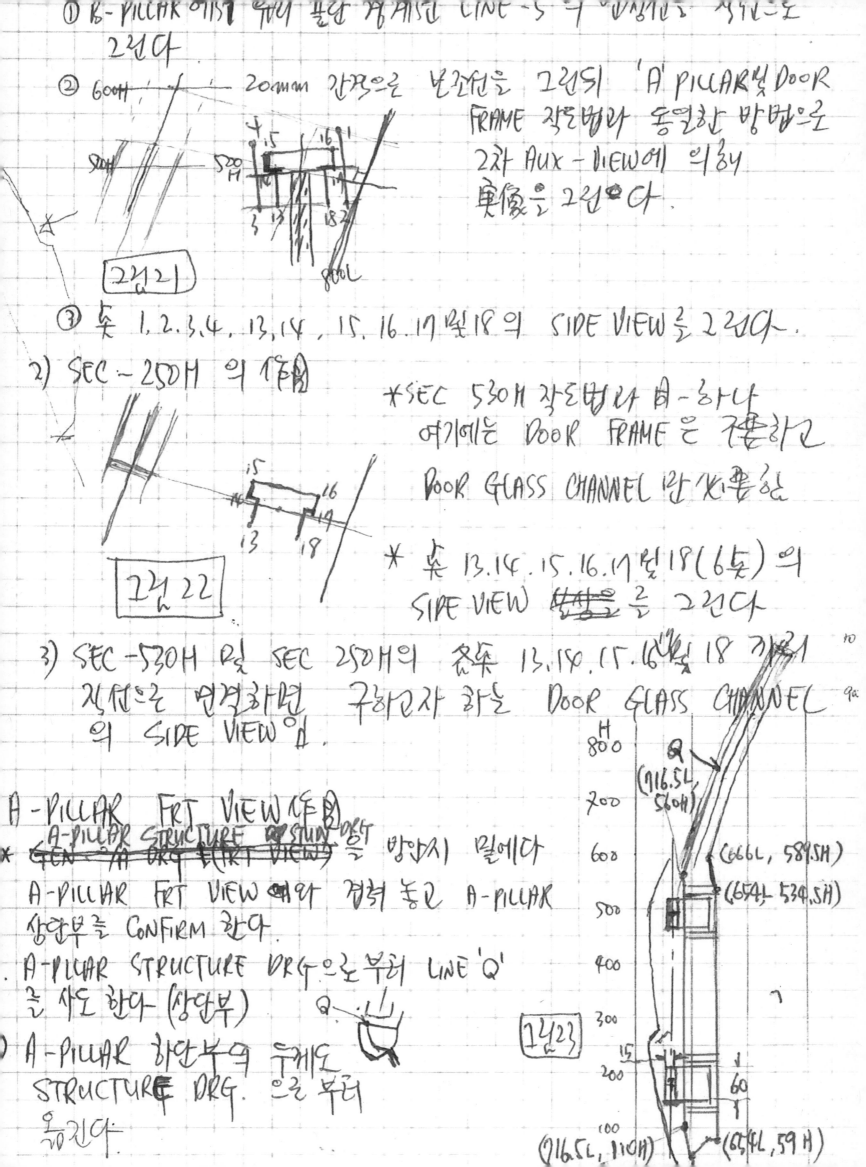

[그림 21]

③ 축 1.2.3.4. 13,14, 15.16.17 및 18 의 SIDE VIEW 를 그린다.

2) SEC-250H 의 作圖

[그림 22]

* SEC 530H 작도법과 동一하나 여기에는 DOOR FRAME 은 除外하고 DOOR GLASS CHANNEL 만 적용한다

* 축 13.14.15.16.17 및 18 (6축) 의 SIDE VIEW 를 그린다

3) SEC-530H 및 SEC 250H 의 各축 13.14.15.16 및 18 기준의 직선으로 연결하면 구하고자 하는 DOOR GLASS CHANNEL 의 SIDE VIEW임.

A-PILLAR FRT VIEW (作圖)
* A-PILLAR STRUCTURE DRG. (FRT VIEW) 를 밑에 깔다
. A-PILLAR FRT VIEW 에와 겹쳐 놓고 A-PILLAR 상단부를 CONFIRM 한다.
. A-PILLAR STRUCTURE DRG. 으로 부터 LINE 'Q' 를 사도 한다 (상단부)
) A-PILLAR 하단부의 두께는 STRUCTURE DRG. 으로 부터 옮긴다

[그림 23]

H
800   Q
        (716.5L, 56bH)
700
600   (66bL, 589.5H)
500   (65bL, 530.5H)
400
300
15
200   60
100
(716.5L, 110H)   (65bL, 59H)

상단부 INNER PNL & REINF. PNL의 변주됨 FRT VIEW &
SIDE VIEW 상황 (FROM SOLUTION)

* 고려사항

 ① DOOR TRIM PNL 상단부 높이

 ② TAPER 부분의 SOLUTION

 ③ DOOR TRIM PNL 와 같음.

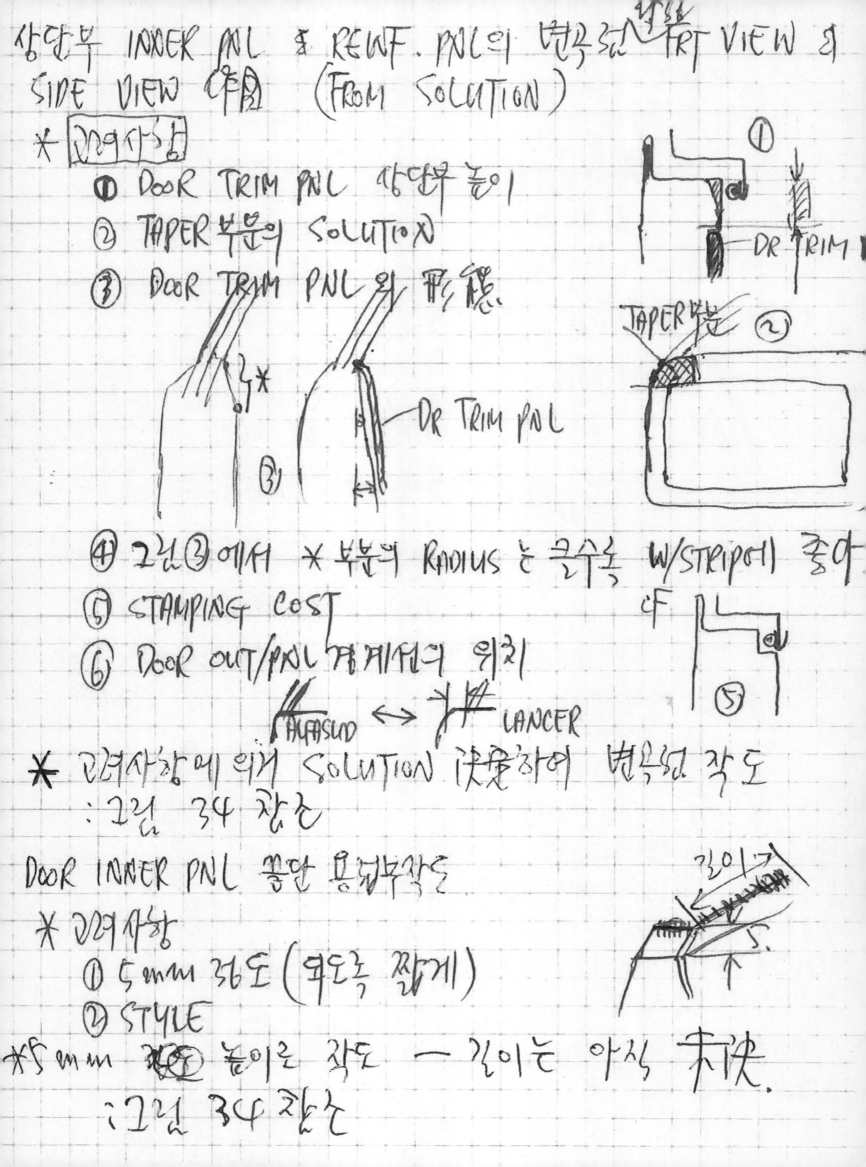

 ④ 그림 ③ 에서 ＊ 부분의 RADIUS 는 클수록 W/STRIP에 좋아.

 ⑤ STAMPING COST

 ⑥ DOOR OUT/PNL 겹쳐지는 위치

  ALFASUD ⟷ LANCER

＊ 고려사항에 의거 SOLUTION 決定하여 변복없 작도
  : 그림 34 참조.

DOOR INNER PNL 끝단 용법부작도

＊ 고려사항
 ① 5 mm 정도 (되도록 짧게)
 ② STYLE

＊5 mm 높이은 작도 — 길이는 아직 未決.
  : 그림 34 참조.

The handwritten notes on the left and center show meeting minutes.

Left note:
- 4) PROTOTYPE 用 MM... 2台는 R.H. DRIVE 도착예정이요 TEST用... 하도록 한다.
- 5) BRAKE SYSTEM 1台 BRAKE SYSTEM 의 ... 는 理解도 키우...
- 6) INSTRUMENT CLUS... 가. CLUSTER 의 ... I.D. 에서 D... 나. 계기류 COMP...
- 7) TORINO 에서 제작... SYSTEM 을 정립... 한다. TORINO TEA... 別로 PART NO. ...EERING 까지
- 8) NEW PROJECT CAR 레반 업무를 추가... ENGINEERING 협정한다.
- 9) ENGINEERING CON... 英国 AUSTIN M... TEAM 과 ENGI... TEAM 構成 ...
- 10) EMBLEM 1台 차량 명칭및 EMBL...

Center note:
ITALDESIGN SIRP S.p.A.

TORINO 會議 決果 (1974. 2. 7.)

1. 場所: PRINCIPI DI PIEMONTE HOTEL
2. 參席者: 신형동이사, 검주화 차장, 이승복라장, 박랑당라장, 검용우라장 이충구대리
3. 會議内容.
   1) COMMUNICATION件. (TORINO vs KOREA)
      가. 업무연락및 레반 업무연락은 영국 LONDON을 경유토록하고 URGENT 업무연락은 직접 TELEX를 보내도록한다.
      나. REPORT는 WEEKLY BASE로 TORINO 업무진행 현황을 보고토록 하고 本社에서 MASTER SCHEDULE 이 작성된 以后에는 SCHEDULE FILL UP를 위한 BACK DATA 로써 EVENT別로 업무진행 決果를 수시 보고토록한다.
   2) TORINO (某 것들) 업무 확대건.
      본래의 업무 와 日本지역에서 수행예정인 BODY ENGINEERING 의 일부업무및 BODY CONST LINE의 METHOD 업무를 추가 한다!
      가. MASTER MODEL FOLLOW UP : TORINO TEAM 5名+ 1名은 6.7月頃부터 I.D.업무 수행후 일본지역의 INNER M/MODEL 제작업무에 참여토록하고 Die 제작업무에 조언토록 한다.
      나. METHOD OF JIG/FIXTURE : 5名+1名은 (이승복라장 ; 업무 내용에 따라 某것들은 '가', '나' 업무로 겸무토록 할 수 있다) 8月頃까지 ID 업무 수행후 일본지역에서 JIG/FIXTURE METHOD STUDY 업무 (但 JIG/FIXTURE ORDER 업무 까지 로 限定함) 을 수행한다.
   3) CHASSIS PART 局 개발건.
      가. 또 LANCER CHASSIS PARTS (ENG. T/M, Rr AXLE 제외) 는 局 CONTENT % 증가 와 개발 촉진 및 관련 ENGINEER 의 TRAINING 목적으로 100% 國產化 함을 원칙으로 한다.
      나. 금년 末 까지 國產化 하기로 하고 예정되는 PARTS 는 LIST UP 하여 K.D 도입토록 한다.

이탈디자인 파견 기간 업무 진행 방식을 기록한 회의록
Meeting minutes that describe the work plan during the dispatch to Italdesign

이탈디자인에서 진행한 설계 연수와 '이 대리 노트'

현대자동차가 포니를 개발하기 위해 결성한 다국적 드림팀과의 계약 조건에는 양산을 전제로 한 인적 교류, 즉 파견 과정이 포함돼 있었다. 현대자동차는 자사의 엔지니어를 이탈리아 토리노에 1년간 파견해 설계 도면 그리는 법과 프로토타입 제작 기초를 배우도록 했다. 당시 파견자 중 한 명이던 이충구 전 사장(당시 대리)은 이탈디자인에서 보고 익힌 내용을 꼼꼼하게 수기(手記)로 기록했다. 훗날 '이 대리 노트'로 불린 설계 연수 보고서는 당시 신차 개발 과정에서 중요한 지침서로 쓰였을 뿐 아니라, 이후 현대자동차의 신차 개발 프로세스 기틀을 다지는 데에도 중요한 자료로 활용되었다.

"당시 이탈디자인 스튜디오는 토리노 교외에 있었습니다. 13m짜리 커다란 제도판 두 개 위에 100mm 간격의 그리드 라인이 그려진 제도 용지가 쫙 깔려 있는 곳이었죠. 저는 작업자 두 분이 설계하는 걸 눈여겨보면서 매일매일 작업 과정을 노트에 기록했어요. 자동차 설계에 대해 조금이라도 알아야 물어볼 게 생기는데, 아는 게 아예 없으니 그냥 있는 그대로

Design training at Italdesign and manager Lee's notes

The terms of the contract with the multinational dream team for the development of the Pony included the assignment of personnel, on the premise of mass production. Hyundai sent its engineers to Turin, Italy, for a year to learn how to draw blueprints and learn the basics of prototyping. Hyundai's former president Chung-goo Lee (deputy manager at the time) was one of the dispatchers, and he meticulously recorded by hand what he saw and learned at Italdesign. The design training report, later referred to as 'The Notes of Manager Lee' was not only referenced as an essential guideline in the new car development process at the time but was also used as a useful resource in laying the groundwork for Hyundai's new car development process today.

"At the time, the Italdesign studio was located in the suburbs of Turin. It was where drafting paper with grid lines 100 millimeters apart was spread over two large 13-meter drafting boards. I kept an eye on the design of the two workers and recorded the work process in a notebook every day. I needed to know something about car design to ask questions. However, I didn't know anything, so I copied each one as it is in a notebook, in case I need to refer to it in the future. I wrote down everything down to small details, such as drafting supplies, paperweights, and drafting tables from Italdesign. Not only the design room but also the contents of the master model production room. Thanks to this, I could include the overall content of the

하나하나 노트에 옮겼습니다. 나중에라도 찾아볼 수 있게요.
이탈디자인의 제도용품, 문진, 제도 테이블 같은 세세한 것까
지 참고할 만한 건 모두 기록했습니다. 설계실은 물론이고 마
스터 모델 제작실 진행 내용까지도요. 덕분에 이 노트에 포니
개발 프로세스에 관한 전반적 내용이 담길 수 있었습니다."
(이충구 전 현대자동차 연구개발본부 사장)

1년 남짓 지속된 이탈리아 파견은 자동차 설계의 기본 개념조
차 없던 이들이 도면 그리는 법 등 자동차 설계의 기초를 배워
가는 과정이었다. 그러나 이 과정은 순탄치 않았다. 연수 과
정에서 가장 어려웠던 점은 언어 장벽이었다. 이탈리아 기술
자와 영어로 의사소통하기 어려웠을 뿐 아니라, 생소한 자동
차 부품이나 기술 용어도 영어와 이탈리아어가 달라 어려움
이 가중되었다. 이런 상황에서 파견자 모두가 업무를 분담해
작업 내용을 꼼꼼히 기록했고, 일과가 끝난 밤에 다 같이 모여
서로 보고 들은 걸 공유하면서 작업 내용을 점검하고 정리해
나갔다. 고달픈 나날이었지만 성과는 있었다. 숙련된 엔지니
어들이 일하는 모습을 어깨너머로 보고 배우며 설계 업무 기
초를 다질 수 있게 된 것이다.

Pony development process in this notebook."
(Chung-goo Lee, former President and Head of
R&D Division, Hyundai Motor Company)

The one-year dispatch to Italy was a chance for
those completely uneducated on car design to
learn the basics, including how to draw blueprints. However, this process was not easy. The
most challenging part was the language barrier.
Not only was it difficult to communicate with
Italian technicians in English, but unfamiliar
terms related to automotive parts or technologies were different between English and Italian,
further increasing communication difficulties.
In the midst of these difficulties, the dispatched
workers meticulously recorded the work details.
At night, when the workday was over, everyone
gathered to share what they saw and heard,
checking and organizing the work contents. The
days were tough, but it paid off. They could learn
from experienced engineers, laying the groundwork for design work.

cc MR C.H. TURNBULL & MR P. SLATER
MR J.W. JEONG
THE HYUNDAI MOTOR COMPANY   CONFIDENTIAL   (1)

NOTES COVERING VISIT OF K. BARNETT TO ITAL DESIGN -
24 JUNE 1974 TO 5 JULY 1974.

1) PLACES VISITED IN ADDITION TO ITAL DESIGN INCLUDED!
F.E.A CONVERSO - SEVERAL VISITS TO CHECK PROGRESS & ENSURE
    ADEQUATE LIAISON FOR CORRECTION OF MODELS &
    DRAWINGS.
TECNO STUDI - TO REVIEW UNDERBODY LAYOUT & DETAILING. ALL
(25 JUNE)   WORK IS TO ISOMETRIC STANDARDS.
COGGIOLA, COACH BUILDER - 26 JUNE - TO VIEW WORK IN
    PROGRESS ON HYUNDAI COUPE. MODEL COMPLETED IN
    PLASTER. PANEL JIGS BEING FITTED TO MODEL
LAMET - DIE DESIGN & MANUFACTURING CO. - (28TH JUNE)
FONTANA - (2 JULY) - TO VIEW PRESENTATION MODEL & PROTOTYPE
    PANEL MANUFACTURE IN PROGRESS.
DEA - (4 JULY) - BRIEF VISIT & TO MAKE CONTACT WITH UK
    REPRESENTATIVE - MR. D.K. WEBSTER
POLITECNICO TORINO (4 JULY) - DISCUSS IN DETAIL STATIC TESTS
    OF 'LANCER' & HYUNDAI BODIES.

2) OTHER PERSONS VISITING I.D. DURING THIS PERIOD
    WERE MR. J. CROSTHWAITE - 24-27 JUNE
        MR. D. WILLETT } 26 - 28 JUNE
        MR. B.C. KIM }
        MR. S.K. CHAEGAL - 24 JUNE - 28 JUNE.

3) POINTS ARISING FROM NOTES OF VISIT TO ITAL DESIGN BY
    MR. WILLETT & MR. MANGHAM - 11 & 12 MAY 1974
3.1 Ref. page 3. REGARDING STATIC TESTING OF LANCER &
    HYUNDAI PROTOTYPE No 5 BODIES.
    THESE BODIES SHOULD BE TESTED WITHOUT WINDSHIELD OR
    BACKLIGHT. FRONT SUSPENSION CROSSMEMBER TO BE FITTED. ALL
    DOORS, BONNET & TRUNK LID TO BE IN A SLIGHTLY OPEN
    POSITION, NOT CLOSED & LOCKED. LOAD
    IN ADDITION TO TORSION & CENTRAL, BEAM TESTS, WE MUST
    ALSO CARRY OUT A REAR-END BEAM LOAD TEST TO GIVE A
    COMPARISON WITH CORTINA DATA. ALSO, STATIC TESTS ON FRONT
    & REAR DOORS TO BE CARRIED OUT.
    TORSION TESTS ON BOTH BODIES, WITH WINDSHIELD & BACKLIGHT, & FRONT
    SUSPENSION CROSS-MEMBER FITTED, & WITH ALL DOORS, BONNET &
    TRUNK LIDS LOCKED MAY BE CARRIED OUT IF TIMING PERMITS.
    I.D. ARE TO PROVIDE COSTS FOR THE COMPLETE TEST
    PROGRAM INCLUDING MANUFACTURE OF TEST FIXTURES
    THE TESTS HAVE BEEN DISCUSSED IN DETAIL WITH I.D.,

CONFORM WITH U.S. STANDARDS
LOCATED ON CANTRAIL, WHICH
PROBLEM IS STILL UNDER
6.10 I HAVE RESERVATIONS REGAR
    IN USE (0.7 MM) IN USE
    TESTS MAY ESTABLISH WHETHER
6.11 I HAVE ASKED MR. J.W. JEONG
    DURING PROTOTYPE BUILD. A
    LANCER UNDERFRAME, A COMPLE
    POSSIBLE UNTIL BUILD OF PROT
6.12 A SUMMARY OF GAUGE MAT
    EITHER IN THE PARTS LIST, OR
    5.7) WILL BE HELPFUL IN ASSES
    DEVELOPMENT TESTS.
6.13 FOR INFORMATION, THE LANCE
    IS 226.9 Kg (500 LB), BROKEN
        BODY LESS DOORS - 177.
        2 FRONT DOORS   - 17.
        2 REAR DOORS   - 13.
        BONNET   - 11.
        TRUNK LID   - 5.
        DOOR HINGES   - 3.
    THE FRONT & REAR ENGIN
    BE WEIGHED.
6.14 MY VISIT TO DEA. WAS VERY
    WITH MY MEETING WITH POLI
    MORNING, I AM REASONABL
    EQUIPMENT THROUGH THE W
    MACHINE) & PRIOR KNOWLED
        I CONSIDER THAT THE P
    (Eg L&K) EQUIPMENT SHOU
    PURPOSES ONLY, NOT FOR STYL
    MODELS OR DIES, FOR STYLING
    MORE SUITABLE
    THE ELECTRONIC PACKAGE F
    IS TOO SOPHISTICATED TO REMAIN DORMANT FOR LONG
    PERIODS, AND FUTURE PURCHASE SHOULD BE PHASED FOR DELIVERY
    TO MEET REQUIREMENTS FOR FUTURE MODEL PROGRAMS
    THE WEAK PART OF THESE SYSTEMS IS THE ELECTRONIC PACKAGE.
    IF HYUNDAI BUY SUCH EQUIPMENT, IT IS ESSENTIAL THAT THE VENDOR
    TRAIN A HYUNDAI ENGINEER IN ORDER TO DIAGNOSE THE FAULTY
    MODULE VIA TELEX.
6.15 I DISCUSSED DESIGN ROOM EQUIPMENT WITH MR. J.W. JEONG
    WE WERE SHORT OF CATALOGUES FOR DETAILED SPECIFICATION,
    & I ATTACH COPIES FOR FORWARDING TO HIM.
        I HAVE ALSO ASKED HIM TO OBTAIN DETAILS OF I.D. PICTOGRAPHIC

CO-OPERATIVE AS EXPECTED.
FOR ALTERATIONS ARE REAC
FOR PROGRAM EXTENSION & IN
THEREFORE HAVE GENERALLY TO
BY MR. JEONG VIA THE GOOD
ENGINEER, SNR BALTERI, WHO IS
TO HOW MUCH CAN BE DONE INT
BE KEPT TO A MINIMUM.
7.7 AT PRESENT, I.D.
    A PROMISE FROM SNR MANTI
    PROTOTYPE No 1 WILL BE KEPT
    DAY & NIGHT!
7.8 SNR. MOLINERI OF I.D. HAS
    INFORMATION REGARDING HYU
    PUBLICITY MATERIAL FOR THE TUR
    COURSE, BE VETTED BY HYUNDAI
    THE SHOW IS STILL SOME TIM
    POSTAL DIFFICULTIES MUCH TIM
    BE SET IN HAND NOW. I HAVE
    REPRINT OF THE AUTOCAR INTE
    STARTER (COPY ATTACHED). WILL
    FORWARD TO SNR. MOLINERI.
7.9 THE POOR POSTAL SERVICES IN
    PERSONAL DIFFICULTIES FOR HY
    DUE TO LATE ARRIVAL OF MAIL,
    WITH THEIR FAMILIES, CREATING
    MEANS BE FOUND FOR OVERCOM

6.19 THE DRAWINGS OF DESIGN CE
    WITH MR. JEONG, & ARE BEING
    SUGGESTIONS. FURTHER DISCUSSIO
    DEVELOPMENT AREA ARE NECESSARY.

6.20 FUTURE DOCUMENTS SHOULD HAVE A DISTRIBUTION LIST
    ATTACHED, SO THAT ALL PERSONS CONCERNED ARE
    INFORMED OF DECISIONS AFFECTING THEIR WORK.

현대자동차는 조지 턴불을 영입하면서 영국 신문에 광고를 내 자문 역할을 해줄 외국인 기술자 6명을 계약직으로
채용했다. 이 이미지는 포니와 포니 쿠페 프로토타입 제작 현황을 수기로 기록한 출장 보고서로 차체 설계 파트의
수석 엔지니어였던 케네스 바넷이 작성했다.
When George Turnbull was scouted, Hyundai also advertised with British papers to hire
six engineers for contract positions, where they would serve as advisors. The above image
depicts a hand-written business trip report prepared by Kenneth Barnett, Chief Body Design
Engineer, detailing the preparation of the Pony and Pony Coupe prototypes.

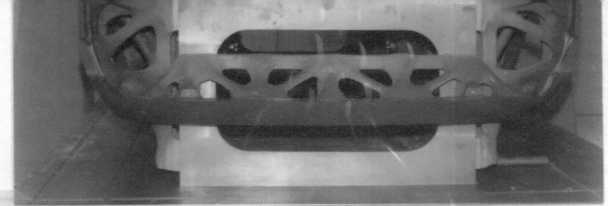

① CUBE에 조립된
상태의 MASTER
MODEL FRONTAL
VIEW.

① Master model mounted on
cube. (Frontal View)

② FRONT QUARTER
VIEW
; 'DEA' MEASURING
MACHINE 으로 FRO
-NT DOOR OUTER
PANEL 의 'L'하단부
를 CHECK 하는 장경

② Frt. Quarter View :
Frt. door outer panel is being
checked using 'DEA'.

포니 마스터 모델 제작 과정을 기록한 사진첩 일부
**Part of a picture album detailing the production
process of the Pony master model**

③ CUBE에 조립되어
'DEA' MEASURING
MACHINE 의 정반
위에 얹어 놓은
MASTER MODEL 의
REAR VIEW

③ Master model mounted on
Cube (Rear View)

④ REAR UPPER
VIEW.

④ Master model
(Rear Upr. View)

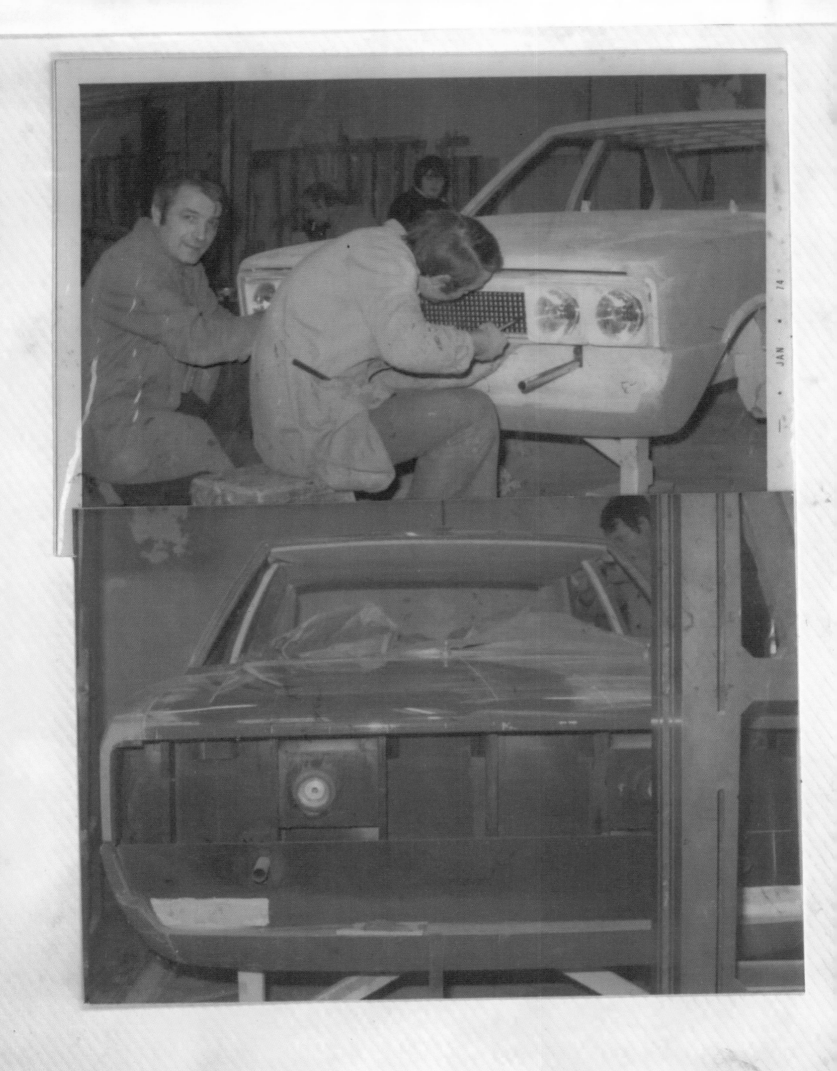

포니 마스터 모델 제작 과정을 기록한 사진첩 일부
Part of a picture album detailing the production
process of the Pony master model

JAN • 74

이탈리아 토리노에서 촬영한 포니 프로토타입
Photos of the Pony prototype taken in Turin, Italy

토리노 모터쇼에서 최초 공개된 포니와 포니 쿠페

다음 수순은 모터쇼 출품 준비였다. 이탈디자인과 계약 당시 독자 모델 최초 공개 시기를 이탈리아 토리노에서 열리는 '제55회 국제자동차박람회'로 확정한 현대자동차는 기한 내에 프로토타입 제작을 완료하기 위해 전력을 다했다. 토리노 모터쇼는 당시 가장 권위 있고 규모가 큰 세계적인 모터쇼로, 현대자동차 최초의 독자 모델 데뷔 무대로 손색이 없었다. 현대자동차는 모터쇼 일정에 맞춰 차명 국민 공모도 진행했다. 1974년 7월 18일부터 8월 25일까지 진행된 공모전에 총 5만 8,000여 통의 엽서가 쇄도했을 만큼 참가 열기도 뜨거웠다. 이처럼 전 국민적 관심 속에 탄생한 이름이 바로 '포니'였다.

1974년 10월 30일 토리노 모터쇼에서 첫선을 보인 포니와 포니 쿠페에 대한 반응은 기대 이상이었다. 16개국, 65개 사에서 최신 차량 245대를 출품했는데 유수 기업의 경쟁차를 제치고 포니와 포니 쿠페에 가장 많은 관심이 집중된 것이다. 전 세계를 강타한 오일쇼크로 소형차를 선호하는 당시 상황에서 포니와 포니 쿠페는 높은 실용성과 혁신적 디자인을 겸비한 모델로 호평받았다. 그러나 가장 크게 주목받은 점은 한국이라는 개발도상국이 대량생산이 가능한 독자 모델 보유 국가에 합류했다는 사실이었다. 현지 언론에서 많은 관심을 표명하며 집중 언급한 내용 또한 이 점이었다. 당시 유럽의 3대 일간지 중 하나인 〈라 스탐파(La Stampa)〉는 1면에 포니 관련 기사를 대서특필하면서 '한국이 자동차 공업국 대열에 진입했다'는 점을 부각했다. 이 외에도 많은 유력 매체가 포니와 포니 쿠페에 대한 호의적인 기사를 쏟아냈다.

"1974년 10월 그날 이후 이탈리아 토리노는 우리에게 더 이상 '이탈리아 북부의 중소 도시'가 아니었다. 포니에게는 잊지 못할 데뷔 무대였으며, 나에게는 고유 모델을 향한 무한한 자

The Pony and Pony Coupe unveiled at the Turin Motor Show

The next step was to prepare for motor show entry. At the time of the contract with Italdesign, Hyundai agreed that the first unveiling of its original model would be at the 55th International Motor Show held in Turin, Italy. The company gave its best to complete the prototype within the deadline. The Turin Motor Show was the most prestigious and large-scale motor show at the time. It was an excellent stage in which Hyundai could debut its first independent model. Hyundai also held a public contest for the name of the car in line with the motor show schedule. Many people were passionate about giving a name to Korea's first independent model — approximately 58,000 postcards flooded in. The name 'Pony' was born amid national interest.

The response to the Pony and Pony Coupe, which debuted at the Turin Motor Show on October 30, 1974, was beyond expectation. That year, the Turin Motor Show exhibited 245 new vehicles from 65 companies in 16 countries. Most attention was focused on the Pony and Pony Coupe, beating out competitors from leading manufacturers. The Pony and Pony Coupe, unveiled when the preference for small cars was high due to the oil shock that hit the world, received favorable reviews as their designs combined practicality and innovation. However, what attracted the most attention was that Korea, a developing country, had joined the list of countries capable of mass producing its own model. This was what intrigued the interest and focus of local media. *La Stampa*, one of Europe's three major daily newspapers at the time, featured an article

토리노 모터쇼에 출품된 포니를 다룬 해외 언론 기사
Overseas media coverage of the Pony at the
Turin Motor Show

about the Pony on the front page, emphasizing that Korea had entered the ranks of automobile manufacturing countries. In addition, many influential media had poured out favorable articles about the Pony and Pony Coupe.

"Since that day in October 1974, Turin, Italy, has ceased to be a small town in northern Italy for us. It was an unforgettable debut stage for the Pony. For me, it was a place that gave me the boundless confidence toward our own model and a source of hope that allowed me to take my first steps toward the world." (Se-yung Chung, former Chairman of Hyundai Motor Company)

After the Turin Motor Show, the company's reaction to the Pony project changed from pessimistic to an optimistic view. Even those who were initially pessimistic about developing an independent model in a developing country came together and actively jumped into establishing a Pony mass production system, constructing a plant and pioneering export markets. This dramatic change in attitude and great interest also stemmed from the fact that the Pony was the result of a moving story created by overcoming many adversities with a sincere heart. In light of past experiences, the Pony has these elements like overcoming limitations, the manifestation of human potential that surpasses the impossible, and the incredible leaps made by passion.

신감을 확인해 준 자리이자 세계를 향해 첫발을 내딛게 해준 희망의 발원지였다." (정세영 전 현대자동차 회장)

토리노 모터쇼를 계기로 포니 프로젝트에 대한 사내 반응은 비관론에서 희망 섞인 관측으로 완전히 바뀌었다. 개발도상국에서 대량 양산형 고유 모델을 개발한다는 도전적 행보에 처음에는 부정적이었던 사람들마저 합심해 포니 양산 시스템 구축, 완성차 공장 건설, 수출 판로 개척 등에 적극적으로 뛰어들게 된 것이다. 이러한 극적인 태도 변화와 큰 관심은 포니가 간절한 마음으로 수많은 역경을 딛고 만들어낸 감동적인 결과물이라는 사실에서 비롯되기도 했다. 과거 경험에 비추어볼 때 예상되는 한계의 극복, 불가능에 대한 예측을 뛰어넘는 인간의 잠재성 발현, 열정이 빚어낸 놀라운 도약…. 포니에는 바로 이런 요소가 깃들어 있었던 것이다.

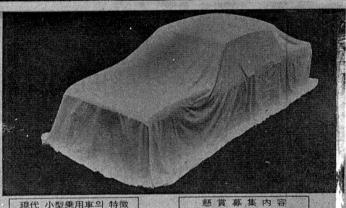

国内最初의 韓国産 乗用車에 부칠 車名과 심볼 마크를 募集 합니다

— 海外市場에서 쉽게 通用될 수 있는 이름을 —

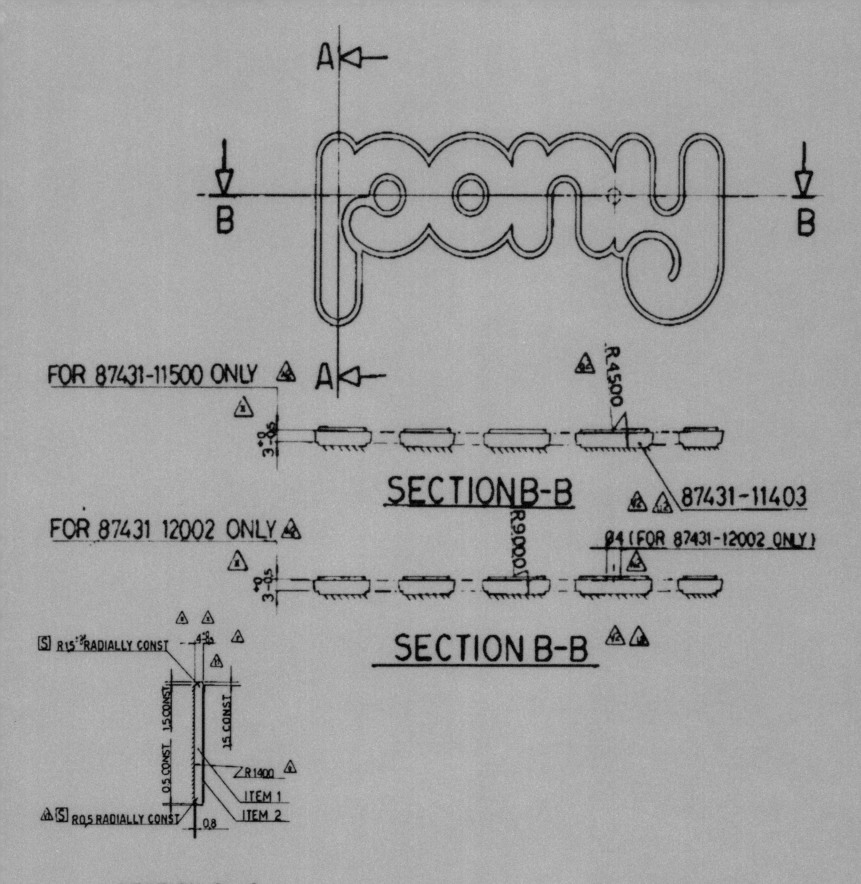

FOR 87431-11500 ONLY

FOR 87431 12002 ONLY

SECTION B-B

SECTION B-B

87431-11403

R4500

R9000

B4 (FOR 87431-12002 ONLY)

S R15 RADIALLY CONST

S R0.5 RADIALLY CONST

R1400

ITEM 1
ITEM 2

SECTION A - A

주 기 : 1. 재질 : ITEM 1 : 알루미늄 다이캐스팅 규격번호 (JIS H 5302) ADC-5
ALT 알루미늄판 규격번호 (JIS H 4000)
ITEM 2 : 양면 접착테이프 규격번호 MS 711-8
2. 표면처리 : 해칭부위 : 헤어라인은 마스타 스타링 샘플에 순할것
ALT : 헤어라인 없는 백색 무광택
해칭외 부위 흑색 무광택 페인트 규격번호 MS 651-4
3. 기입되지 않은 치수는 마스타 스타링 샘플에 순할것

NOTE 1. MATERIL : ITEM 1 : ALUMINUM ALLOY TO SPEC NO JIS H 5302, ADC-5
ALT ALUMINUM PLATE TO SPEC NO JIS H 4000
ITEM 2 DOUBLE COATED - PRESSURE SENSITIVE ATPE TO SPEC NO MS 711-8
2. FINISH HATCHED AREA : HAIRLINES TO MATCH MASTER STYL'G SAMPLE
ALT MAT WHITE WITHOUT HAIRLINES
REMAINDER MAT BLACK PAINT TO SPEC NO MS 651-4
3. DIMS NOT SHOWN TO MATCH MASTER STYL'G SAMPLE

포니 레터링 엠블럼 도면
Pony lettering emblem drawing

포니의 차명은 국민 공모를 통해 탄생했다. 당시 전국에서 아리랑, 무궁화, 휘닉스 등 수많은 이름이 응모되었는데, 현대자동차는 젊은 감성의 차명이 중요하다는 판단 아래 공모 엽서를 정리하던 아르바이트 여대생들의 의견을 수렴했다. 그 결과 여대생들의 선호도가 가장 높고 해외에서도 발음하기 용이한 '포니'가 차명으로 결정됐다.

The name "Pony" was chosen through a public contest. Submissions included Arirang (A representative Korean folk song), Mugunghwa (Korea's national flower), and Phoenix. Hyundai thought that it should select a name that appeals to the younger generation, so it collected opinions on naming from part-time female college students who sorted out the contest postcards. As a result, the name "Pony", which proved popular among the students and was easier for customers in overseas markets to pronounce, was adopted.

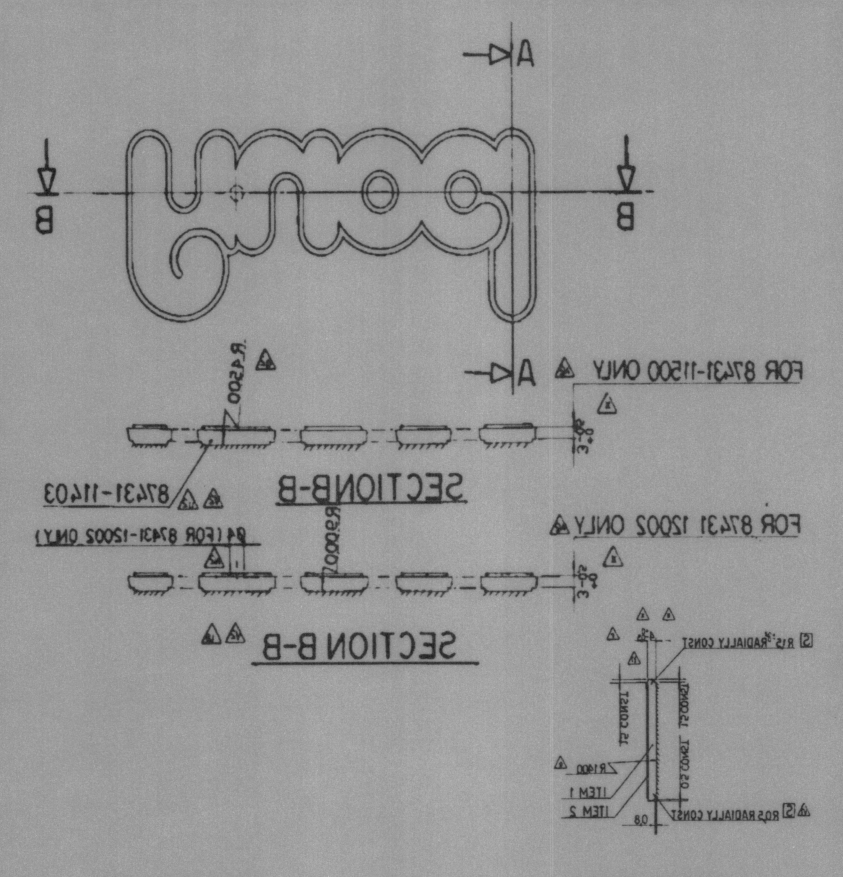

SECTION B-B

SECTION B-B

R6000

R15° RADIALLY CONST

1S CONST

0.2 CONST

R1500

ITEM 1
ITEM 2

R05 RADIALLY CONST

0.8

SECTION A - A

NOTE 1. MATERIAL : ITEM 1 : ALUMINUM ALLOY TO SPEC NO JIS H 5302, ADC-5
ALT ALUMINUM PLATE TO SPEC NO JIS H 4000
ITEM 2 DOUBLE COATED - PRESSURE SENSITIVE ATPE TO SPEC NO MS 711-8
2. FINISH HATCHED AREA : HAIRLINES TO MATCH MASTER STYL'G SAMPLE
ALT MAT WHITE WITHOUT HAIRLINES
REMAINDER MAT BLACK PAINT TO SPEC NO MS 651-4
3. DIM'S NOT SHOWN TO MATCH MASTER STYL'G SAMPLE

포니 레터링 엠블럼 도면

Pony lettering emblem drawing

수많은 이름이 응모되었으나, 현대자동차는 젊은 감각의 차명이 중요하다는 생각에서 아래
모든 응시를 분류하던 아르바이트 여자대학생들의 의견을 수렴했다. 그 결과 여대생들이
선호도가 높고 해외에서도 발음하기 용이한 '포니'가 차명으로 선정됐다.

The name "Pony" was chosen through a public contest. Submissions
included Arirang (a representative Korean folk song), Mugunghwa
(Korea's national flower), and Phoenix. Hyundai thought that it should
select a name that appeals to the younger generation, so it collected
opinions on naming from part-time female college students who
sorted out the contest postcards. As a result, the name "Pony",
which proved popular among the students and was easier for
customers in overseas markets to pronounce, was adopted.

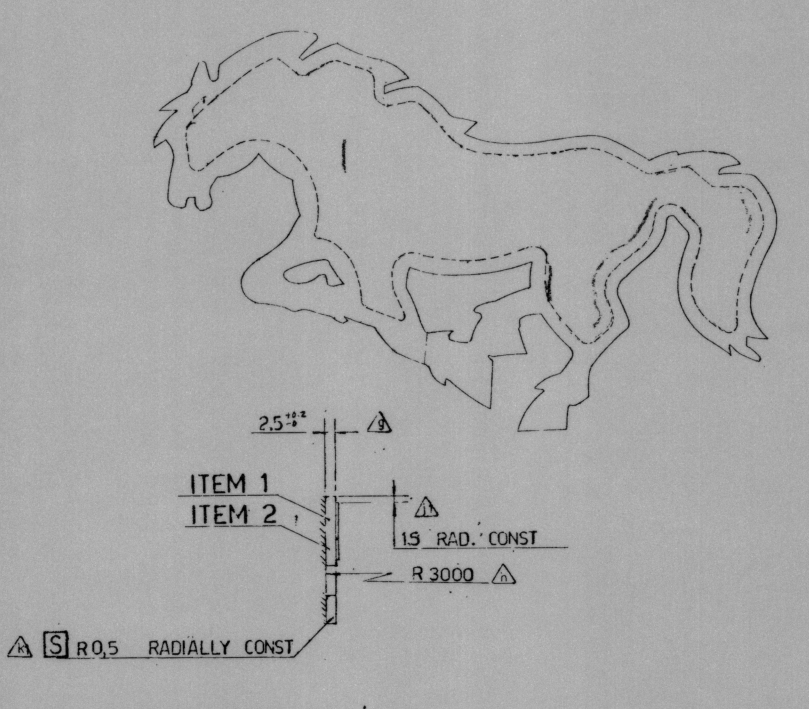

$2.5^{+0.2}_{-0}$

ITEM 1

ITEM 2

1.5 RAD. CONST

R 3000

S R 0,5 RADIALLY CONST

SECTION A-A

주 기 : 1.재질 :ITEM 1: 알루미늄 다이캐스팅 규격번호 (JIS H 5302) ADC-5.
ATE : 알루미늄판 규격번호 (JIS H 4000)
ITEM 2 : 양면 접착테이프 규격번호 (MS 711-8)
2.표면처리: 해칭부위; 헤어라인은 마스터 스타일링 샘플에 준할것.
ALT : 헤어라인 없는 백색 무광택.
해칭외 부위 :검정 페인트 규격 번호 MS 651-4
3.양날쎈개 접착 테이프(ITEM 2)를 부착과여 대상할것.
4.흠집및 날카로운 부위를 고를것.
5 아노다이즈 규격번호 MS 633-2 (피막두께; 최소 0,008mm)

NOTE : 1. MATERIAL : ITEM1:ALUMINUM! ALLOY TO SPEC NO. JIS H 5302, ADC-5.
ALT :ALUMINUM PLATE TO SPEC NO. JIS H 4000.
ITEM 2: DOUBLE COATED-PRESSURE SENSITIVE TAPE TO SPEC NO MS 711-8.
2. FINISH:HATCHED AREA:HAIRLINES TO MATCH MASTER STYL'G SAMPLE.
ALT:MAT WHITE WITHOUT HAIRLINES.
REMAINDERS : MAT BLACK PAINT TO SPEC NO MS 651-4
3 EMBLEM TO BE SUPPLIED ON ADHESIVE TAPE (ITEM2)
4 REMOVE BURRS AND SHARP EDGES
5 ANODIZE TO SPEC NO MS 633-2 (COAT Th ; 0,008mm MIN).

말 형상 엠블럼 도면
Horse shape emblem drawing

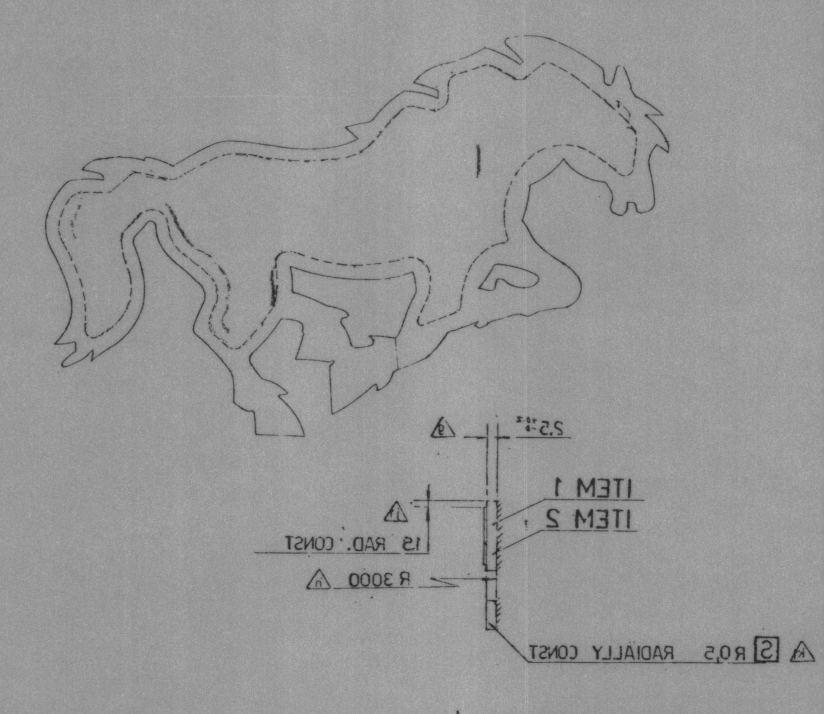

SECTION A-A

ITEM 1
ITEM 2

2.5 ±0.2

15 RAD.: CONST

R 3000

R 0.5 RADIALLY CONST

NOTE: 1. MATERIAL: ITEM 1: ALUMINUM: ALLOY TO SPEC. NO. JIS H 5302, ADC-5.
ALT: ALUMINUM PLATE TO SPEC NO. JIS H 4000.
ITEM 2: DOUBLE COATED-PRESSURE SENSITIVE TAPE TO SPEC NO. MS 711-8.
2. FINISH: HATCHED AREA: HAIRLINES TO MATCH MASTER STYLE SAMPLE.
ALT: MAT WHITE WITHOUT HAIRLINES.
REMAINDERS : MAT BLACK PAINT TO SPEC NO. MS 651-4
3. EMBLEM TO BE SUPPLIED ON ADHESIVE TAPE (ITEM 2)
4. REMOVE BURRS AND SHARP EDGES.
5. ANODIZE TO SPEC. NO. MS 633-2 (COAT TH: 0.008 mm MIN).

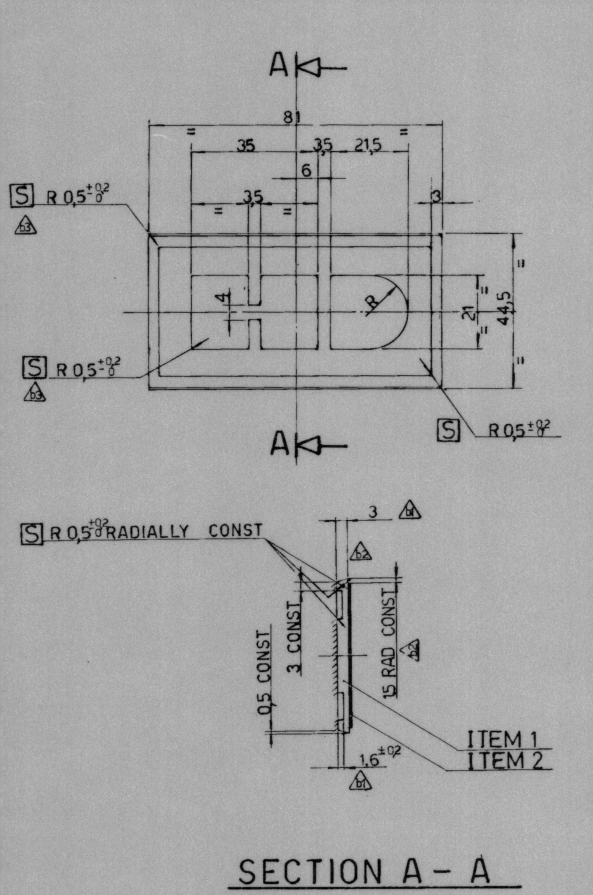

A ← | ← A (section markers)

81
35 | 3,5 | 21,5
6
3,5
3
4
R
21
44,5

S R 0,5 ±0,2 /0
b3

S R 0,5 ±0,2 /0
b3

S R 0,5 ±0,2 /0

S R 0,5 ±0,2 /0 RADIALLY CONST
0,5 CONST
3 CONST
15 RAD CONST
3
1,6 ±0,2
ITEM 1
ITEM 2
b2
b1

SECTION A – A

주기:1:2대 컬

△a.ITEM 1:알루미늄 다이개스팅 규격번호(JIS H 5302)ADC-5.
ALT:알루미늄판 규격번호(JIS H 4000).
ITEM 2 알 실유테이프
ALT:해어라인 제작부위:해어라인은 규격번호 MS 711-8.
ALT:해어라인 없는 백색 무광택
△c.2표면처리:제작부위:해어라인은 마스터 스타일링 색플에 준할것.

NOTE:1. MATERIAL
△a.ITEM 1:ALUMINUM ALLOY TO SPEC NO JIS H 5302, ADC-5.
ALT:ALUMINUM PLATE TO SPEC NO JIS H 4000.
ITEM 2:DOUBLE COATED PRESSURE SENSITIVE TAPE TO
SPEC NO MS 711-8.
△c.2.FINISH:HATCHED AREA:HAIRLINES TO MATCH MASTER STYLG SAMPLE.
ALT:MAT WHITE WITHOUT HAIRLINES.
REMAINDERS : MAT BLACK PAINT TO SPEC NO MS 651-4.

해당부위 금속배드크 규격번호 MS 651-4.
3엔블럼은 점착테이프(ITEM2)를 부착하여 공급할것.
4버트 및 날카로운 부위를 제거할것.
△a.5.아노다이즈 규격번호 MS 633-2 (피막두께, 최소 0,008mm)

3.EMBLEM TO BE SUPPLIED ON ADHESIVE TAPE (ITEM 2).
4.REMOVE BURRS AND SHARP EDGES.
△a.5.ANODIZE TO SPEC NO MS 633-2 (COAT Th;0,008mm MIN).

HD 로고 엠블럼 도면
HD logo emblem drawing

토리노 모토쇼에서 처음으로 선보인 HD 로고는 울산 종합 자동차 공장 건설 후
현대자동차의 공식 로고로 사용되었다. 백색 바탕은 '평화와 복지'를, 이니셜의 청색은
'진취적 기상'을, 달리는 자동차 형태로 도안한 HD 이니셜은 '현대차의 중단 없는
행진'을, 청색 사각형 테두리는 '전 사원의 화합과 단결'을 의미했다.

The HD logo, showcased for the first time at the Turin Motor Show, was
adopted as the official logo of the Hyundai Motor Company after the
Ulsan Plant was built. The white background represents "peace and
welfare", the blue represents "enterprising spirit", the HD initials in the
form of a speeding car represent 'Hyundai Motor Company's "onward
advance", and the blue rectangular frame represents "harmony and
unity among Hyundai's people".

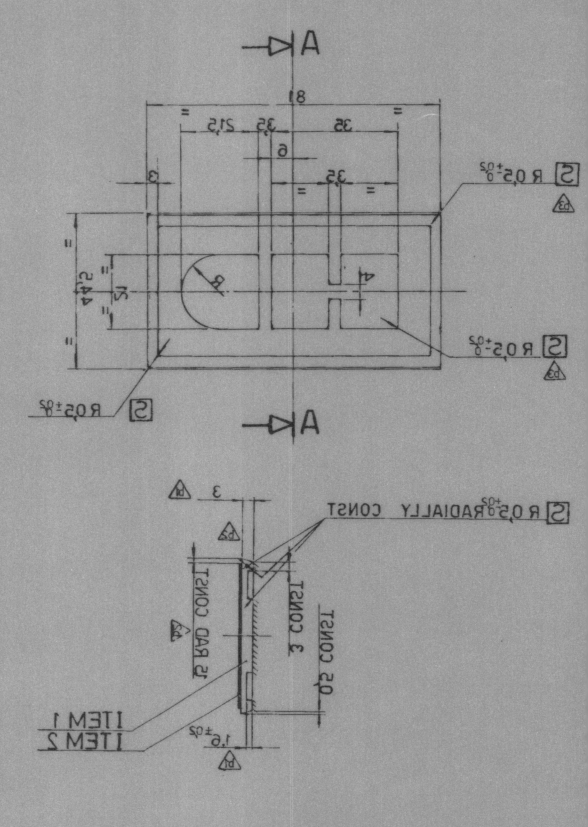

SECTION A-A

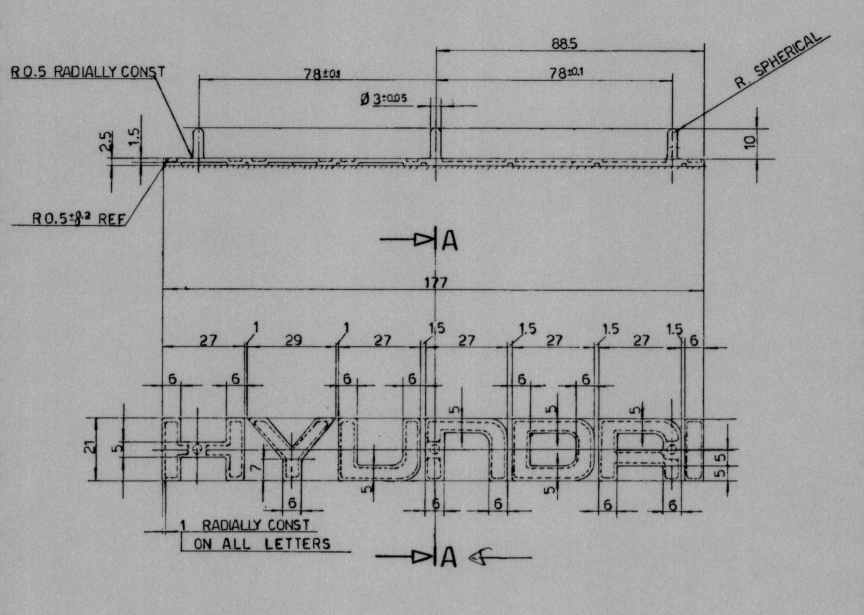

R 0.5 RADIALLY CONST

R 0.5 ±8.2 REF

88.5

78 ±0.1

78 ±0.1

R. SPHERICAL

Ø 3 ±0.05

2.5   1.5

10

▷|A

177

27   1   29   1   27   1.5   27   1.5   27   1.5   27   1.5   6

6   6   6   6   6   6   6

21   5   5   5   5

7   5   5   5   5   5.5

6   6   6   6   6

1 RADIALLY CONST
ON ALL LETTERS

▷|A ◁

NOTE:
1 MATERIAL:-FOR 87411-11100 : ZINC ALLOY DIE CASTING TO SPEC NO MS145-2
          -FOR 87411-11000 : ABS TO SPEC NO MS 225-1 TYPE ABS 90-20B
2 FINISH:
     - FOR ZINC ALLOY DIE CASTING(87411-11100)
        HATCHED SURFACE TO BE CHROMECOATED TO SPEC NO MS 612-10 TYPE6 AND REMAINDERS
        TO BE SATIN BLACK TO MATCH STYLING SAMPLE
     - FOR ABS(87411-11000)
        HATCHED SURFACE TO BE CHROMECOATED TO SPEC NO MS625-2 AND REMAINDERS
        TO BE SATIN BLACK TO MATCH STYLING SAMPLE
3 MARKED THUS * R 0.5 8² TO BE APPLIED TO ALL EDGES

HYUNDAI 로고 엠블럼 도면
HYUNDAI logo emblem drawing

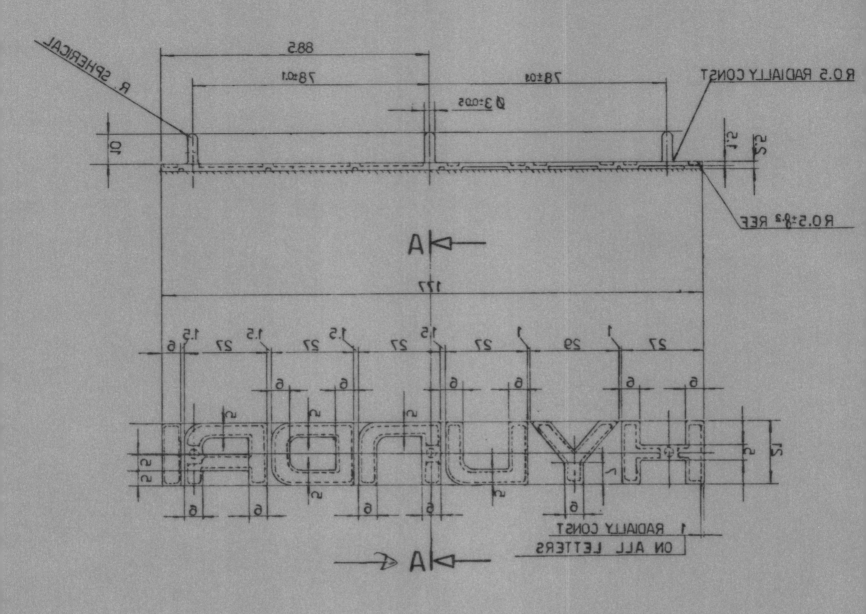

R. SPHERICAL

R.0.5 RADIALLY CONST

88.5

78±0.1

□3±0.05

10

2.5

1.5

R.0.5±0.2 REF

A

177

1.5 1.5 1.5 1.5 1.5 1
6   27   27   27   29   27
1.5

2

12

1 RADIALLY CONST
ON ALL LETTERS

A

주 기.1.재 질 :-FOR 87411-11100 : 아연다이캐스팅의 재료규격 MS.145-2
            -FOR 87411-11000 : ABS 재료규격 MS 225-1 TYPE ABS 90-20B.

2. 표면처리 :
   -아연다이캐스팅(87411-11100) 빗금친 표면은 재료규격 MS 612-10 TYPE 6의 크롬에 맞추어 처리하며 나머지 부분은
    무광블랙은 스타일 견본에 맞출것.
   -ABS(87411-11000) : 빗금친 표면은 재료규격 MS 625-2에 맞추어 크롬코팅할 것이며 나머지 부분은 무광블랙은 스타일견본에 맞출것.

3. 부호 *R 0.5⁺0.² 는 모든 모서리에 적용할것.

NOTE:
1 MATERIAL:- FOR 87411-11100 : ZINC ALLOY DIE CASTING TO SPEC NO MS145-2
           -FOR 87411-11000 : ABS TO SPEC NO MS 225-1 TYPE ABS 90-20B
2 FINISH:
   - FOR ZINC ALLOY DIE CASTING(87411-11100)
   HATCHED SURFACE TO BE CHROMECOATED TO SPEC NO MS612-10 TYPES AND REMAINDERS
   TO BE SATIN BLACK TO MATCH STYLING SAMPLE
   - FOR ABS(87411-11000)
   HATCHED SURFACE TO BE CHROMECOATED TO SPEC NO MS625-2 AND REMAINDERS
   TO BE SATIN BLACK TO MATCH STYLING SAMPLE
3 MARKED THUS *R 0.5⁺0.² TO BE APPLIED TO ALL EDGES

HYUNDAI 로고 엠블럼 도면
HYUNDAI logo emblem drawing

대한민국을 전 세계 아홉 번째 자동차 독자 모델 생산국에
진입하게 만들어준 포니(위)와 토리노 모터쇼에서 포니와
함께 공개돼 호평을 받은 포니 쿠페(아래)

With the Pony, Korea became the 9th country
worldwide to produce its own proprietary
model (Top)
Unveiled next to the Pony at the Turin Motor
Show, the Pony Coupe model garnered positive
acclaim (Below)

토리노 모터쇼에 출품된 포니, 포니 쿠페와 함께 기념사진을
촬영한 조지 턴불 부사장, 정세영 당시 사장, 조르제토
주지아로 디자이너(왼쪽부터)
George Turnbull, Se-yung Chung, and Giorgetto
Giugiaro taking a commemorative picture
with the Pony and Pony Coupe at the Turin
Motor Show

우리 손으로
길을 다져나가다

Paving the way
with our own hands

수많은 시행착오 끝에 완성한 한국형 양산 프로세스

1975년 1월 이탈디자인으로부터 설계 도면과 프로토타입을 인수하면서 현대자동차는 포니의 양산 준비를 본격화했다. 부품 생산, 생산 설비 구매와 설치, 생산 라인 기술자 훈련 등 처음 접하는 수많은 업무를 준비하는 과정 역시 난관의 연속이었다. 생각지도 못한 문제가 드러났고, 짧은 시간 내 해결책을 찾기 위해 수시로 머리를 맞대야 했다.

이탈디자인이 작업한 도면을 기반으로 양산을 본격화하는 과정에서 직면한 가장 큰 문제는 도면 형태였다. 이탈디자인에서 받은 도면 대부분이 어셈블리 도면(assembly drawing)이어서 실제 제작하기 위한 상세 부품 도면(part drawing)은 없었던 것이다. 당시 부품 산업이 발달한 유럽 등 선진국에서는 어셈블리 도면만 있어도 부품업체가 자동차 제조사와 협의해 가면서 상세 도면을 만들었다. 그러나 당시 한국에는 제대로 된 부품업체가 없던 시절이라 선진국과 같은 방식으로는 부품 제작이 불가능했다. 게다가 미쓰비시의 엔진, 변속기, 섀시 도면은 일본 규격으로 제작된 반면 이탈디자인의 차체와 의장 도면은 이탈리아 규격으로 그려져 있어 규격과 표기 방식에 차이가 있었다. 결국 한국 실정에 맞는 상세 도면과 품질 테스트 방식 등을 새롭게 만들어야 한다는 사실을 뒤늦게 깨달은 것이다.

이와 같이 양산을 준비하면서 어려운 문제에 봉착했을 때 현대자동차 직원들은 외국인 자문단의 도움을 받으며 문제를 하나하나 해결해 나갔다. 일례로 부품 도면의 경우 조지 턴불과 함께 온 영국의 차체 디자인 기술자를 통해 도면을 검수하고 출도(出圖)하는 방법을 배워나갔다.

그러나 기술 자문만으로 모든 문제를 해결할 수는 없다. 자문단도 차량을 처음부터 개발한 경험이 없었기에 설계에서 생산으로 이어지는 실질적 작업은 현대자동차 직원이 주

Korea's mass production process, after numerous trials and errors

In January 1975, Hyundai took over the Pony's design drawings and prototypes from Italdesign, and began preparing for its mass production. However, preparing for multiple new mass production tasks, such as parts production, the purchase and installation of production equipments, and training production line technicians, was also a series of difficulties. The company encountered numerous unforeseen circumstances, and many issues frequently required solutions within a limited timeframe.

The biggest challenge for the full-scale mass production based on the Italdesign drawings was the form of the drawings, most of which were of assembly and none containing detailed parts for actual production. In developed countries such as Europe, where the parts industry was advanced, it was possible to manufacture parts even if there were only assembly drawings because parts manufacturers made detailed drawings in consultation with automobile manufacturers. However, at that time, there were no proper parts manufacturers in Korea, so it was impossible to manufacture them like in developed countries. In addition, Mitsubishi's engine, transmission, and chassis drawings were made with Japanese standards while Italdesign's car body and design drawings were made with Italian standards, so there was a difference in specifications and notation. Ultimately, it became evident that there was a need to create detailed drawings tailored to the Korean situation, alongside a new method for quality testing.

With the assistance of foreign advisory

도적으로 결정하고 검증하면서 진행해 나가야 했다. 모든 개발 과정이 새롭고 처음 경험하는 일이라 수없이 시행착오를 겪어야 했지만, 한국 실정에 맞게 규격과 프로세스를 체계화하는 과정을 통해 설계에서 양산으로 이어지는 구체적 로드맵을 그리고 부품 국산화 계획도 수립할 수 있었다. 앞이 보이지 않을 만큼 막막하던 길이 조금씩 또렷해지기 시작한 것이다.

groups, Hyundai's employees successfully resolved complex problems that arose during their preparations for mass production one by one. For example, in the case of parts drawings, they learned how to inspect and publish the drawings from body design engineers who had flown in from England with George Turnbull.

However, technical consultation alone could not solve every problem. Since these advisory groups had no experience in developing vehicles from scratch, the process of design to production had to be carried out by Hyundai employees themselves. At the same time, Hyundai employees had to take the lead in making decisions and verifying them. The entire development process was new and unfamiliar, so there was a lot of trial and error. Nevertheless, by systematizing standards and processes to suit the Korean situation, a detailed road map from design to mass production and a plan for the localization of parts could be established. Gradually, the road that once looked dark and hopeless began to show hope and possibilities.

포니의 레이아웃 도면(위)과 보디 얼라인먼트 도면(아래)
The Pony's layout (top) and body alignment
drawings (below)

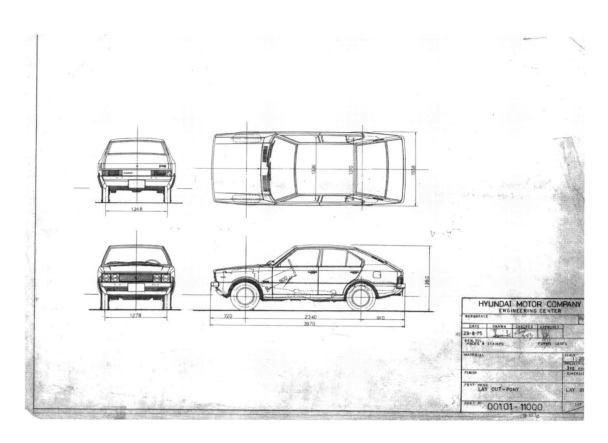

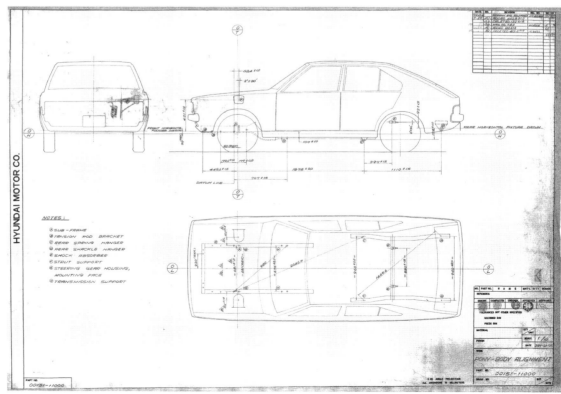

부품 국산화를 통한 자동차 산업 인프라 구축

자동차를 생산하기 위해서는 부품 산업이 뒷받침되어야 한다. 하지만 포니 개발 당시 한국의 자동차 부품 산업 기반은 매우 열악했고, 신차 개발에 필요한 부품업체 또한 거의 없는 상황이었다. 독자 모델 개발과 함께 부품 국산화가 목표였던 현대자동차는 포니의 부품 국산화율을 90%로 정하고 이를 달성하기 위해 국내 부품업체 실태를 전면 조사했다. 그리고 생산 능력이 있는 업체를 엄선해 선정된 업체에는 기술 협력 뿐 아니라 해외 전문 기술 도입 알선, 자본 제휴 등 지원을 아끼지 않겠다는 계획을 세웠다. 현대자동차는 이 계획을 실현하기 위해 1974년 4월 일일이 업체를 순회하며 최종 선정 작업을 벌였고, 6월 말 160개 업체를 1차 적격 업체로 정하고 각 업체 대표를 울산 공장으로 초청해 종합 자동차 공장 건설과 고유 모델 개발에 대해 설명하고 협조를 요청했다.

1974년 6월 섀시 부품부터 본격적으로 개발하기 시작했다. 미쓰비시로부터 엔진, 변속기, 리어 액슬, 플랫폼 레이아웃 등의 도면을 제공받았고, 그 외 현가·조향·제동장치, 배기·냉각 시스템 등 모든 도면은 현대자동차 기술실에서 설계했다. 그해 10월 현대자동차 기술실에서 설계한 도면 출도(出圖)가 완료되었는데, 섀시의 모든 부품을 도면에 따라 국산화할 수 있도록 100% 도면화했으며, 각 부품 설계 사양에는 검사 기준과 기술 시험까지 포함했다. 1975년 1월에는 이탈디자인이 보낸 차체 및 플로어 부품 최종 설계 도면이 도착해 부품 개발을 가속화했다. 업체가 부품을 시험 생산하면 품질관리부가 품질 검사를 철저히 했고, 품질이 떨어지는 부품의 경우 끈질긴 지도를 통해 개선해 나갔다. 외국에서 부품을 가져다 조립하던 기존과 달리 부품 기술 자료와 설계 제공 등 전 부품 생산을 온전히 책임져야 하는 상황이라 모든 과정에 엄청난 집중력을 발휘해야 했고, 무거운 책임감을 갖고 작업

Advancing the automotive industry through the localization of parts

An auto parts industry is necessary to support the production of automobiles. However, during the development of Pony, Korea's auto parts industry was in its infancy, and there were hardly any companies producing the necessary parts for new car development. Hyundai aimed to localize parts and build its own model, setting the target for the Pony's parts localization rate at 90% and reassessed the actual conditions of domestic parts manufacturers to achieve this goal. In addition, it set up a plan to carefully select companies with production capacity and provide support such as technical cooperation, bringing in international expertise, and capital alliance. Hyundai toured these companies one by one in April 1974 and conducted the final selection process. At the end of June, 160 eligible companies were selected in the first round and company representatives were invited to the Ulsan plant to explain the construction of a comprehensive automobile plant and the development of an independent model, and asked for cooperation.

Full-scale parts development began in June 1974 with the chassis. Blueprints for the engine, transmission, rear axle, and platform layout were provided by Mitsubishi. Hyundai's technical department drew all other blueprints including the suspension, steering, braking, exhaust, and cooling systems. In October, the drawings prepared by Hyundai's technical department were finalized. All parts of the chassis were drafted 100% to be localized, and the design specifications of each component included inspection

에 임했다. 그해 현대자동차는 포니를 생산하고 종합 자동차 공장을 건설하면서 전국의 429개 업체를 계열화했는데, 이는 그 자체로 한국 자동차 부품 공업 발전의 시작이자 자동차 산업 생태계를 형성하는 계기로 평가될 만한 일이었다.

standards and technical test specifications. In January 1975, parts development was accelerated as the final drawings for the body and floor parts arrived from Italdesign. When a vendor produces a pilot part, the quality control department conducts a thorough inspection. Parts with insufficient quality were then improved through persistent quality guidance. Unlike previously where parts were imported from overseas and assembled, full responsibility had to be taken for the entire production of parts. This includes providing technical data and designs, where every step of the process requires meticulous attention and came with a heavy responsibility. That year, Hyundai formed an affiliation with 429 companies across the country while during the production of the Pony and the construction of the automobile plant. This result can be regarded as the beginning of the Korean auto parts industry's development in addition to being the trigger to form an auto industry ecosystem.

주행 및 내구성 테스트와 품질관리

현대자동차가 포니를 출고하기 전 많은 시간을 투자한 부분은 주행 및 내구성 테스트였다. 이와 더불어 한국의 도로 실정에 맞는 차를 개발하기 위한 테스트를 꼼꼼히 하면서 품질을 개선해 나갔다. 현대자동차는 이탈리아에서 가져온 프로토타입과 국내 기술자들이 자체 제작한 시제품을 활용해 1년 동안 성능 테스트를 진행했다.

당시만 해도 지금 같은 종합 주행 시험장이 없던 시절이라 주행 테스트는 공장 내에서 진행하거나 울산에서 서울까지난 일반 도로를 활용했고, 때로는 울산공항 활주로를 빌려서 진행했다. 그리고 시험 결과에 따라 부품의 형상이나 재질을 바꿔가면서 성능을 향상시키고 내구성을 높여나갔다. 비포장도로, 오르막길 등 다양한 환경의 도로에서 주행 테스트를 거듭하며 차체를 보강하고 문제점을 개선하는 과정도 거쳤다.

현대자동차는 이와 같이 숱한 테스트를 통해 품질을 향상시키기 위한 노하우를 터득해 나갔다. 일례로, 당시만 해도 비포장도로가 대부분이다 보니 차체의 틈새를 통해 먼지가 들어오는 차량이 많았다. 이를 해결하기 위해 현대자동차는 먼지 유입 여부를 시험하는 더스트 터널 설비를 도입했다. 1년에 걸쳐 진행한 다양한 성능 테스트 중 특히 남산 오르막길 주행 테스트의 성공은 기념비적이라 할 만하다. 여러 번에 걸쳐 진행한 테스트에서 차체가 자꾸 깨지는 바람에 이를 보완하고 덧붙이다 보니 점점 무거워졌고, 힘이 달려서 남산 오르막길 주행이 어려울지도 모른다는 걱정이 커졌다. 직접 테스트에 참여한 정세영 회장이 "이 차가 남산을 못 올라가면 우리 망한다!"는 말을 대놓고 했을 정도였다. 그러나 우려와 달리 포니는 남산 오르막길을 거뜬히 올라갔다. 나중에 이유를 알고 보니 국내에서 만든 포니 엔진이 미쓰비시의 기존 엔진보다 출력이 2마력이나 더 높았기 때문이었다. 자동차 생산

Driving and durability testing and ongoing quality control

Hyundai invested a significant amount of time in conducting driving and durability tests before releasing the Pony. In addition, its quality was improved by meticulously conducting tests to develop a car suitable for Korean road conditions. Hyundai conducted performance tests for a year using prototypes brought over from Italy and also those made by local engineers.

At the time, there was no comprehensive proving ground, so every driving test was conducted in the plant or on general roads from Ulsan to Seoul, sometimes even by renting the runway at Ulsan Airport. The forms and materials of parts were then changed to improve performance and ensure durability, depending on the test results. The body was reinforced, and problems were addressed through repeated driving tests on roads in various conditions, such as unpaved roads or uphill.

The company slowly accumulated its quality improvement skills through lots of trial and error when going through testing. For example, back then, most of the roads were unpaved, so dust would get in through gaps in the bodywork. To address these issues, Hyundai introduced a dust tunnel facility to test dust inflow. Among the numerous driving tests conducted throughout the year, the success of the Namsan uphill driving test was a monumental achievement. There were concerns that the power might not be sufficient to drive the car up Namsan, as the car got heavier with improvements and reinforcements. It was to the point that then-President Se-yung Chung, who participated in the

경험이 많은 미쓰비시가 정해진 기준치 이내 수준으로만 만들면 된다는 생각으로 각 부품을 제작한 반면, 엔진을 처음 생산하는 현대자동차는 정밀도에 심혈을 기울임으로써 엔진 출력이 오히려 더 개선되는 결과가 나온 것이다.

test himself, openly stated, "If this car can't climb the Namsan slope, we're doomed!" However, the Pony went up the Namsan hill, easing everyone's worries. Later, Hyundai discovered the Pony's engine produced 2 horsepower more than Mitsubishi's original engine, which made the uphill test possible. With much experience in automobile production, Mitsubishi manufactured its parts with the idea that each part only needed to be made to fall within the predetermined standard. On the contrary, Hyundai, which produced its first-ever engine, improved its power by focusing more on precision.

우리 손으로 우리 실정에 맞게 길을 개척하다

Paving the way with our own hands

포니와 경쟁 차 브리사의 연비 비교 시험 보고서
(1975년 7월)
A fuel efficiency comparison report for the Pony and the competing model, Brisa (July 1975)

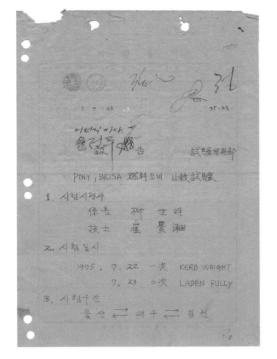

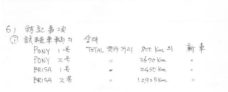

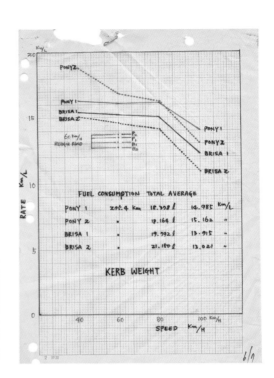

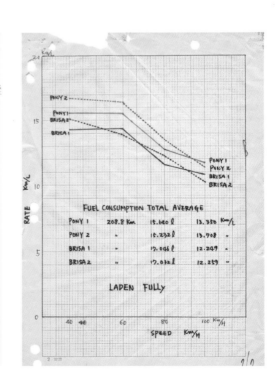

포니가 개척한
자동차 양산의 길

The road to automobile
mass production
pioneered by the Pony

포니 생산 기지, 울산 종합 자동차 공장 건설

포니를 개발하는 동안 이를 생산하기 위한 완성차 공장 건설도 차근차근 진행되었다. 울산시 염포동 일대의 땅 약 198만 3,400m²(60만 평)를 자동차 공장 예정지로 승인받아 정밀 지질 검사부터 측량, 토지 매입 등을 신속하게 진행했고, 1974년 9월부터 완성차 공장 건설 공사에 본격 착수했다.

양산차 공장을 완공하기 위해서는 외형 못지않게 내실을 갖추는 것이 중요했다. 국내 최초의 양산차 공장 건설과 생산 체계 구축을 위해 공장 건설 전반에 걸쳐 자문을 해줄 전문가로 조지 턴불 부사장을 위촉했고, 미쓰비시와는 공장 배치와 내부 설계에 대한 용역 계약을 체결했다. 조지 턴불 부사장은 공장 건설에 필요한 공학적·기술적 자문과 생산 설비 구매 관련 조언을 해주었으며, 현대자동차는 그의 이름을 빌려 생산 설비 업체와 협의를 시작할 수 있었다. 제조 공정과 공법, 기계 장비 선정 등의 공장 설계는 미쓰비시가 담당했다. 이는 기존에 체결한 가솔린엔진 기술 협조 계약과는 별도로, 프레스·조립·주물·엔진 등 12개 시설의 배치와 각 라인의 세부 설계 등을 포함한 것이었다. 1974년 7월에 이루어진 이 계약에 따라 미쓰비시는 자사 기술자를 현대자동차에 파견해 설계 작업에 착수했고, 이듬해 2월 설계를 최종 확정했다. 이를 토대로 단조 공장을 시작으로 프레스·조립·주물·엔진 공장을 순차적으로 착공했다.

공장 설계와 공정 구축은 해외 전문가의 도움을 받았지만 토목, 건축 등 공장 건립과 설비 도입 및 설치는 내부 인력이 주도했다. 국내 기계공업이 초기 단계라 국산 공작기계와 계측기의 정확도가 떨어져 설비 대부분을 수입할 수밖에 없었지만 어디서 무엇을 수입해야 할지, 어떤 회사의 어떤 제품이 좋은지 알아보는 건 모두 내부 직원의 몫이었다. 직원들은 해외 연수 시 전수받은 설비 구매 관련 지식 및 노하우를 바탕

Construction of the Pony production base, Ulsan Comprehensive Automobile Plant

While the Pony was being developed, the construction of a complete vehicle production plant also proceeded step by step. After receiving approval for a land area of approximately 1,983,400m² in the Yeompo-dong area of Ulsan as a site for an automobile plant, the entire process from detailed geological inspection to surveying and purchasing land was quickly carried out. Thus, in September 1974, the construction of a mass-produced automobile plant began in earnest.

To complete the automobile plant, it was important to not only have an impressive exterior but also a stable and solid internal structure. To build the first mass-production automobile plant in Korea and establish a manufacturing system, George Turnbull was appointed as a Vice President to advise on the plant construction, and a service contract was signed with Mitsubishi for plant layout and interior design. Vice President George Turnbull gave engineering and technical advice needed for the plant construction and purchase of manufacturing equipment. By leveraging his reputation, Hyundai Motor was able to initiate discussions with equipment manufacturers. A service contract had been signed with Mitsubishi which was responsible for designing the plant, including the manufacturing process, construction method, and mechanical equipment selection. This was a separate contract from the existing gasoline engine technology cooperation contract, which included arranging 12 facilities such as press, assembly, casting, and engine factories and a detailed design of each

완공을 앞둔 울산 종합 자동차 공장
The Ulsan Comprehensive Automobile Plant
just before its completion

으로 필요한 설비 목록을 작성한 후 영국·프랑스·일본 등으로
날아가 기계 장비 회사들과 협상을 진행했다. 한편 설비 발주
자금 제한은 직원들의 어려움을 가중시켰다. 프랑스·영국·일
본 등에서 들여온 차관은 해당 국가의 설비를 구매하는 데만
사용할 수 있었기 때문이다. 이에 따라 자동차 보디 제작 전
용 프레스기와 금형 기계는 프랑스에서, 엔진 가공과 보디 스
탬핑, 주물 가공, 디젤엔진, 단조, 금형 등 각 공장과 기술 센터
시설재는 영국에서 수입했으며, 주조·단조 공장 건설에 필요
한 시설재는 일본에서 들여왔다.

facility. According to this contract concluded in
July 1974, Mitsubishi dispatched its engineers
to Hyundai to begin the design work which it
finalized in February of the following year. Based
on this, the construction of press, assembly,
casting, and engine factories began sequentially,
starting with the forging plant.

While the plant design and process construction were assisted by overseas experts,
internal personnel led the plant construction,
including civil engineering and construction as

1975년 6월부터는 주조·단조 공장을 시작으로 수입한 생산 설비의 설치 작업에 돌입했으며, 1975년 11월 엔진 공장을 마지막으로 기계 설치 작업을 마무리했다. 그리고 1975년 12월 1일 포니 생산 기지이자 해외 수출 기지가 될 완성차 공장을 완공했다. 약 1년 3개월 만에 8만 대 규모의 종합 자동차 공장 건설을 완수한 것이다. 이는 당시 세계적으로 유례를 찾아보기 힘든 최단기간 건설 기록이었다.

well as the introduction and installation of facilities. Since the domestic machinery industry was in its infancy, most of the equipment had to be imported due to the inaccuracy of domestic machine tools and instruments. Nonetheless, it was entirely up to the internal staff to find out where to import what and which brands were good. Employees drew up a list of necessary equipment based on the knowledge and expertise of equipment purchases they had received during overseas training and then flew to England, France, and Japan to negotiate with mechanical equipment companies. On the other hand, the restrictions on budget for equipment orders added to the employees' difficulties. This was because the loans from France, England, and Japan could be used to purchase facilities in those countries only. Accordingly, press and die machines dedicated to car body production were imported from France; engine processing, body stamping, casting processing, diesel engines, die, and other facilities for each plant and technology center were imported from the UK; and facility materials for the construction of the casting and forging plant were imported from Japan.

In June 1975, the installation of imported production facilities began with the foundry and forging shop and in November 1975, the engine plant was completed. On December 1, 1975, the complete vehicle manufacturing plant, which would be the Pony's production base and an overseas export base, was completed. This comprehensive automobile plant with a capacity of 80,000 units was completed in about 1 year and 3 months, the shortest construction period of its time, a record not seen elsewhere in the world.

No. 168

올해, 사 쌓들이 산 더미처럼 쌓여져 왔다.

12월 4일

국제박람회에 출품됐던 포니차가 공장

1 파 차이에 첫 선을 보였다. 멀리서 보

니 서쪽(깐)은 빨산색, 앞면의 모양은 좋은

쪽인데, 뒷면은 꽁지 빠진 ~~꿩 모양~~ 꿩처럼 짧은것

같았다. 국제박람회 출품이 끝나고 제 집

을 찾아 온것을 알았다. 앞으로 이 포

니를 우리의 손으로 만들어, 세계각국 ~~으로~~

접시접을 보내야 되겠구나!

(10×20)

No. 268

11월 20일 30

종합 자동차 공장은 착공 1년 3개월 만에 준공되었다. 종합공장이 마침내 완공되어 오늘 오후 2시 45분경, 종합공 장의 핵공장인 주조공장에서 역사적인 용탕(쇳물)이 전기로에서 나왔다. 쇳물을 주입한 후 공장장님이 하 간부님들을 모 시고 고사를 지내고, 현장 인원들은 작 업이 끝난 후 술과 떡을 먹었다. 현대에 주물공장을 기다리며 일기를

(10×20)

울산 공장에서 기술기사로 근무한 김경수 씨가 포니 생산을 위한 완성차 공장 건설 과정을 꼼꼼하게 기록한 일기다. 대한민국 최초로 자동차 독자 모델을 생산한다는 긍지와 애사심이 느껴지는 자료로, 포니 생산 준비로 분주했던 공장 안팎의 생생한 현장을 글과 그림으로 정성스럽게 기록했다.

Gyeong-su Kim, a production line worker working in the Ulsan Comprehensive Automobile Plant then, kept the record meticulously of how the plant was prepared for Pony manufacturing. Kim's pride at being part of the team that would bring Korea's first proprietary model to life and his love for the company are evident in his words and pictures drawn with care. The diary describes the work done in the plant to prepare for mass production of the Pony.

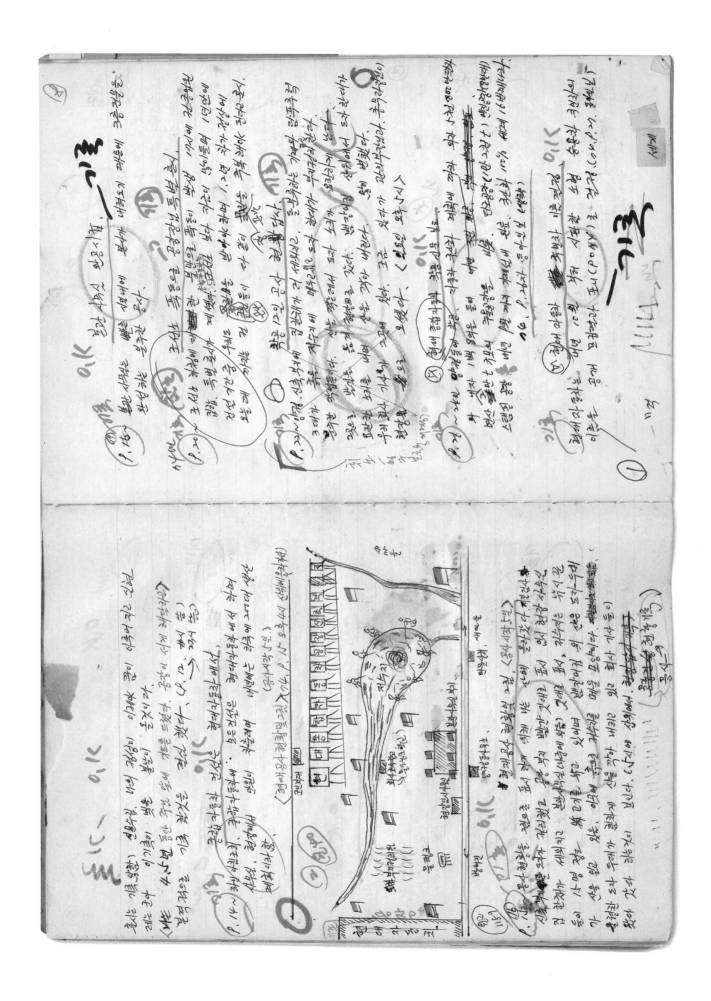

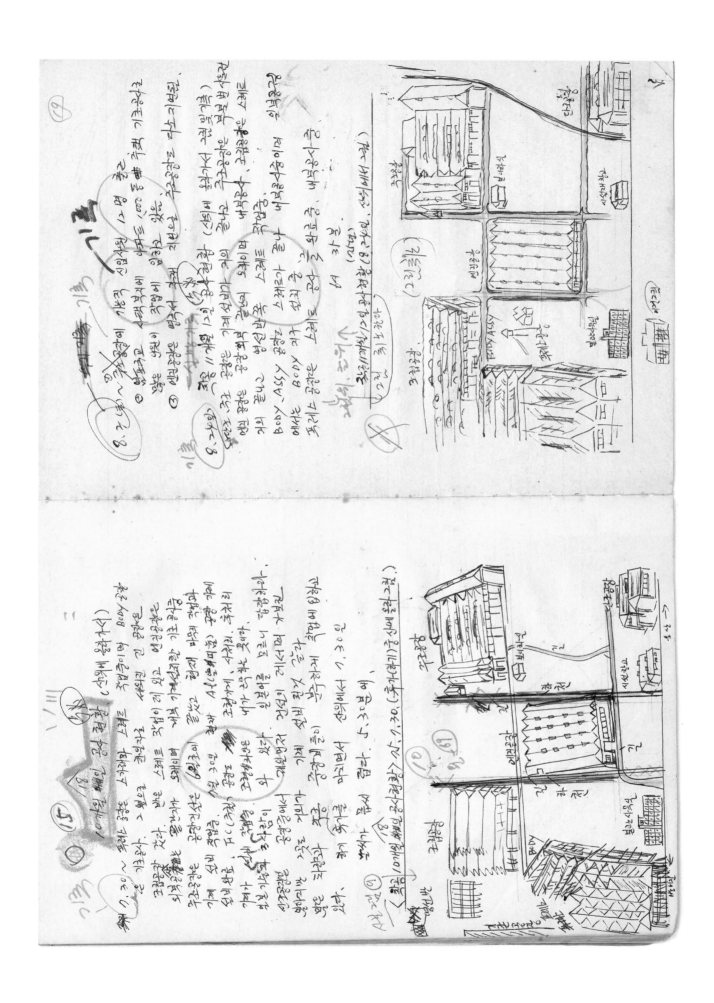

울산 종합 자동차 단조 공장
**The forging shop within the
Ulsan Comprehensive Automobile Plant**

현대자동차는 일본의 쇼와(昭和)금형공업으로부터 단조 공장 설비와 생산에 대한 기술
지도를 받았다. 당시 쇼와금형의 나치 고문은 오른손이 절단되는 사고로 실의에 빠져
고문직을 고사했으나 "우리가 산 것은 당신의 오른손이 아니라 머리입니다. 우리를
지도해 주십시오"라는 당시 공장 직원들의 말에 용기를 얻고 성심껏 지도했다고 한다.
직원들의 배움에 대한 열정과 인간적 감화가 기술 훈련의 기회를 연 것이다.

Hyundai Motor Company acquired both the forging facilities and
instruction in the use of forging technology from Japan's Showa
Corporation. At that time, Hyundai sought to enlist the help of Nachi,
an engineer from the Showa Corporation. Though he initially refused
the position due to the loss of his right hand from an industrial accident,
he finally accepted an advisory position after being encouraged by the
workers in the plant with these words: "What we asked for was not your
right hand, but what is inside your head. Please share that with us."
The workers' passion and humanity opened up opportunities for learning.

울산 종합 자동차 단조 공장
The forging shop within the
Ulsan Comprehensive Automobile Plant

짧은 시간 내에 안정화 이룬 포니 생산 라인

현대자동차는 각 공장의 대부분 기능공이 기계 가공 기초가 없는 상황에서 한국에 처음 소개되는 기계 설비를 능숙하게 다룰 수 있을 때까지 많은 노력을 기울였다. 기계 설치, 시운전, 시험 절삭, 시제품 생산에 이르기까지 모든 공정을 익히기 위한 강도 높은 훈련이 이어졌다. 완성차 공장 완공 이전인 1973년 11월 초에는 미쓰비시 교토 제작소에 3개월간 엔진 분야 연수생을 보냈고, 기술 연마에 필요한 전문가를 영입하기도 했다. 하지만 미쓰비시는 현대자동차 연수생들에게 그리 호의적이지 않았다. 자사 기술이 유출되지 않을까 미쓰비시가 항상 신경을 곤두세우고 있었기 때문이다. 기술 약자로서 연수 과정에서 겪은 경험은 빠른 시일 내에 자력으로 독자 모델을 생산하고 독자 기술을 개발하겠다는 현대자동차의 각

Rapid stabilization of the Pony production line

Hyundai had put considerable effort into their plant technicians to become proficient in handling machines introduced to Korea for the first time, as most of them had no background in their use. Intensive training took place for the workers to learn all processes, from machine installation, commissioning tests, and trial cutting to manufacturing pre-production cars. In early November 1973, before the completion of the automobile plant, Hyundai dispatched trainees to the Mitsubishi Kyoto Plant for engine training for three months and recruited experts who could provide technical guidance to nurture skilled workers. However, the overall atmosphere at Mitsubishi at the time of training was not very favorable to Hyundai trainees because Mitsubishi was (and continues to be) on edge worrying about possible technology espionage. Being technologically inferior to its counterpart during the training process further strengthened Hyundai's determination to produce its model and develop its technology as soon as possible.

Even after the engine training, Hyundai selected 200 technical personnel and sent them to overseas technical partners for training that lasted as short as one month or as long as a year or more until the end of 1975, when the comprehensive automobile plant was completed. Also, Hyundai began training about 2,000 technicians a year by job type and stage. As a result, the proficiency of the technicians steadily improved, and the Pony production line quickly stabilized. However, for jobs requiring an exceptionally high level of technology, service provision contracts were signed with overseas companies to provide

오를 더욱 굳건하게 만드는 계기가 되었다.

현대자동차는 엔진 기능공 연수 이후에도 종합 자동차 공장을 완공한 1975년 말까지 기술 요원 200여 명을 선발해 해외 기술 제휴사에 보내 짧게는 1개월, 길게는 1년 이상 연수를 시키는 한편, 연간 2,000여 명의 기능공을 대상으로 직종별·단계별로 훈련에 돌입했다. 그 결과 기능공의 숙련도는 꾸준히 향상됐고, 포니 생산 라인도 빠르게 안정화되었다. 그러나 고도의 기술을 요하는 부분은 따로 해외 기업에 용역을 발주하거나 과감하게 기술 연수를 의뢰했다. 대표적인 예가 금형 작업이었다. 차체를 찍어내는 금형은 제작하는 데 시간이 엄청 오래 걸리는 데다, 금형이 빨리 완성된다 하더라도 정확히 맞추는 작업만 6개월 이상 걸리기 때문에 1976년 초에 포니를 양산하는 건 실현 불가능한 계획이라는 것이 조지 턴불 부사장의 견해였다.

현대자동차는 이 문제를 타개하기 위해 신속하게 일본 금형 회사를 물색하기 시작했다. 그리고 오기하라 철공소와 거래하게 됨으로써 금형 제작 기간을 대폭 줄일 수 있었다. 이전까지 차 부분별로 금형을 만들던 오기하라는 포니를 통해 처음으로 차 전체 금형을 제작, 사세를 확장하게 되면서 열성적으로 금형을 만들었다. 일본에서 금형 완성품이 도착한 후 턴불 부사장이 지켜보는 가운데 하나하나 맞춰보니 한 치의 오차도 없이 맞아떨어졌다. 금형 때문에라도 공장 완공 후 양산하기까지 최소 2년 이상 더 필요하다고 주장했던 턴불 부사장은 이후 양산 스케줄에 대한 언급은 일절 하지 않았다. 현대자동차의 열정과 추진력을 인정할 수밖에 없었던 것이다. 개발, 생산, 구매 등 다양한 부문의 임직원들이 국내 최초 독자 모델을 만든다는 자부심을 가지고 프로젝트에 임한 결과였다. 그리고 마침내 1975년 12월 포니 시작품 생산을 시작으로 1976년 2월 국내 시장에 본격 출고되었다.

for technical training without hesitation. A representative example of this was body stamping dies. It takes a lot of time to make a press die for stamping a car body, and even if the die is completed quickly, it usually takes more than six months to precisely match it. Turnbull, therefore, expressed the opinion that mass production of the Pony by early 1976 was an unfeasible plan. Hyundai quickly started looking for a Japanese press die company to overcome this problem. Among them, through a transaction with Ogihara Iron Works, it was possible to drastically reduce the period of die production. Ogihara, which had been making dies for separate parts of a car up before that, created dies for an entire car for the first time through the Pony. As business expansion became possible, Ogihara enthusiastically took part. After the dies arrived, each die was matched individually under Vice President Turnbull's watch, and they fit seamlessly. Turnbull, who insisted that at least two more years were needed from plant completion to mass production considering the dies alone, did not comment on the mass production schedule after that. He had no choice but to acknowledge the passion and drive of Hyundai employees in various sectors, such as development, production, and purchasing, working on the project with pride in making Korea's first independent model. And finally, starting with producing the Pony's pre-production models in December 1975, the Pony was released to the domestic market in earnest in February 1976.

The arrival of Pony marked the beginning of a new era and a decisive turning point for the Korean automotive industry. With the Pony,

"자동차 생산이 100% 국산화되면 그에 따라 우리나라 기계 공업이 발전한다는 생각에, 또 그것으로 국가에 기여해야 한다는 일념으로 나는 설립 이후 지금까지 자동차에 막대한 투자와 노력을 쏟아왔다."

"I have invested a tremendous amount of money and effort because I believe that if we can produce all automobile parts domestically, Korea's machine industry will develop in tandem. This was my way of contributing to the development of my country."

정주영 선대회장 Founding Chairman Ju-yung Chung

포니의 등장은 한국 자동차 산업의 새 시대를 여는 일대 사건이자 결정적 전환점이었다. 한국은 포니를 통해 미국, 영국, 프랑스, 이탈리아, 독일, 일본, 스웨덴, 체코에 이어 세계에서 자국 브랜드의 고유 모델을 대량생산하는 아홉 번째 국가가 되었다. 이 국가들은 공통적으로 자국 고유 모델을 해외로 수출했는데, 이는 곧 수출에 대한 의사 결정을 자주적으로 할 수 있다는 점에서 의미가 크다. 이로써 현대자동차는 좁은 내수 시장을 넘어 해외 수출을 통해 규모의 경제를 실현할 수 있는 새로운 길을 열게 되었다. 그뿐 아니라 완성차 공장을 준공하고 국산차 생산을 본격화함으로써 외국 자동차 기업의 조립 생산자에서 벗어나 그토록 열망하던 독자적 자동차 제조사 대열에 합류하게 되었다. 이는 자동차 생산 경험이 많고 시장 지배적 위치에 있던 거대 글로벌 기업과의 종속 관계를 거부하고 아시아 개발도상국의 신생 회사가 추구한 독자 노선의 결과라는 점에서 매우 의미 있는 성취였다.

포니의 양산은 비단 자동차 산업뿐 아니라 대한민국 경제가 한 단계 진일보했음을 보여주는 사건이었다. 1960년대부터 폐허가 된 사회를 재건하기 위해 국가 주도로 경제개발 5개년계획을 진행했지만, 이는 도로 건설 위주의 사회간접자본 구축에 초점이 맞춰져 있었고, 고도 경제 성장기로 진입하기 위해서는 민간에서 비롯되는 경제적 동력이 필수적이었다. 특히 중·장기적 경제성장 동력을 만들기 위해서는 일상 소비재 생산 위주의 경공업 중심 국가에서 거대 생산 시스템을 갖춘 중공업 중심 국가로 전환할 필요가 있었다. 현대자동차의 양산차 공장 건설은 대한민국이 중공업 중심 국가로 한 단계 발전하는 데 기여한 민간 주도 프로젝트였다는 점에서 시대의 절실한 요구에도 부응하는 일이었다.

무엇보다도 포니의 양산은 창업주가 굳게 믿고 있었던 '사람이 지닌 가능성과 잠재력'을 입증한 것으로, 고유 모델

Korea became the 9th country in the world to mass-produce its own (native brand) model after the United States, UK, France, Italy, Germany, Japan, Sweden, and Czech Republic. What these countries had in common was that they exported their own models abroad. As such, mass-produced independent models are significant in that brands can make decisions about exports independently, which is why Hyundai forged a new path to realize economies of scale by exporting overseas beyond the limited domestic market. In addition, Hyundai was able to break away from being an assembly producer of foreign automobile companies and join the ranks of independent automakers, which it had longed for, by building the complete vehicle manufacturing plant and producing domestic cars in earnest. This was a significant achievement in that it was the result of the decision to take a separate pursued by a new company from a developing country in Asia, having rejected a subordinate relationship with a giant global company who had extensive experience in automobile production and a dominant market position.

The mass production of the Pony was an event that showed that the Korean economy as well as the automotive industry had taken a step forward. Since the 1960s, the state-led five-year economic development plan has been carried out to rebuild the society in ruins. Still, these plans were centered on building social overhead capital with a focus on road construction. On the other hand, economic power derived from the private sector was essential to embark on a phase of high economic growth. In particular, to create a mid-to-long-term economic growth

출시라는 사명감을 가지고 혼신의 노력을 다한 국내 기술자들이 이룩한 결과였다. 우수한 기술자들의 헌신에 힘입어 자사 첫 고유 모델을 출시한 현대자동차는 자동차 제조에 이어 수출이라는 또 다른 개척의 길에 들어서게 된다.

engine, it was necessary to transform from a light manufacturing producing daily consumer goods to a country that focuses on heavy manufacturing with massive production capabilities. Therefore, the construction of Hyundai's mass-production automobile plant was a private sector-led project that helped Korea move forward as a heavy industrialized nation, responding to the desperate needs of the times.

Above all, the mass production of the Pony is proof of the human possibilities and potential that the founder, Ju-yung Chung, firmly believed in, a result by the efforts of domestic engineers with a mission to develop and produce an independent model. After launching its first independent model, Hyundai was set to embark on another unprecedented journey in automobile exports thanks to the dedication of its talented engineers.

현대자동차의 첫 고유 모델 포니 1호 차 차체 생산 광경
(1975년 10월)
The production process involved in creating the
body of the first Pony (October 1975)

포니 생산 라인 중 프레스 공정
The stamping process in the Pony's production line

포니 생산 라인 중 차체 조립 공정
The welding process in the Pony's production line

포니 생산 라인 중 도장 공정
The painting process in the Pony's production line

포니 생산 라인 중 의장 공정
The assembly process in the Pony's production line

포니 생산 라인 중 의장 공정
The assembly process in the Pony's production line

포니 생산 라인 중 검수 공정
The inspection process in the Pony's production line

출고센터에서 출고를 기다리는 형형색색의 포니
The Pony in various colors waiting for shipment
at the delivery center

험로를 뚫고
세상을 질주하다

Tackling rough
terrain and
conquering the
world

포니는 대한민국 대중에게 이동의 자유로움을 선사한 첫 국민차였다. 또한 해외에 수출된 첫 국산차로, 현대자동차는 포니의 수출길을 개척하면서 예상치 못한 험로에 빠지기도 했다. 그러나 이 험로를 헤쳐나가는 과정은 현대자동차가 선도적 글로벌 브랜드로 성장하고 대한민국이 세계적 자동차 공업국으로 발돋움하는 원동력이 되었다.

The Pony was Korea's first car for the people, providing Koreans with the freedom of mobility. It was also the first domestically produced car to be exported overseas, facing unexpected hardships along the way. However, overcoming these challenges propelled Hyundai into a leading global brand and fueled South Korea's rise as a world-class automotive powerhouse.

마이카 시대의 개막

1960년대 정부가 주도한 경제개발 5개년계획으로 시작된 대한민국의 산업화는 1970년대에 이르러 소비재를 중심으로 한 경공업에서 조선·철강·자동차 등 중화학공업 중심의 산업으로 한 단계 진화했다. 전 세계가 '한강의 기적'* 이라 부르는 대한민국의 급격한 경제성장이 시작된 것도 이때부터다. 현대자동차가 창립된 1967년 1인당 국민소득은 150달러, 포니가 출시된 1976년 830달러, 포니2가 출시된 1982년 1,973달러[8]로 가정경제 수준이 빠르게 향상되면서 거주 환경과 라이프스타일에 큰 변화가 생겼다. 구매력을 갖춘 중산층이 늘어나면서 이들을 겨냥한 아파트 건설 붐이 일었고, 대한민국 최초의 신도시라 할 수 있는 강남 개발이 본격화되었다. 도시화의 진척과 아파트의 유행은 시민들의 라이프스타일이 전통적 좌식 문화에서 현대적 입식 문화로 바뀌는 데에도 큰 영향을 끼쳤다. 그로 인해 침대, 소파, 싱크대 등 입식 가구가 주거 환경에 급속도로 자리 잡으면서 집 안 풍경이 서구적으로 바뀌었고, 구매력 증가로 텔레비전과 세탁기 등 가전제품이 일상 깊숙이 들어왔다. 당시 사회적 맥락에서 이러한 생활 풍경의 변화는 중산층 문화의 등장으로 요약할 수 있다.

포니는 이렇게 변화의 욕구로 충만한 사회 환경과 구매력을 갖춘 중산층 소비자들의 등장과 맞물려 출시되었다. 높은 가성비는 물론이고, 해외로 수출된 첫 국산차라는 타이틀까지 가진 포니는 출시되자마자 이유 있는 판매 돌풍을 일으키며 성공 신화의 전조를 보여주었다. 출시 첫해 국내에서 1만 대 이상의 판매고를 올리며 상승세를 탄 포니는 1977년 1만9,847대, 1978년 3만8,411대, 1979년 4만6,971대의 판매고를 기록, 3년 연속 국내 승용차 시장에서 50% 이상의 점유율을 차지했다. 그 결과 포니는 1978년 12월 국내 최초로 단일 차종 10만 대 생산을 돌파하는 성과를 거뒀다.

'한강의 기적'은 1960-1970년대 한국의 경이적인 경제성장을 일컫는 상징적인 용어로 세계대전의 패전국 독일이 전후에 일으킨 경제성장을 '라인강의 기적'으로 부르는 것에 비유했다. 20세기 초 36년간의 식민 지배와 1950년 발발한 한국전쟁으로 원조 경제에 의존했던 대한민국은 1962년 시작된 경제개발5개년계획을 기점으로 불과 20여 년에 초고속 경제성장을 이룩했다. 1962년 당시 대한민국의 국내총생산(GDP)은 23억 달러였으나 1979년에는 640억 달러로 28배가 늘어났으며, 같은 시기 1인당 국민소득은 87달러에서 1,693달러로 20배가량 증가했다.[7]
The "Miracle on the Han River" refers to South Korea's remarkable economic growth during the 1960-70s, drawing a parallel with Germany's post-war economic recovery, Miracle on the Rhine. South Korea embarked on a rapid development journey starting with the five-year economic plan in 1962. South Korea's gross domestic product (GDP) skyrocketed from $2.3 billion in 1962 to $64 billion in 1979, a 28-fold increase, while the per capita income rose from $87 to $1,693, a 20-fold increase.[7]

Ushering in the era of car ownership

Korea's industrialization was jumpstarted by the government-led, five-year economic development plan during the 1960s. In the 1970s, the industrial development underwent a shift from light industries to heavy and chemical industries such as shipbuilding, steelmaking, and automotive. It was around this period that the country's rapid economic growth, often referred to as the "Miracle on the Han River,"* began. In 1967, when Hyundai Motor Company was founded, Korea's GDP per capita was merely $150. By 1976, when the Pony was launched, the GDP per capita shot up to $830. It jumped to $1,973 in 1982, when the Pony2 arrived.[8] This rapid improvement in household economies led to significant changes in living environments and lifestyles. The growth of the middle class with purchasing power spurred an apartment construction boom and the development of Gangnam, South Korea's first new town. Urbanization and the popularity of apartments had a profound impact on shifting lifestyles from traditional floor sitting to modern standing culture. This change brought western-style furniture, like beds, sofas, and kitchen cabinets, into homes, transforming the interior landscape. The increased purchasing power also ushered in household appliances like televisions and washing machines into daily life. These lifestyle changes can be summarized as the emergence of middle-class culture within the social context of the time.

The Pony was launched amid a society filled with a desire for change and the emergence of middle-class consumers with purchasing pow-

이 같은 포니의 판매 호조에는 우수한 상품성과 경제성이 결정적 역할을 했다. 그중에서도 탁월한 내구성은 포니의 최대 인기 요인이었다. 외국에서 들여온 부품을 조립해 판매하는 경쟁 차와 달리, 포니는 비포장도로율이 높고 험로가 많았던 당시 국내 도로 환경에 맞춰 개발해 주행 테스트까지 완료한 만큼 한국 지형에 최적화되어 있었다. 특히 하루에 400km 이상 주행해도 제 성능을 충분히 발휘할 정도로 차체가 탄탄하고 내구성이 좋았던 까닭에 포니는 택시로도 인기가 높았다. 게다가 효율성 높은 엔진을 탑재해 연비 또한 우수했다. 출시 당시 차량 부품의 90%를 국산품으로 장착해 A/S가 용이한 데다 차량 정비 시 부품 가격도 타사에 비해 저렴해 조립 생산 방식으로 제작된 경쟁 차와 비교해 보유 경제성이 월등히 높은 것도 장점이었다.

자동차 시장이 빠르게 성장하는 과정에서 진화하는 고객의 니즈에 기민하게 대응한 것도 포니의 지속적 판매 성장을 이끈 요인이었다. 현대자동차는 엔진 타입을 다양화해 가솔린 외에도 경제성 높은 LPG 모델의 포니를 개발했으며, 적재성이 우수한 포니 픽업, 실내 공간을 확장한 포니 왜건, 스포티한 포니 3도어 등 다양한 파생 모델을 출시했을 뿐 아니라 오너 드라이버를 위해 자동변속기를 장착한 포니 오토매틱 모델도 선보여 소비자 선택의 폭을 넓혔다. 또한 수요층 다변화를 위해 오렌지색, 황금색, 은색, 하늘색, 곤색 등 밝고 화사한 컬러도 과감하게 도입했다.

이처럼 포니의 급격한 판매 신장으로 한국 사회에 승용차가 빠르게 대중화되었고, 중산층 가정에도 자가용 보유가 일반화되면서 이른바 '마이카' 시대가 열렸다.

"세상도 변해서 요즘은 시골길을 터덜대며 달리는 마차에 사람이 가득 타는 미풍(美風)을 볼 기회가 드물어졌다.

er. With its high cost-effectiveness and the title of being the first domestically produced car to be exported overseas, the Pony immediately sparked a sales frenzy, heralding the beginning of a legendary success story. In the year of its launch, the Pony recorded more than 10,000 vehicles in domestic sales, followed by sales volumes of 19,847 in 1977, 38,411 in 1978, and 46,971 in 1979. It secured over 50% of the domestic passenger car market share for three consecutive years. As a result, in December 1978, the Pony became the first Korean car to achieve the milestone of producing over 100,000 units.

The Hyundai Pony's impressive sales were significantly driven by its excellent quality and affordability. Especially its durability was a key factor in its popularity. Unlike its competitors, which assembled imported parts, the Pony was developed specifically for Korea's challenging road conditions, with high rates of unpaved roads and rough terrain, and underwent extensive road testing to ensure optimal performance. Its robust body and durability allowed it to perform well even when driven over 400km a day, making it a popular choice for taxis. Additionally, it featured an efficient engine that offered excellent fuel economy. At the time of launch, 90% of the car's parts were domestically produced, making after-sales service convenient and spare parts more affordable compared to its assembly-based competitors. This contributed to the Pony's superior cost-effectiveness in ownership.

Another significant driver of the Pony's continued growth in sales was Hyundai's swift adaptation to evolving customer needs

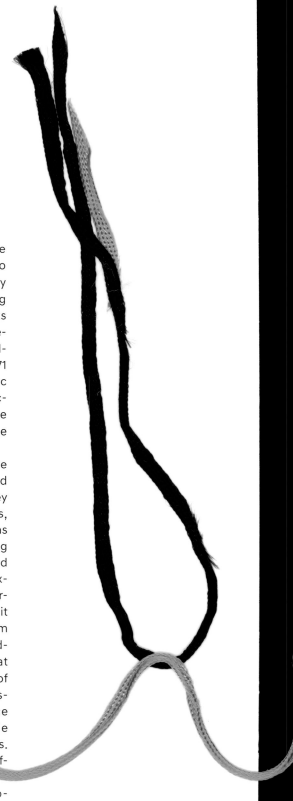

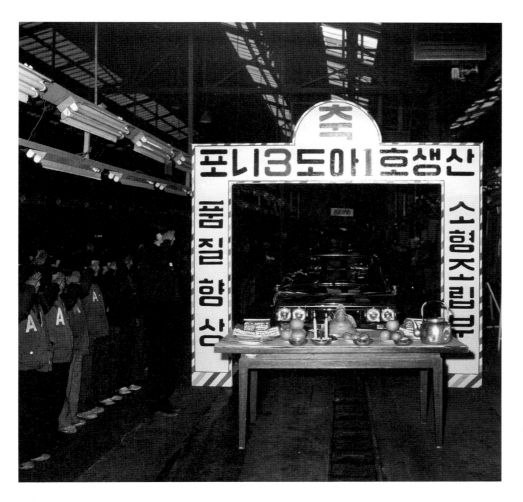

포니 3도어 1호 차 생산(1980년 3월)
Production of the 1st Pony 3-door (March 1980)

in the rapidly growing automotive market. For instance, Hyundai diversified engine types, developing not only gasoline models but also cost-efficient LPG versions of the Pony. The company also released various derivative cars such as the light cargo capable Pony Pickup, the roomier Pony Wagon, and the sporty Pony 3 Doors. Furthermore, they expanded the range of consumer choices by releasing the Pony Automatic model, equipped with an automatic transmission for drivers who prefer the convenience of non-shifting. Another bold move to diversify consumer segments was the introduction of bright and vibrant colors such as orange, gold, silver, sky blue, and dark blue.

This strategic approach led to a rapid increase in Pony sales, accelerating the popularization of passenger cars in Korean society. It ushered in the era of private car ownership among middle-class families, marking the beginning of the so-called "my car" era.

"Times have changed, and it has become a rarity to spot a horse-driven carriage filled with passengers rumbling down a countryside path. Instead, what's emerging is the so-called "My Car" era. This marks the beginning of a new class known as private car owners. (An article published in The Dong-a Ilbo on October 6, 1977)

그 대신 차차 머리를 들기 시작한 것이 이른바 '마이-카'다. 자가용족이라고 하는 새로운 계층이 등장하기 시작한 것이다." (동아일보 1977년 10월 6일 자 기사)

도시화가 진행되면서 흙먼지로 가득했던 비포장도로는 아스

Urbanization eventually transformed the dusty, unpaved paths into asphalt-covered roads and cars replaced horse-drawn carriages The launch of the Pony transformed not only the landscape of roads but also how the public experienced mobility. In the early 20th century, cars were

팔트가 깔린 포장도로가 되었고, 도로에는 우마차 대신 자동차가 지나게 되었다. 포니 출시로 도로 풍경은 물론 대중의 이동 경험 양상이 변화한 것이다.

　　20세기 초 한국에 자동차 문화가 열린 시기에 자동차는 부유층의 전유물로 여겨졌으나, 이제 막 형성되기 시작한 한국 중산층은 포니를 통해 보다 쉽게 마이카의 꿈을 실현할 수 있었다. 포니의 등장으로 자가용은 중산층 편입을 상징하는 아이콘이 되었으며, 마이카 붐은 자동차가 일상의 이동을 돕고 활동 반경을 확장하는 '대중의 발'로서의 역할을 하게 만들었다. 이는 자동차 산업이 모두가 더 풍요로운 삶을 누리는 나라가 되는 데 기여할 것이라고 한 정주영 선대회장의 현대자동차 설립 당시 꿈이 결실을 보는 풍경이기도 했다.

considered a luxury for the wealthy in Korea. However, the emerging middle class found the dream of owning a car more accessible with the introduction of the Pony. The Pony popularized car ownership as a status symbol for the middle class, and the resulting surge in demand for automobiles made them a more accessible means of transportation for a broader population. This reflected the vision of Founding Chairman Chung who believed the automobile industry could contribute to a more prosperous life for everyone.

포니 10만대 생산 기념 행사(1978년 12월)
Celebration of the Pony's production exceeding
the 100,000 mark (December 1978)

Chapter 3

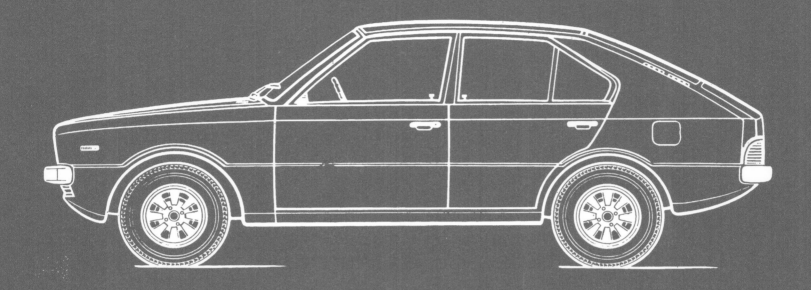

일 반 제 원 표

항 목	내 용	제 원
일 반 제 원	전 장	3, 970 m m
	전 폭	1, 558 m m
	전 고	1, 360 m m
	축 거	2, 340 m m
	전 윤 거 (전)	1, 278 m m
	(후)	1, 248 m m
	최 저 지 상 고	174 m m
	트 렁 크 용 적	420 ℓ
	차 량 중 량	870 k g
	승 차 정 원	5 명
	차 량 총 중 량	1,145 k g
	축 중 (전)	540 k g
	(후)	605 k g
엔 진	형 식	4 CYL – IN – OHC
	내 경 × 행 정	73×74 m m
	배 기 량	1, 238 c c
	압 축 비	9. 0
	최 대 출 력	80ps / 6,300 r. p. m.
	최 대 토 – 크	10. 8kg – m / 4,000 r. p. m
	연 료 소 모 율 (최대부하시)	210g / ps – H (3,000 r. p. m.)
	공 회 전 속 도	650∼750 r. p. m.
점 화 계 통	점 화 타 이 밍	4° BTDC / 700 r. p. m.
	점 화 순 서	1 – 3 – 4 – 2
	스 파 크 프 러 그 간 격	0.7∼0.8 m m
	회 전 방 향	시 계 방 향
	디 스 트 리 뷰 터 포 인 트 간 격	0.45∼0.55 m m
연 료 계 통	기 화 기 형 식	스 트 롬 버 그 2 벤 츄 리 수 직 형
	벤 츄 리 직 경	21 m m, 27 m m
	쵸 – 크	수 동 식
	연 료 펌 프	다 이 어 후 램 식
	연 료 탱 크 용 량	4 5 ℓ
	연 료 휠 터	캐 트 릿 지 형
윤 활 계 통	윤 활 유 용 량	4 ℓ
	오 일 펌 프	트 로 코 이 드 기 어 형
	오 일 압 력 스 윗 치 작 동 압 력	0.3kg / cm² 이 하

포 니
주 유 계 통 도

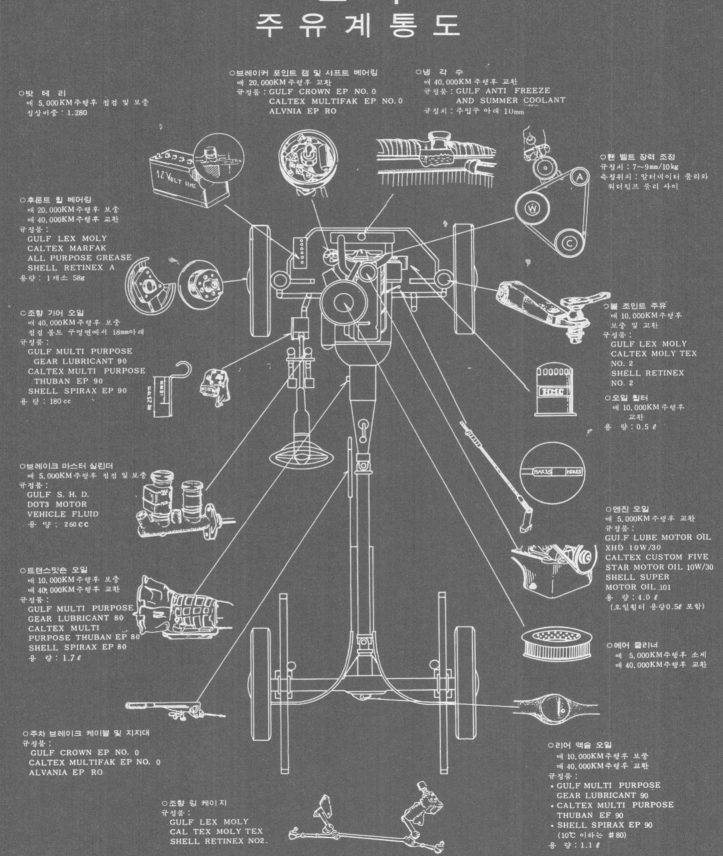

○밧 테 리
매 5,000KM주행후 점검 및 보충
정상비중 : 1.280

○브레이커 포인트 캠 및 샤프트 베어링
매 20,000KM주행후 교환
규정품 : GULF CROWN EP NO. 0
CALTEX MULTIFAK EP NO. 0
ALVNIA EP RO

○냉 각 수
매 40,000KM주행후 교환
규정품 : GULF ANTI FREEZE
AND SUMMER COOLANT
규정치 : 주입구 아래 10mm

○팬 벨트 장력 조정
규정치 : 7~9mm/10kg
측정위치 : 알터네이터 풀리와
워터펌프 풀리 사이

○후론트 휠 베어링
매 20,000KM주행후 보충
매 40,000KM주행후 교환
규정품 :
GULF LEX MOLY
CALTEX MARFAK
ALL PURPOSE GREASE
SHELL RETINEX A
용량 : 1개소 58g

○조향 기어 오일
매 40,000KM주행후 보충
점검 볼트 구멍 면에서 18mm아래
규정품 :
GULF MULTI PURPOSE
GEAR LUBRICANT 90
CALTEX MULTI PURPOSE
THUBAN EP 90
SHELL SPIRAX EP 90
용 량 : 180cc

○볼 조인트 주유
매 10,000KM주행후
보충 및 교환
규정품 :
GULF LEX MOLY
CALTEX MOLY TEX
NO. 2
SHELL RETINEX
NO. 2

○오일 휠터
매 10,000KM주행후
교환
용 량 : 0.5ℓ

○브레이크 마스터 실린더
매 5,000KM주행후 점검 및 보충
규정품 :
GULF S. H. D.
DOT3 MOTOR
VEHICLE FLUID
용 량 : 260cc

○엔진 오일
매 5,000KM주행후 교환
규정품 :
GULF LUBE MOTOR OIL
XHD 10W/30
CALTEX CUSTOM FIVE
STAR MOTOR OIL 10W/30
SHELL SUPER
MOTOR OIL 101
용 량 : 4.0ℓ
(오일휠터 용량0.5ℓ 포함)

○트랜스밋숀 오일
매 10,000KM주행후 보충
매 40,000KM주행후 교환
규정품 :
GULF MULTI PURPOSE
GEAR LUBRICANT 80
CALTEX MULTI
PURPOSE THUBAN EP 80
SHELL SPIRAX EP 80
용 량 : 1.7ℓ

○에어 클리너
매 5,000KM주행후 소제
매 40,000KM주행후 교환

○주차 브레이크 케이블 및 지지대
규정품 :
GULF CROWN EP NO. 0
CALTEX MULTIFAK EP NO. 0
ALVNIA EP RO

○리어 액술 오일
매 10,000KM주행후 보충
매 40,000KM주행후 교환
규정품 :
• GULF MULTI PURPOSE
GEAR LUBRICANT 90
• CALTEX MULTI PURPOSE
THUBAN EF 90
• SHELL SPIRAX EP 90
(10℃ 이하는 #80)
용 량 : 1.1ℓ

○조향 링 케이지
규정품 :
GULF LEX MOLY
CAL TEX MOLY TEX
SHELL RETINEX NO2.

★혼 스윗치

다기능 스윗치의 끝부분에 스윗치가 부착되어 있으며 누르
면 경적이 울립니다.
또한 점화 스윗치를 껏을 때에도 혼은 작동됩니다.

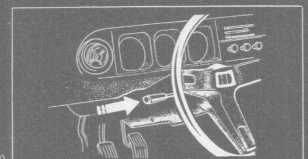

〈그림 14〉

★실 내 등

이등은 실내 천정 중앙에 설치되어 있으며 스윗치는 렌즈의
우측에 있읍니다. 스윗치를 앞쪽으로 밀면 항상 불이 켜
지며 뒷쪽으로 밀면 도어를 열었을 때만 불이 켜집니다. 중
간 위치에 놓으면 등은 항상 꺼져있읍니다.

★점등 스윗치

이 점등 스윗치는 점화스윗치에 관계없이 아래와 같이 1단,
2단으로 당겨집니다.

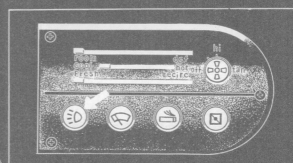

〈그림 15〉

	1 단계	2 단계
헤드램프	×	○
주 차 등	○	○
테일램프	○	○
번호판등	○	○

이 스윗치를 우측으로 1단 돌리면 주차등 우측만 점등되며
2단으로 돌리면 좌우측 모두 점등되며 3단을 돌리면
　　　좌측만 점등됩니다.　　　　【주】 주차등을 끄지 않는
상태에서 1단계및 2단계로 당겨지지 않습니다.

〈그림 16〉

★와이퍼 스윗치

이 스윗치는 점등 스윗치와 나란히 있읍니다.
먼저 점화 스윗치를 "ON"에 위치 시킨뒤 강우량 상태에 따
라 저속 및 고속으로 선택 사용하실 수 있읍니다. 또한 스
윗치를 끄면 자동적으로 와이퍼가 원위치로 돌아 갑니다.
● 와셔 펌프
　이 펌프는 클럿치 패달 왼쪽에 설치되었으며 발로 밟으
　면 전면 유리창에 세척수가 분사됩니다.

【주】
전기식 와셔 스윗치를 부착하였을 때에는 와셔를 20초이상
사용하지 마십시요. 용액이 없는 경우에 계속 사용 하시면
모터 고장의 원인이 됩니다.

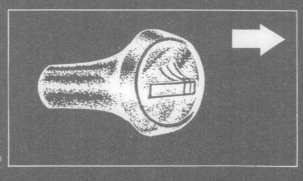

〈그림 17〉

★씨거 라이터

보턴을 안으로 눌러 두었다가 찰칵 소리와 함께 튀어 나올
때 뽑아서 사용하십시요. 씨거 라이터는 그림 ON위치에서
작동합니다.

〈그림 18〉

냉각된 엔진	가열된 엔진	주
1. 점화키이를 ON위 치로 하고 2. 악셀레이터 페달을 깊숙히 밟는다. 3. 페달을 서서히 놓는다. 4. 점화키이를 ST-ART위치로. 시동 안되면 재반복한다. 5. 시동을 한 뒤에는 약1분동안 저속 공회전 시킨뒤 운행한다.	1. 점화키이를 ON위 치로 하고 2. 악셀레이터 페달을 ⅓~½ 정도로 밟는다. 〈주〉페달을 펌프질 하지 말것 3. 점화키이를 ST-ART위치로 하여 가동되면 ON위치로 한다.	만약 시동이 안되면 1. 페달을 깊숙히 밟고 2. 점화키이를 ST-ART위치로 하여 3. 엔진이 시동되면 페달을 놓고 점화키이를 ON위치로 한다.

〈주〉 시동후에는 저속 공회전 상태로 약 1 분정도 엔진을 가동시켜 엔진을 워밍업 한뒤에 운행하시기 바랍니다.

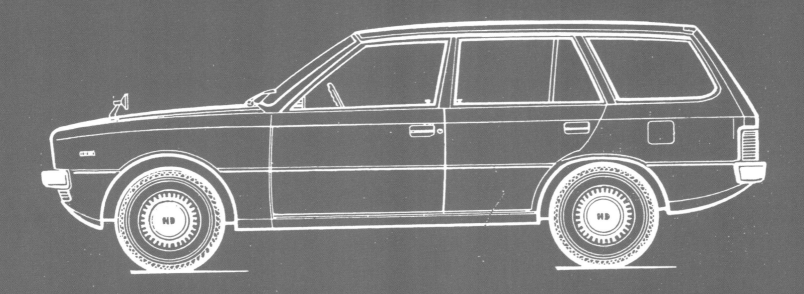

★ 히터 및 통풍 조절장치

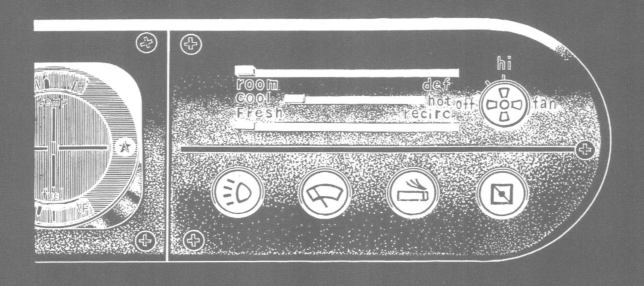

(1) 실내 통풍 방향 조절 레버	room ←──────→ def (실내난방) (윈드쉴드글래스의 서리제거)
(2) 온도 조절 레버	cool ←──────→ hot (저온) (고온)
(3) 통풍 조절 레버	fresh ←──────→ recirc (신선한 외부공기 유입) (환풍) (내부공기순환)
(4) 홴 스윗치	off ──→ 중간 ←──→ hi (멈춤) (약함) (강함)

★히터 사용방법

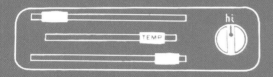

● 사용하지 않을때.

● 실내공기를 급 가온할때.

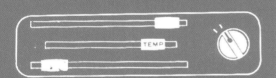

● 정상적인 온방상태.

● 윈드쉴드 글래스에 서리를 제거할때.

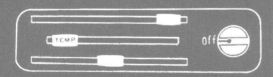

● 홴을 가동하여 신선한 공기를 강제 환풍시킬때.

● 홴을 정지한 상태에서 신선한 공기로 자연환풍시 _때

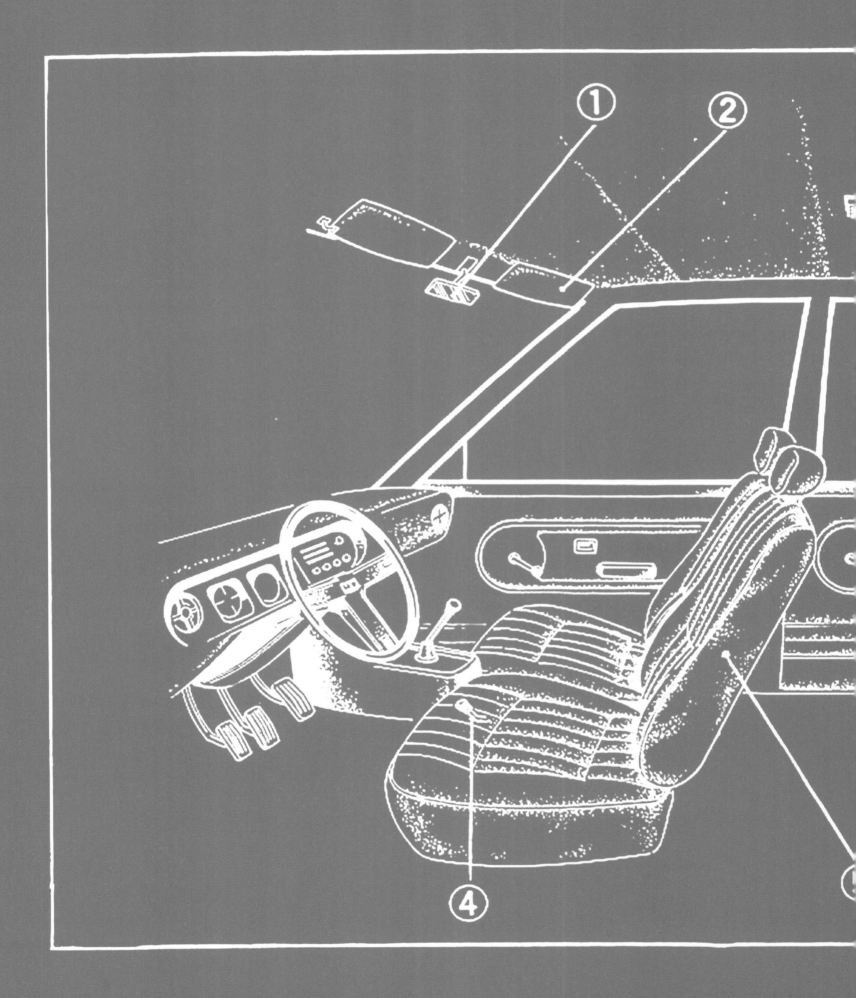

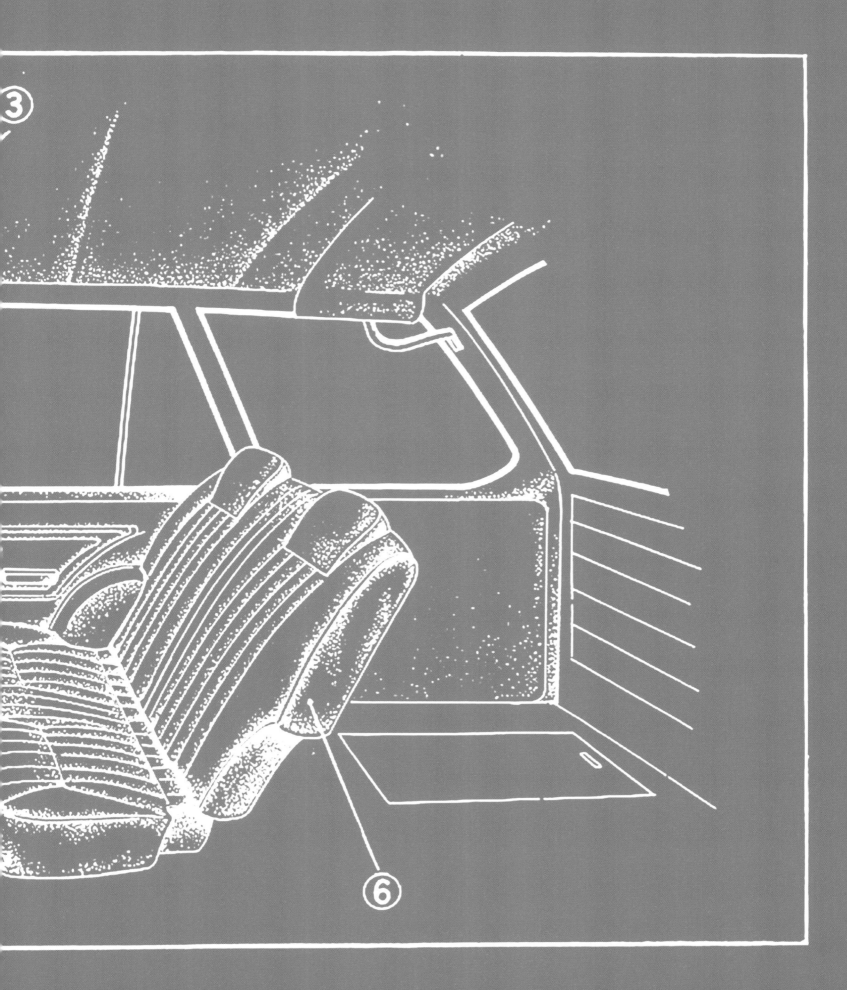

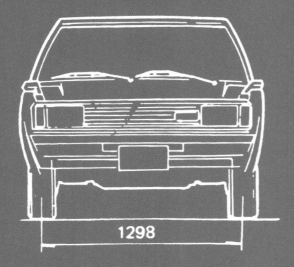
1298

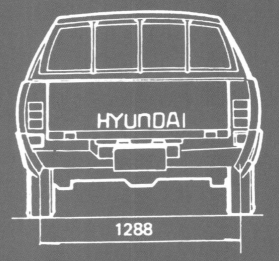
1288

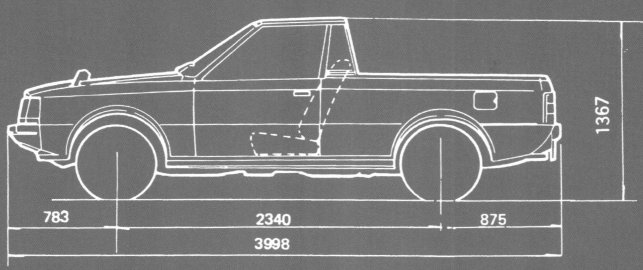
783   2340   875
3998
1367

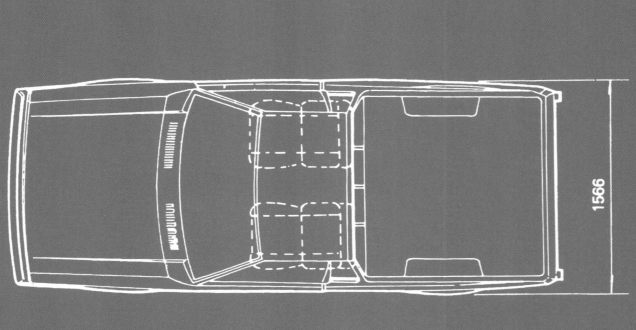
1566

〈그림 4〉

〈그림 5〉

〈그림 6〉

〈그림10〉

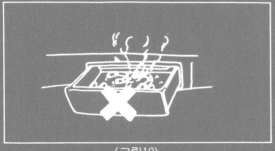

〈그림11〉

〈그림12〉

2. 긴 언덕길을 내려올때 엔진브레이크를 병행하여 사용하시기 바라
   며, 계속적으로 브레이크 페달을 사용하여 제동을 걸면 베이퍼록
   이나 훼이드 현상이 발생되어 제동효율이 떨어지게 됩니다.
   젖은 노면이나 눈길 주행시 급격한 엔진브레이크의 사용을 삼가해
   주십시오. 〈그림 4〉

3. 고속주행중 타이어가 터지거나 파열되는 경우 핸들을 힘껏쥐고 서
   서히 제동을 걸어 속도를 늦추십시오. 급제동을 하는 경우 핸들이
   심하게 움직이게 되어 위험합니다.

4. 안전벨트를 필히 착용하여 주십시오. 〈그림 5〉

★ 안전주행

1. 차내의 테일게이트내에 연료가 들어있는 용기나 휘발성 물질이 있
   는 용기는 가능한 넣지 마십시오.
   증발가스에 인화되어 폭발할 우려가 있읍니다. 〈그림 6〉

5. 재떨이를 사용하신 후에는 필히 닫아 주십시오. 열려있는 경우 담
   배 불로 인해 타부위에 옮겨붙게 되어 화재 위험이 있읍니다.
   〈그림10〉

【주】 1. 재떨이를 자주 비워 담배꽁초가 쌓이지 않도록 하십시오.
     2. 재떨이에 종이등의 가연성 물질을 넣지 마십시오.
        예) 껌종이, 휴지.
     3. 성냥 및 담배 불은 필히 끈후 재떨이에 넣으십시오.

★ 어린이 탑승시

1. 어린이는 뒷좌석에 태우도록 합시다.
   앞승객석에 어린이가 앉아 운전장치, 장비 등을 움직이게 되면
   안전운행에 위협을 받게 되어 뜻밖의 사고가 일어날 위험이 있읍
   니다. 〈그림11〉

2. 뒷도어를 확실하게 닫고 도어에 마련된 안전 자물쇠고리를 바깥쪽
   으로 당겨 어린이가 차 안에서 문을 열 수 없도록 해야 합니다.
   〈그림12〉

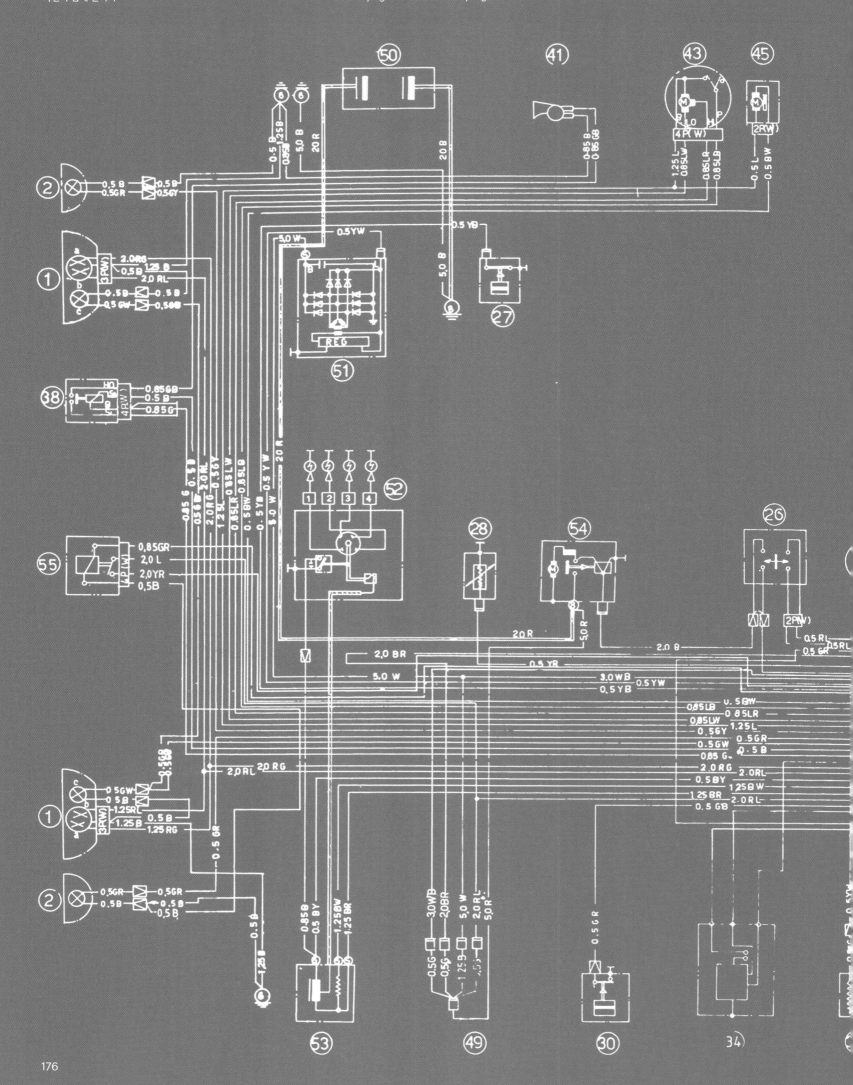

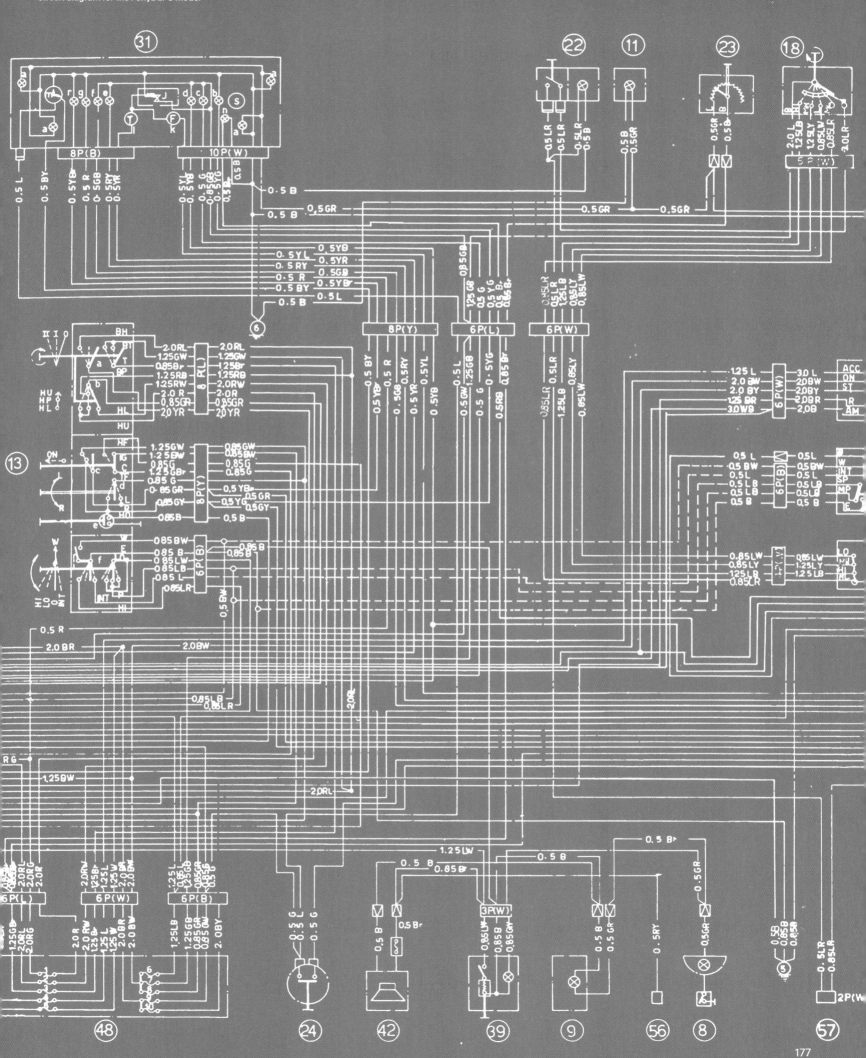

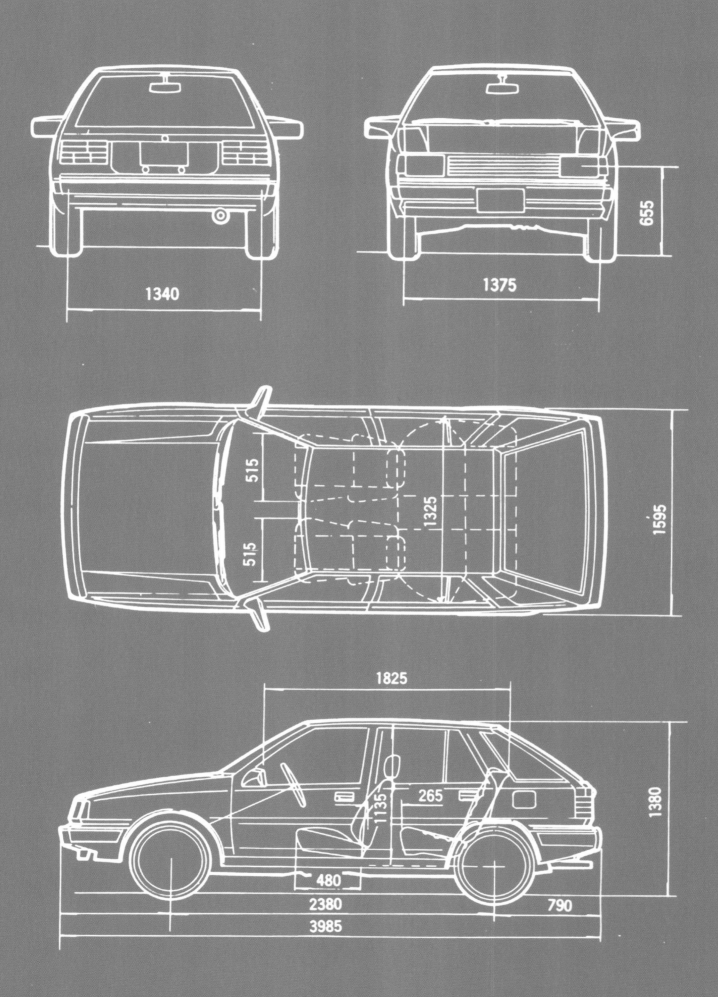

귀하의 포니엑셀

포니엑셀과 함께 현대자동차의 가족이 되신 것을 환영합니다.

그동안 폐사 기술진의 각고의 노력끝에 세계적으로 선풍을 일으키고 있는 전륜 구동방식의 차량이 국내 최초로 개발되어 금번 포니엑셀을 고객 여러분에게 자신있게 소개하게 된 것을 충심으로 기쁘게 생각하는 바입니다.

최신형 5도어 스타일, 보다 우아하고 미려한 외관, 최고의 안정성, 내구성, 안락성 및 경제성 등 승용차가 필요로 하는 모든 것을 구비한 포니엑셀은 귀하의 품위를 높여줄 것이며, 항상 귀하의 마음을 흡족하게 하여 드릴 것 입니다.

본 책자에는, 귀하의 차가 언제나 최상의 상태에서 충분한 성능을 발휘할 수 있도록 하기 위해, 올바른 운전법과 일상시의 점검 조정법 및 차량 취급시의 주의사항에 대해서 알기 쉽게 설명되어 있읍니다.

귀하의 차량을 운행하시기 전에, 본 책자를 처음부터 끝까지 잘 숙지하여 조작하신다면, 항상 최대의 성능과 최상의 경제성 및 안정성을 얻으실 수 있읍니다.

귀하께서 수리작업이나 고장진단을 필요로 하실 경우, 현대자동차 써비스(주)의 각 사업소나 지정정비공장에 오시면, 완벽한 품질검사를 거친 HMC순정부품과 최신장비로써 귀하의 차량을 성심껏 보살펴 드릴 것입니다.

본 책자가 귀하에게 보다 많은 도움이 되시길 빌며, 항상 폐사의 차량을 애용하여 주심에 재삼 감사드립니다.

1985 년   2 월

현대자동차주식회사   763 - 0211
정비관리부   763 - 0311
   763 - 0411

※ 1. 정비 관계 내용을 더 상세히 알고자 하실때는 포니엑셀 정비지침서가 별도로 마련되어 있으니 참조하시기 바랍니다.

2. 본 책자에 수록된 사양 및 제원은 폐사 설계변경에 따라 사전통보없이 변경될 수도 있아오니, 그점 양지하시기 바랍니다.

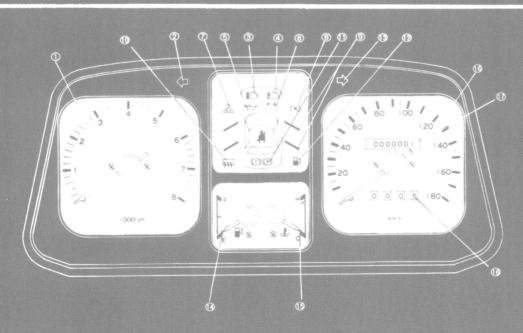

(1) 타코메터
(2) 방향지시 표시등 (좌측)
(3) 원등 표시등
(4) 근등 표시등
(5) 오일 압력 경고등
(6) 충전 경고등
(7) 비상 경고등
(8) 쵸우크 경고등
(9) 도어 경고등
(10) 뒷유리 예열 경고등
(11) 브레이크 경고등
(12) 잔유 연료량 경고등
(13) 방향지시 표시등 (우측)
(14) 연료 계기
(15) 냉각수 온도계기
(16) 속도계
(17) 적산 거리계
(18) 구간 주행거리계

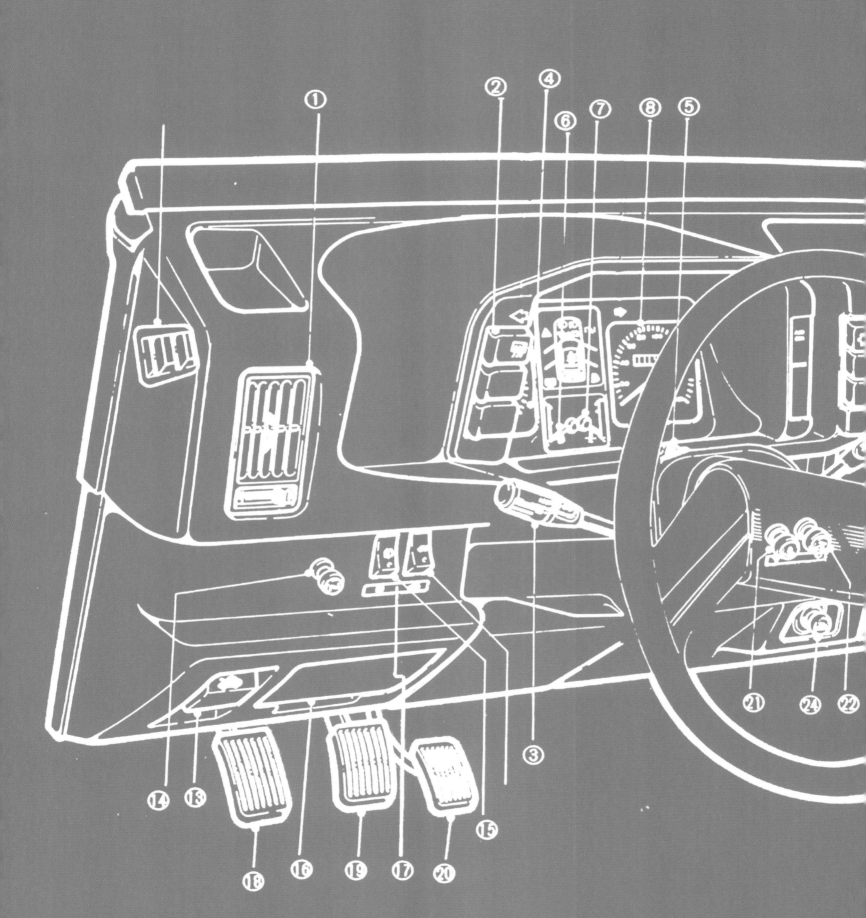

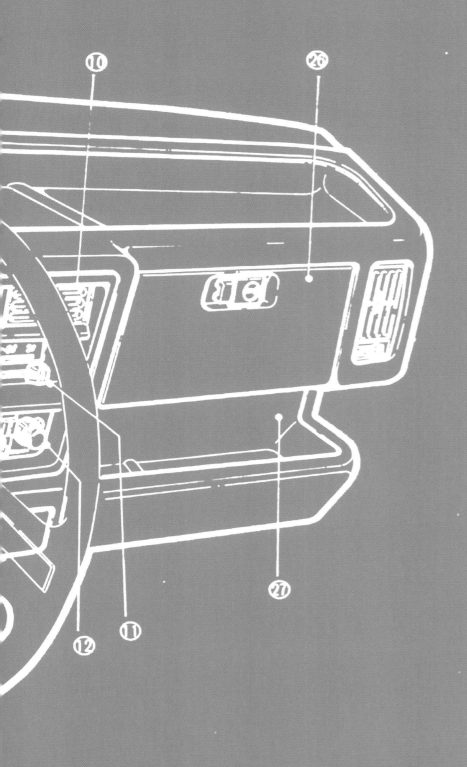

(1) 사이드 통풍구

(2) 뒷유리 서리제거 스윗치

(3) 다기능 스윗치

(4) 타코메터

(5) 비상경고등 스윗치

(6) 연료계

(7) 온도계

(8) 속도계

(9) 에어콘 스윗치

(10) 중앙 통풍구

(11) 송풍기 스윗치

(12) 라디오

(13) 본네트 개폐기

(14) 쵸우크 스윗치

(15) 뒷유리 와이퍼/와셔 스윗치

(16) 휴즈박스

(17) 조명 박스

(18) 클러치 페달

(19) 브레이크 페달

(20) 악셀레이터 페달

(21) 계기판 조명 조절기

(22) 인터미턴트 와이퍼 스윗치

(23) 윈드쉴드 와이퍼 와셔 스윗치

(24) 시가라이터

(25) 재떨이

(26) 글로브 박스

(27) 화물선반

(28) 옆유리습기 제거장치

수출을 위해 선적 중인 포니
Ponies being loaded on a shipping vessel for export

祝 한국의 포니 수출 祝

담대한 도전이 낸
바닷길, 수출길

An export route over
the sea, forged by an
audacious challenge

해외 수출의 포문을 연 포니

포니가 국내 시장에서 좋은 반응을 얻는 동안에도 현대자동차의 눈은 세계시장을 향해 있었다. 창립 당시부터 수출은 회사의 핵심 경영 목표 중 하나였는데, 이는 자원이 부족하고 좁은 국토마저 남북으로 분단되어 시장 규모가 협소한 대한민국의 경제 자립을 위해서는 수출이 필수라고 생각했기 때문이다. 특히 독자 모델 개발을 결정하면서 수출은 생존을 위한 지상 과제로 부상했는데, 포니가 개발된 1970년대 중반 대한민국 자동차 시장은 연간 3만~4만 대 규모로 보잘것없었기에 규모의 경제를 달성하기 위해서라도 해외 진출은 반드시 필요했다. 고유 모델의 디자인을 의뢰할 때 서구적 스타일링을 요구한 것도 애초부터 수출을 염두에 두었기 때문이다.

1974년 토리노 모터쇼에서 포니가 공개된 후 세계 각지에서 수입 문의가 쇄도하자, 현대자동차는 1975년부터 1976년까지 약 1년 동안 수출 시장 개척을 위한 해외 시장 조사를 진행했다. 자동차 비생산국 중에서도 당시 1인당 국민소득이 500달러* 전후로 포니의 수출 가능성이 높은 아시아, 중남미, 중동, 아프리카 지역 국가를 우선 조사 대상으로 선정한 현대자동차는 해당 지역에 임직원을 파견해 각국의 자동차 공업 수준, 자동차 판매 및 경쟁 동향, 판매 채널 등 해외 시장 진출을 위한 기초 정보를 수집했다. 그러고는 이 조사 결과를 바탕으로 장·단기 수출 전략을 수립했다. 단기적으로는 현재 포니 사양으로 수출이 가능한 국가, 완성차 수입 관세가 낮은 국가, 자동차 생산 시설이 미비한 국가 등을 대상으로 우선 수출 전략을 구체화하고, 장기적으로는 선진국에 대한 시장 조사를 진행한 후 1978년부터 현지 진출 전략을 수립하는 것으로 설정했다.

이에 따라 현대자동차는 1976년 하반기부터 포니 수출을 목표로 세계 각지에서 현지 대리점 발굴 및 판촉 활동 등을 펼쳤다. 그 결과 1976년 2월 사우디아라비아에 진출한 현

The Pony opens the door to export

Even as the Pony was well-received in the domestic market, Hyundai Motor had its sights set on the global market. From the very start, exporting was one of the company's core management objectives. This was due to the belief that exports were essential for South Korea's economic independence, given its limited resources and small market size, exacerbated by the division of the Korean peninsula. Especially with the decision to develop an independent model, exports became a crucial mission for survival. In the mid-1970s when the Pony was developed, the South Korean car market was minuscule, with annual sales of only 30,000 to 40,000 units. Thus, international expansion was necessary to achieve economies of scale. Moreover, the request for a Western styling when designing the model meant that Hyundai had exports in mind from the beginning.

After the Pony was unveiled at the 1974 Turin Auto Show and inquiries for import flooded in from around the world, Hyundai conducted global market research from 1975 to 1976 to explore and develop export markets. Hyundai first focused on non-automobile producing countries with a per capita GDP around $500*, where the Pony had high export potential. These countries included regions such as Asia, Latin America, the Middle East, and Africa — where Hyundai dispatched employees to gather basic information for market entry, including sales volume, potential competitors, distribution network, and more. Based on this research, Hyundai established both short and long-term export strategies. In the short term, they focused on

*
1974년 기준 1인당 국민소득은 대한민국 550달러,
에콰도르 830달러, 미국 7,980달러였다.[9]
Korea's per capita income in 1974 was $550,
as compared to Ecuador's $830 and the United
States' $7,980.[9]

에콰도르 야구아 자동차와의 포니 수출 계약 현장
(1976년 7월)
An export contract being signed with YAGUA
Motor Co. of Ecuador (July 1976)

대건설에 포니 15대를 업무용 차량으로 시험 수출한 데 이어, 같은 해 7월 에콰도르에 포니 5대를 수출하는 데 성공하며 자동차 수출의 포문을 연 것이다.

"에콰도르로 처음 수출하며 우리가 보낸 것은 단지 다섯 대의 포니뿐만은 아니었다. 포니를 선적한 컨테이너선이 드넓은 태평양을 건너는 동안 세계를 향한 우리의 꿈, 오대양 육대주를 향한 현대의 야망도 함께 실려갔던 것이다."[10] (정세영 전 현대자동차 회장)

포니 수출 첫해인 1976년에 현대자동차는 중동, 중남미, 아프리카 등지에 포니와 포니 픽업 1,019대를 수출했고, 이듬해인 1977년에는 30개국에 7,224대를, 1978년에는 40개국에 1만8,202대를 수출했다. 수출 지역도 중동, 중남미, 아프리카, 아시아, 유럽 등지로 지속 확대했다.

countries where the current Pony specifications could be exported, where import tariffs on finished cars were low and where car production facilities were underdeveloped. The long-term strategy called for in-depth research on developed markets to establish concrete systems for export from 1978 onward.

In accordance with this strategy, Hyundai established authorized dealers and promotional activities worldwide to facilitate the Pony's export in the latter half of 1976. The company made its initial foray into car exports by sending 15 Ponies to Hyundai E&C in Saudi Arabia as business vehicles in February 1976. Following this, Hyundai successfully exported five Ponies to Ecuador in July, marking the beginning of their automobile exports.

"Our first export to Ecuador was not just about sending five Ponies. As the container ship crossed the vast Pacific, it also carried our dreams for the world and Hyundai's ambition towards the five oceans and six continents."[10] (Se-yung Chung, former Chairman of Hyundai Motor Company)

In 1976, the first year of its export, Hyundai exported 1,019 Ponies and Pony Pickups to the Middle East, Latin America, and Africa. In 1977, the following year, 7,224 cars were exported to 30 countries, followed by 18,202 to 40 countries in 1978. Exports continued to expand to countries in the Middle East, Latin America, Africa, Asia, and Europe.

험로를 뚫고 개척한 수출길

해외 진출 초창기 현대자동차는 예상치 못한 많은 시행착오를 거치고 난관을 극복하며 수출 시장을 개척해 나갔다. 우선 포니 양산 전 해외 대리점을 발굴하는 것부터 난항이었다. 당시 해외에서 한국의 인지도는 극히 미미했고, 혹시 한국을 안다고 해도 전쟁으로 인한 부정적 이미지가 대부분이었다. 게다가 아직 완성차가 양산되기 전 단계여서 제대로 된 카탈로그가 준비되어 있지 않아 보여줄 것이라고는 포니 사진 한 장밖에 없어 신생 회사인 현대자동차와 신차 포니를 설명하기가 쉽지 않았다. 그런 상황에서 언어 장벽으로 인한 소통의 어려움은 현지 영업 활동 중 당면한 큰 걸림돌 중 하나였다. 중남미, 중동 등 다양한 지역의 판매망을 뚫기 위해서는 원활한 의사소통이 필수였지만 현지인은 영어에, 현대자동차 직원은 현지어에 미숙했던 것이다. 해외 수출 초창기 에콰도르, 이집트, 쿠웨이트 등 남미, 아프리카, 중동 지역에서 체결한 수출 계약은 이러한 난관을 뚫고 이뤄낸 값진 성과였다.

자동차 전용선이 부재했던 것도 초창기 해외 수출의 어려움을 가중시킨 요인이었다. 완성차는 조금만 손상을 입어도 판매에 막대한 지장을 초래하는 까닭에 자동차 전용선에 선적하는 것이 필수다. 하지만 수출 첫해인 1976년에는 물량이 많지 않아 자동차 전용선이 없었던 만큼 부산항이나 울산항에 취항하는 정기선을 활용했고, 이마저도 적당한 선박을 구하기 어려울 때는 가까운 일본으로 보내 환적하는 방법을 택했다. 그러나 이런 방법으로는 시일이 많이 소요돼 약속한 인도 일자를 맞추지 못하는 경우가 종종 발생했다. 이 같은 선적의 어려움은 자동차 수출 물량이 크게 늘어난 1977년 이후 자동차 전용선을 확보하면서 비로소 해소되었다.

수출 이후에도 예상치 못한 난관에 맞닥뜨렸는데, 현지에서 품질 결함 문제가 제기된 것이다. 당시 수출 경험이 전무

Blazing a trail for export

Initially, Hyundai's efforts to expand into export markets faced unexpected issues. The first hurdle was finding overseas dealerships before mass-producing the Pony. At the time, Korea's recognition abroad was extremely low, and if anyone did know about Korea, it was mostly due to a negative image associated with the Korean war. Moreover, since it was a stage before mass production, there was no proper catalog prepared. The only thing to show was a single picture of the Pony, making it difficult to explain the newborn company and the new car. In such circumstances, one of the biggest obstacles faced during local sales activities was the language barrier. To penetrate sales networks in various regions such as Latin America and the Middle East, smooth communication was essential, but locals were not proficient in English, and Hyundai employees were not proficient in the local language. The export contracts concluded in South America, Africa, and the Middle East regions in the early stages of overseas exports, such as in Ecuador, Egypt, and Kuwait, were valuable achievements made by overcoming these obstacles.

The absence of dedicated car carriers also intensified the difficulties of early overseas exports. Since even minor damages to cars can significantly disrupt sales, shipping them on dedicated car carriers is essential. However, in 1976, the first year of exports, the volume was not large enough to justify dedicated car carriers. Therefore, regular liners docking at Busan or Ulsan ports were utilized, and when it was challenging to find appropriate ships, cars were sent to a nearby Jap-

했던 현대자동차는 지금은 필수인 현지 사전 테스트를 진행
하지 못한 채 포니를 수출했고, 그 결과 현지의 가혹한 기후와
지형으로 인해 품질 결함이 발생한 것이었다. 열대기후인 중
동에서는 차가 높은 기온을 견디지 못해 포니의 시트와 플라
스틱 부품이 껍질 벗겨지듯이 갈라지고 변색됐으며, 에어컨
은 제 기능을 못 하고 뜨거운 바람을 연일 쏟아냈다. 한편 남
미에서는 높은 고도로 기압이 낮아져 엔진 출력이 급속히 떨
어지는 일이 발생했다. 이렇게 현지에서 품질 문제가 생길 때
면 현대자동차는 즉시 해당 지역으로 이동 정비반을 급파해
당면 문제를 빠르게 수습하는 데 주력했고, 현지 기후에 적합
한 새로운 부품을 개발하거나 수입품으로 대체하는 방법으로
문제를 해결해 나갔다. 이러한 경험을 토대로 현지 기후나 풍
토에 대한 사전 점검 없이는 야심 차게 진출한 수출 시장에서
살아남을 수 없다는 교훈을 얻었고, 이후 다양한 지역에서 혹
한 및 혹서 등 현지 기후 테스트를 필수로 진행하는가 하면, 사
내 품질 시험 시설을 대대적으로 보완했다. 이렇듯 현대자동
차는 수출길을 개척하는 과정에서 다양한 시행착오를 겪으며
수출을 위한 시스템과 프로세스를 정교하게 다져나갔다.

수출에 대한 경험 부족으로 발생하는 문제 외에 포니
의 해외 수출을 위해 현지에서 동분서주한 수출 담당 직원들
의 고충도 상당했다. 정국이 불안정한 국가에서 일어나는 혁
명이나 쿠데타의 소용돌이에 휘말리거나 말라리아 등 풍토
병에 걸려 심하게 앓는 등 위험한 순간을 겪기도 하고, 당시에
는 요즘처럼 각국을 자유롭게 이동하기 어렵다 보니 해외 장
기 체류로 부모님 임종, 자녀 출생과 성장 과정을 지켜보지 못
한 이도 많았다. 그럼에도 당시 직원들은 우리 기술자의 손으
로 만든 자동차를 세계 시장에 수출함으로써 대한민국의 산
업 증진에 기여한다는 자긍심과 사명감을 품고 어려움을 극
복해 나갔다.

anese port for transshipment. This method often
resulted in delays, making it difficult to meet the
promised delivery dates. The challenges of shipping were finally resolved after 1977, when the
volume of car exports increased significantly, and
dedicated car carriers were secured.

Another unexpected difficulty was the issue
of quality control in the field. As Hyundai had
no export experience at the time, the Pony was
exported without conducting the now-essential
local pre-tests, resulting in quality defects due
to harsh local climates and terrains. For example, in the tropical climate of the Middle East,
the car couldn't withstand the high temperatures. The Pony's seats and plastic parts cracked
and discolored, and the air conditioning failed to
function properly, continuously blowing hot air.
In Latin America, the high altitude caused a de-
crease in air pressure, leading to a drastic drop
in engine output. Whenever quality issues arose
locally, Hyundai promptly dispatched a repair
team to the area to quickly rectify the problem.
They developed new parts suitable for the local
climate or replaced them with imported parts.
Based on these experiences, Hyundai learned
that without pre-checks for local climate and
terrain, it would be impossible to survive in the
ambitious export market. As a result, the company began conducting mandatory local climate tests (including extreme cold and heat) in
various areas, and significantly upgraded their
in-house quality testing facilities. In pioneering
its export path, the various trials and errors that
Hyundai encountered enabled the company to
refine its systems and processes for exporting.

Beyond the challenges caused by a lack of

해외 진출 초창기에는 자동차 전용선의 부재로 크레인을 이용해
정기선에 선적했다. 이러한 어려움은 수출 물량이 많아지고 한국 국적의
전용선이 마련된 1977년 이후부터 해소되었다.

In the early days of expanding overseas, cars were
loaded onto regular liners using cranes due to the lack of
dedicated car carriers. These challenges began to ease
after 1977, when the volume of exports increased and
dedicated Korean carriers became available.

"마케팅 활동, 대리점 관리, 딜러의 불만 해소 등 단 한 가지도 쉬운 것이 없었어요. 그런데도 만물박사처럼 해결사 역할을 해야 하는 게 힘들었죠. 하지만 해외에서 수출 신용장을 받아 오면 생산 일감이 늘어나 국내 공장이 더 잘 돌아갈 수 있다는 사명감으로 열심히 뛰었습니다." (신현규 부사장, 전 해외판매부 중미 지역 담당자로 현대자동차 워싱턴사무소장 역임)

당시는 기업 활동이 국가 경제의 자립과 밀접한 관련이 있었던 개발도상국 시절이었기에, 포니의 수출은 현대자동차라는 기업은 물론 직원 개인의 입장에서도 국가 경제 발전을 도모한다는 사회적 함의를 품고 있었고, 임직원들 역시 이를 분명히 인지하고 수출길 개척에 헌신했다.

experience, Pony's overseas export team faced significant difficulties in the local market as well. During the turbulence of revolutions and coups in unstable countries, some experienced dangerous moments, with malaria or other epidemic diseases. Moreover, as it was difficult to travel freely between countries like today, many missed critical family moments such as a parent's death or their children's birth and growth due to long-term stays abroad. Despite these challenges, Hyundai's employees carried a sense of pride and mission in contributing to the enhancement of South Korea's industry by exporting cars crafted by our engineers to the global market, and they persevered through these hardships.

"Marketing, managing dealership, and resolving dealer complaints were all challenging tasks. Being a problem solver like a jack-of-all-trades was tough, but driven by the mission that obtaining export letters of credit from overseas would increase production orders and improve domestic factory operations, we worked diligently." (Hyun-kyu Shin, former regional manager of Latin America Overseas Sales Department, later served as Head of the Washington D.C. Office, Hyundai Motor Company)

At that time, Korea was still a developing country and corporate activities were closely connected with the country's economic performance. Thus, the export of the Pony had social implications for Hyundai as a firm and its staff as individuals. Hyundai's employees remained mindful of this mission to develop the nation's economy in their work to find new export opportunities.

선적 대기 중인 포니
Ponies awaiting shipment

칠레 수출을 위해 선적 중인 포니(1978년 5월)
Ponies being loaded for export to Chile (May 1978)

수출 1만 대 돌파를 축하하는 플래카드가 눈에 띈다.
A banner celebrating the company's 10,000th unit to be exported
can be seen in the picture.

하역 중인 포니
Ponies being unloaded

바레인 시내를 주행하는 포니
The Pony driving through a city center in Bahrain

해수 테스트 중인 포니
The Pony undergoing seawater immersion test

제동 테스트 중인 포니
The Pony undergoing brake test

비포장도로에서 주행 테스트 중인 포니
The Pony undergoing a test drive on unpaved roads

영국 MIRA에서 off-spoke 충격 테스트 중인 포니(1977년 2월)
The Pony undergoing an off-spoke crash test at MIRA
(February 1977)

HYUNDAI
44409508
ECE 12
TEST 2

MIRA

유럽 진출을 위한 품질 테스트

지구촌 곳곳을 발로 뛰며 수출 지역을 넓혀 나간 현대자동차는 이어 선진 시장 진출을 위한 준비에 착수했다. 선진 시장인 미국은 전 세계에서 가장 큰 시장답게 규제도 가장 까다로웠기에 현대자동차는 미국 진출의 전초기지로서 유럽 진출 계획을 먼저 진행했다. 유럽 진출을 위한 가장 큰 관문은 유럽 지역의 자동차 안전 기준 통과였다. 당시 자동차 산업 초기 단계였던 한국에는 품질 테스트를 할 시설과 시스템이 부재했기에 엄격한 EEC(European Economic Community, 유럽경제공동체) 안전 규정 충족을 위해 해외 시설에 의존할 수밖에 없었다. 이에 현대자동차는 안전 규정 테스트 기관인 영국의 MIRA(Motor Industry Research Association)에 포니 12대를 보내 테스트를 맡겼다. 고유 모델을 처음 개발해본 현대자동차로서는 생소한 시험 항목과 까다로운 규정이 많았지만, 우려와 달리 포니는 각종 테스트를 무사히 통과했고, 특히 정면 충돌 테스트에서는 단번에 합격점을 받았다. 다만 유럽의 품질 기준을 맞추기 위해 안전벨트, 램프류, 시트 등 다양한 품목의 부품을 새로 개발해야 했고, 여러 번의 테스트를 거치며 발견한 문제는 다시 제작하거나 수정·보완해 재시험 치르기를 반복했다. 그러고는 마침내 1977년 9월, MIRA의 각종 테스트에서 최종 합격하고 EEC 인증을 받음으로써 유럽 진출의 꿈을 실현할 수 있었다.

현대자동차는 테스트를 진행하는 동시에 1977년부터 다년간 제네바, 브뤼셀, 암스테르담 등에서 열리는 모터쇼에 적극 참가하며 유럽 내 포니의 인지도를 높여나갔다. 동시에 진출 대상국 선별 작업도 진행했는데, 자국 브랜드가 강세인 데다 규제 기준도 높은 서유럽이나 혹한 테스트가 필수인 북유럽은 후순위에 두고, 네덜란드 등 베네룩스 3국을 우선 진출 대상국으로 선정했다. 이들 나라는 자동차 수요가 연간 30

Quality tests for European expansion

After circling the world to expand its export channels, Hyundai began preparing to enter developed markets. The U.S., being the largest market globally, had the most stringent regulations. Therefore, Hyundai decided to first pursue expansion into Europe as a stepping stone to entering the U.S. market. The biggest challenge for entering Europe was meeting the region's car safety standards. At that time, Korea, still in the early stages of its automotive industry, lacked the facilities and systems for quality testing, necessitating reliance on overseas facilities to meet the strict European Economic Community (ECC) safety regulations. Hyundai's solution was to send 12 Ponies to the Motor Industry Research Association (MIRA), a British consulting organization for automotive technologies, for testing. Despite being new to developing its own models and facing many unfamiliar test items and stringent regulations, the Pony successfully passed various tests, notably receiving immediate approval in the frontal crash test. However, it was necessary to develop new components such as seat belts, lamps, and seats to meet Europe's quality standard. After multiple tests and addressing issues through redesigns or modifications, Hyundai finally passed all tests at MIRA and received ECC certification in September 1977, realizing its dream of entering the European market. While conducting tests, Hyundai actively participated in motor shows held in Geneva, Brussels, Amsterdam, and other cities from 1977 — enhancing the Pony's visibility in Europe. Simultaneously, the company also worked on selecting target countries for expansion. Coun-

네덜란드에서 촬영한 포니 화보
A pictorial cut of the Pony taken in the Netherlands

만~40만 대 규모로 적지 않은 데다 자국 자동차 브랜드가 없어 수입 제한 규정이 엄격하지 않았으며, 영어가 통용되고 항구가 발달해 유럽 시장 진출 거점으로서 적합한 환경을 갖추었기 때문이었다.

1978년 7월 네덜란드에 현지법인 HMH(Hyundai Motor Holland B.V)를 설립한 현대자동차는 유럽 진출을 위한 행보를 본격화했다. 제2차 오일쇼크 및 현지 환율 약세로 1981년 5월 철수할 때까지 HMH는 유럽 각국에서 일어나는 문제에 대응하는 현지 대표 창구 역할과 함께 유럽 내 수출 물량과 수출 국가를 지속적으로 확대하는 전초기지 역할을 담당

tries in Western Europe, where domestic brands were solid and regulatory standards were high, and the Nordic countries, where cold weather testing was essential, were given a lower priority. Instead, the three Benelux countries (Belgium, the Netherlands, and Luxembourg) were selected as the primary target countries for expansion. These countries, with an annual car demand of 300,000 to 400,000 units and no domestic car brands, had less strict import restrictions. Additionally, the widespread use of English and well-developed ports made them

했다. 이처럼 선진 시장인 유럽 진출과 해외 법인 운영 경험을 통해 현지 테스트 및 법규 인증, 딜러 관리, 제품의 현지화, A/S 등 해외 영업 노하우를 축적한 현대자동차는 이후 국내외 수출 조직망을 정비하면서 점차 글로벌 브랜드로서 면모를 갖춰나갔다. 일례로 수출 시장을 확대하고자 진행한 1979년 1월 노르웨이 한지(寒地) 테스트 합격은 훗날 현대자동차가 캐나다 등 혹한 지역에 진출하는 데 경험적 자산이 되었다.

suitable as a gateway for entering the European market.

In July 1978, Hyundai established its local subsidiary, HMH (Hyundai Motor Holland B.V.), in the Netherlands and began full-scale expansion into Europe. Despite facing challenges such as the second oil shock and local currency depreciation, HMH served as a local representative addressing issues across European countries and acted as a forward base for continuously expanding export volumes and countries until its withdrawal in May 1981. Through its experience in entering the advanced European market and operating overseas subsidiaries, Hyundai accumulated foreign sales expertise including local testing, regulatory certification, dealer management, product localization, and after-sales service (A/S). This experience helped Hyundai refine its domestic and international export networks, gradually establishing itself as a global brand. For instance, passing the cold climate test in Norway in January 1979 became an experiential asset for Hyundai's later expansion into cold regions like Canada.

영국 MIRA에서 충돌 테스트 중인 포니(1977년 3월)(위)
제47회 제네바 국제 자동차 박람회에 참가한 포니(1977년 3월)(아래)
The Pony undergoing a crash test at MIRA (March 1977; top)
The Pony's appearance in the 47th Geneva International Motor
Show (March 1977; below)

현대자동차는 포니의 유럽 진출을 위해 각고의 노력을 기울였다.
Hyundai dedicated considerable efforts across different areas to
ensure the success of the Pony in the European market.

네덜란드 도로를 주행 중인 포니
The Pony driving on a road in the Netherlands

파리의 중심가 상젤리제 거리를 달리고 있는 포니
The Pony at Champs-Élysées, the heart of Paris

런던 거리를 주행 중인 포니
The Pony driving through London

수출 시장 확대를 위해 진행한 노르웨이 한지(寒地) 테스트
Cold weather testing undertaken in Norway to expand Hyundai's potential export market

1979년 1월 포니는 노르웨이 윈터 테스트에 합격했다. 이 경험을 바탕으로
현대자동차는 캐나다 등 혹한 지역으로 수출 시장을 확대할 수 있었다.
In January 1979, the Pony successfully completed its winter test in
Norway. This experience helped Hyundai expand into Canada and
other markets with cold weather conditions.

위기 상황에서도 멈추지 않은 도전

현대자동차는 유럽 진출을 위한 다양한 테스트를 진행하며 미국 시장 입성을 위한 준비도 함께해 나갔다. 자동차의 본고장이자 세계에서 가장 큰 시장인 미국 시장 진입은 글로벌 브랜드로 도약하기 위해 반드시 통과해야 할 관문이었다. 그러기 위해서는 까다롭고 엄격하기로 소문난 FMVSS(Federal Motor Vehicle Safety Standard, 미 연방 자동차 안전 기준) 인증을 획득해야만 했다. 이에 1978년 현대자동차는 배출가스 대응은 미국의 올슨(Olson), 내장 부분은 일본의 세케이(Sekkei), 보디 부분은 미국의 칼스팬(Calspan) 등 각 분야에서 전문 기술을 보유한 회사와 제휴해 각종 테스트를 수행하면서 부족한 상품성을 보완해 나갔다.

하지만 1979년 4월 다양한 테스트를 종합해 본 현대자동차는 포니를 FMVSS에 맞추는 작업까지는 완수했으나, 미국 진출은 아직 시기상조라는 결론을 내린다. FMVSS에 맞출 경우, 배출가스 제어를 위한 부가 장치 장착이 필요해 가격 경쟁력을 갖추기 어려울뿐더러 각종 규제 수준을 빠르게 충족한다 해도 그 시점에선 이미 포니 모델 자체가 시장 트렌드에 뒤처지는 모델이 될 것이라는 우려 때문이었다. 이에 따라 미국 진출을 위한 방침도 세계적으로 수요가 빠르게 늘고 있던 전륜구동 모델을 새로 개발해 추진하는 방향으로 변경되었다. 비록 미국 진출 계획은 미뤄졌지만, 까다로운 법규와 기준을 충족하기 위해 진행한 수많은 테스트 과정은 선진 시장 기준에 부합하는 상품으로의 품질 개선뿐 아니라 내부에서 독자적으로 수출을 위한 성능 시험을 추진할 수 있는 노하우를 습득하는 계기가 되었다. 이 경험은 현대자동차가 훗날 포니 엑셀로 미국 시장에 진출하는 데 큰 자양분이 되었다.

한편 1970년대 말까지 국내 자동차 시장과 수출 확대를 이끌며 고속 성장을 거듭하던 현대자동차의 성장세는

Unwavering pursuits even during crisis
As Hyundai established its foothold in Europe, it also continued preparing for the U.S. market. Entering the U.S., the home of automobiles and the world's largest market, was a crucial step to becoming a global brand. To do so, it was necessary to obtain the Federal Motor Vehicle Safety Standards (FMVSS) certification, known for its strict requirements. Therefore, in 1978, Hyundai entered into partnerships with companies that had expertise in related areas, such as the U.S. company Olson for emissions control; the Japanese company Sekkei for the internal-related parts; and the U.S. firm Calspan for the body structure, in order to enhance product quality.

In April 1979, after assessing various tests, Hyundai concluded that while they had managed to adapt the Pony model to meet FMVSS requirements, it was premature to enter the U.S. market. At the time, the concern was that because the Pony required additional devices for emissions control in accordance with FMVSS requirements, it would not only be challenging to offer the car at a competitive price, but also would mean that even if the regulatory standards were quickly met, the Pony model itself might lag behind the market trends at that time. Consequently, the approach for U.S. expansion was revised to develop a new front-wheel-drive model, in line with the rapidly growing global demand. Although the plans for the U.S. market had to be put on hold, the numerous tests to meet the stringent regulations and standards became an opportunity to acquire the know-how to independently conduct performance tests for exports, as well as improve product

1980년대에 접어들며 조금씩 꺾이기 시작했다. 제2차 오일
쇼크로 인한 유가 폭등과 10·26사태로 비롯된 정치적 혼란 때
문에 내수 경제가 불황 국면에 접어든 것이다. 여기에 휘발유
에 대한 특별소비세와 자동차세 인상, 자가용 휴일 주유 금지,
사업용 자동차 신규 등록 불허 등 정부의 강력한 자동차 이용
억제 정책이 더해지면서 국내 자동차 산업 수요는 승용차 기
준 1979년 10만5,348대에서 1980년 6만627대로 전년 대비
60% 가까이 급감했다. 불과 1년 전까지만 해도 호황을 누리
던 국내 자동차업계가 극심한 침체기에 들어선 것이다.

세계적 불황으로 수출 역시 성장세가 꺾이고 겨우 현
상 유지만 하게 되었다. 이처럼 판매가 급격히 감소하고 국
제 금리가 가파르게 오르면서 현대자동차의 경영 상황은 눈
에 띄게 악화해, 1980년 193억 원의 적자에 이어 1981년에도
164억 원의 적자를 기록했다. 설상가상으로 1970년대 말 포
니 10만 대 생산 체제 구축을 위해 차관을 도입해 대규모 설비
투자를 단행한 현대자동차는 갑작스레 높아진 금리와 환율
로 부채 비율이 1978년 264%에서 1980년 675%로 급증, 자
금 상황이 더욱 경색되었다. 당시 경영난은 상당히 심각해 현
대자동차는 부도 직전의 상황까지 내몰렸다. 경영 위기가 심
각해지자 현대자동차는 긴축재정을 실시하는 한편, 장기 전
략으로 추진해 온 투자 계획을 전면 재조정하는 등 위기 관리
체제에 돌입했다. 이에 따라 미국, 유럽 등 선진 시장을 겨냥
해 1976년 초부터 약 5년간 계속해 온 포니 쿠페 양산 프로젝
트는 시장성이 낮다는 판단 아래 전면 백지화되었다. 또한 인
원과 조직을 재정비하고 원가 절감과 생산성 향상을 위한 노
력을 멈추지 않았다.

당시 현대자동차는 위기를 극복할 수 있는 감량 경영
을 다각도로 실천해 나가는 동시에, 기업의 장기적 생존을 위
해 미래 투자에도 지속적인 관심을 기울였다. 대규모 증산

quality to meet advanced market standards.
This experience later served as a significant
driving force when Hyundai entered the U.S.
market with the Pony Excel model.

Hyundai, which had been experiencing rapid growth by leading the domestic car market
and export expansion until the late 1970s, began
to see a slowdown as the 1980s began. Recession, caused by the drastic increase in oil prices
due to the Second Oil Shock and political insta-
bility caused by the assassination of South Korean President Park Chung-hee, hit the domestic
market. When the new government added strict
measures to curtail the use of automobiles, such
as increasing the special excise taxes on gasoline and other car taxes, banning holiday fueling
for private vehicles, and the suspension of new
business vehicle registrations, the demand for
automobiles in the Korean domestic market
dropped to only around 60% of 1979's 105,348
vehicles to 60,627 in 1980. The domestic car
industry, booming just a year before, entered a
severe downturn.

What is more, due to the global recession,
exports also saw a halt in growth, barely maintaining the status quo. Sales plummeted and
international interest rates rose sharply, significantly worsening Hyundai's financial situation.
The company recorded a loss of 19.3 billion KRW
in 1980, followed by a loss of 16.4 billion KRW in
1981. To make matters worse, the company had
borrowed heavily in the late 1970s to build a production system capable of producing 100,000
Ponies per year. Thus, its debt-to-equity ratio
surged from 264% in 1978 to 675% in 1980 due
to the sudden increase in interest and exchange

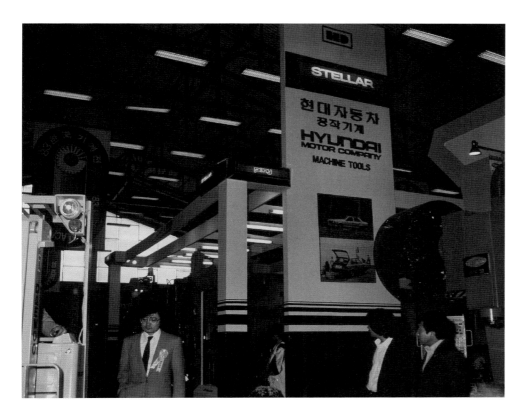

한국 기계 전시회에 트랜스퍼 머신을 출품한 현대자동차 (1983년 10월)
Hyundai exhibits its transfer machine at the Korea Machinery Exhibition (October 1983)

1978년에 발족한 공작기계부는 국내 최초로 트랜스퍼 머신을 개발함으로써 다양한 가공 장비를 만들 수 있는 기술을 확보하고 주도적으로 프로젝트 일정을 관리 할 수 있게 되었다. Established in 1978, the Machine Tool Department developed the first transfer machine in Korea, securing the technology to make a variety of processing equipment. This enabled the proactive management of the project schedule.

으로 생산 단가를 낮춰야만 수출이 확대돼 경영 위기에서 벗어날 수 있다고 판단한 경영진은 규모의 경제를 실현하고자 30만 대 규모 공장 건설을 계획한 것이 대표적인 예다. 불황에도 불구하고 먼 미래를 내다보고 새로운 성장 전략을 찾아 과감한 투자 계획을 수립한 것이다. 이처럼 현대자동차는 경제 침체기에도 회사 실정에 맞게 지속적으로 계획을 축소하거나 수정하면서 내일의 재도약을 위한 암중모색을 거듭했다. 경제성장률 저하, 급격한 물가 상승, 경상수지 적자 등의 악조건 속에서도 현대자동차는 계획한 목표를 착실히 진행해 나갔는

rates. The financial difficulties became so severe that Hyundai was pushed to the brink of bankruptcy. As the crisis deepened, Hyundai implemented austerity measures and completely reevaluated its long-term investment plans as part of its crisis management strategy. As a result, the Pony Coupe mass production project, which had been underway for about five years since early 1976, for advanced markets such as the United States and Europe, was ultimately abandoned due to low profit potential. Personnel and organizations were adjusted, while the company continued reducing costs and improving productivity.

However, despite implementing various cost-cutting measures to overcome the crisis, Hyundai maintained a continuous interest in future investments for the long-term survival. A typical example was the plan to build a plant capable of producing 300,000 units per year in order to realize sufficient economies of scale. The management believed that lowering production costs through mass production was essential for expanding exports and escaping the management crisis. The company made a bold bid for its future amid an existential crisis. Thus, even during economic downturns, Hyundai continuously adjusted and revised its plans to prepare for a rebound, persistently exploring options suitable for the company's situation. Amidst challenging conditions such as economic slowdown, rapid inflation, and current account deficits, the company steadily progressed towards its goal. One such example of success in these challenging times was the establishment of the Machine Tool Department in 1978. This allowed

데, 1978년 공작기계부를 발족하고 자동차 생산에 필요한 다양한 부품을 직접 만들 수 있는 트랜스퍼 머신 제작에 돌입한 것이 그 대표적인 예다. 트랜스퍼 머신에 대한 선제적 투자는 초창기 발생한 결손 등으로 무모한 투자라는 인식이 없지 않았으나, 불과 몇 년 후 30만 대 공장 건설로 소요량이 크게 늘어난 공작기계를 원활히 공급하는 중요한 동력이 되었다.

또한 그해에 현대자동차는 노후한 포니의 이미지를 타파하고자 포니의 성능과 디자인을 개선한 페이스리프트 모델인 '포니2' 개발에 착수했고, 불황의 여파가 채 가시지 않은 1982년 3월에 이 모델을 출시했다. 포니2는 출시되자마자 판매 돌풍을 일으키며 1982년 7월 단일 차종으로는 국내 최초로 30만 대 생산을 돌파했다. 포니2의 판매 호조는 다년간 지속된 현대자동차의 적자를 단번에 흑자로 전환시켰고, 회사가 경영난에서 벗어나 미래를 위한 투자를 가속화하는 데 크게 기여했다. 경영 위기 상황에서 추진한 과감한 미래 투자가 오히려 지속 성장의 토대를 만든 것이다.

the company to produce its transfer machines capable of producing various parts needed for car production. The initial investment in transfer machines was perceived as reckless due to early losses. However, it became a crucial driving force in smoothly supplying machine tools when demand surged with the construction of the 300,000-unit plant a few years later.

That same year, Hyundai initiated the development of "the Pony2" — a facelift model intended to enhance the car's design and performance, thereby transforming the outdated image associated with the original Pony. The new model was launched in March 1982, when the market was recovering from the recession. Upon its release, the Pony2 quickly became a sales sensation becoming the first Korean car model to exceed the 300,000-production mark in July 1982. Moreover, the Pony2's strong performance turned Hyundai's multi-year losses into a surplus, significantly contributing to the company's recovery from financial difficulties and accelerating investments for the future. Indeed, a bold decision to invest amidst a crisis, in the end laid the basis for the company's continued growth.

포니2 출시에 힘입어 단일 차종으로는 국내 최초로 총누계
생산 대수 30만 대를 돌파한 포니
The Pony becoming the first model to exceed
300,000-units produced in Korea (July 1982)

미래를 내다본 과감한 투자, 'X카 프로젝트'

1981년 10월, 현대자동차는 기자회견을 통해 1985년까지 연간 생산 30만 대 규모의 공장을 짓고 미국 진출을 위한 전륜구동형 소형차를 새로 개발하겠다는 계획(X카 프로젝트)을 발표했다. 현대자동차의 이 프로젝트는 사내외에서 많은 우려를 표명했다. 1981년 당시 국내에 등록된 자동차는 57만 대[1] 수준에 불과했고, 이처럼 협소한 시장 여건을 감안할 때 자칫 기업의 존립 자체를 위협할 수 있는 X카 프로젝트는 누가 봐도 무모할 정도로 모험적이고 야심 찬 결정이었기 때문이다.

그러나 연간 생산 30만 대 공장 준공은 회사의 철저한 수요 예측에 기반한 전략이었다. 현대자동차는 자체 분석을 통해 연간 자동차 30만 대 생산이 가능해질 경우 생산 단가를 20% 가까이 낮출 수 있을 것으로 보았다. 또한 당시 한국의 인구 1,000명당 자동차 보유 대수는 6대, 자가 운전 비율은 30%에 불과했지만 신차 출시 시점인 1985년 말에는 경기가 회복돼 자동차 수요가 빠르게 증가하면서 국내 자동차 시장의 성장 잠재력이 매우 커질 것으로 판단했다. 게다가 이미 전 세계 50여 개국에 포니를 비롯한 완성차를 수출하고 있는 만큼 신차의 품질과 가격 경쟁력이 확보된다면 수출 시장 추가 확대를 통해 경기에 민감한 국내 시장에서 벗어나 회사의 판매 건전성이 높아질 것으로 전망했다. 특히 전륜구동형 신차를 개발해 자동차의 본고장 미국에 수출한다면 진정한 글로벌 메이커로 거듭날 수 있다고 판단했다. 즉 30만 대 공장 준공은 미래를 내다본 투자이자 글로벌 브랜드로서 입지를 더욱 공고히 하겠다는 강력한 의지의 표명이었던 것이다.

제1·2차 오일쇼크를 경험하고 난 후 당시 전 세계 자동차 시장에서는 연비가 좋고 실내 공간이 넉넉한 전륜구동 방식이 주 트렌드로 부상했으며, 폭스바겐 등 독일뿐 아니라 일본 메이커도 대부분 전륜구동 방식을 채택하고 있었다. 그때

A bold step forward into the future, the "X Car" Project

In October 1981, Hyundai announced through a press conference that by 1985, it planned to build a plant capable of producing 300,000 units annually and develop a new FWD vehicle for the U.S. market, known as the "X Car" project. This goal raised considerable concerns both internally and externally. After all, the number of vehicles registered in Korea in 1981 barely reached 570,000.[1] Given such a limited market size, the "X Car" project was seen as an extremely risky and ambitious decision, potentially threatening the very existence of the company.

However, the plans to build a 300,000-unit car plant were based on the company's thorough demand forecasts. Hyundai anticipated the cost of production could be reduced by nearly 20% when they produce 300,000 cars annually. At the time, there were only six cars per 1,000 people and the self-driving rate was merely 30% in Korea. Nevertheless, it was projected that by the end of 1985, when the new car would be launched, the economy would recover. This would lead to a rapid increase in car demand, significantly boosting the growth potential of the domestic car market. Moreover, Hyundai had already exported cars, including the Pony, to over 50 countries worldwide. It was expected that securing the quality and price competitiveness of the new car would allow for expansion into additional export markets, thereby improving the company's sales health by reducing dependence on the economically sensitive domestic market. Particularly, it was believed that developing a new FWD vehicle and exporting it to the United

미쓰비시와의 합작 투자 계약 체결 및 30만 대 공장 건설 기념식에 참석한 미쓰비시 구보 도미오 회장 내외와 정주영 선대회장(오른쪽 첫 번째)(1982년 4월)
Chairman Kubo of Mitsubishi and his wife attending the ceremony to celebrate the signing of the joint venture between Hyundai and Mitsubishi and the construction of the new 300,000-unit plant with Ju-yung Chung (first on the right; April 1982)

문에 북미 수출을 위해 경제적인 전륜구동 모델을 새로 개발하는 건 당연한 선택이었다. 다만 전륜구동은 정교한 기계 가공 기술이 필요한 차세대 기술이었기에, 후발 주자였던 현대자동차는 전륜구동 차 개발을 위해 선진 기업과 기술 제휴를 맺고 새롭게 배워나갈 수밖에 없었다. 이에 현대자동차는 일본 자동차 회사를 견제할 아시아 지역 생산 거점을 구축하기 위해 제휴선을 찾고 있던 폭스바겐과 협상을 시도했다. 그러나 폭스바겐이 과거 포드와 협상할 때와 마찬가지로 자본 참여에 의한 기술 제휴를 주장하며 경영권 참여 의지를 강력히 표명한 데다 연구소 설립 불가 등 현대자동차의 자주권을 침해하는 요구 조건을 내세우는 바람에 협상이 결렬되고 말았다. 이후 르노, 알파로메오 등과 이어진 교섭에도 결과는 마찬

States, the homeland of automobiles, would allow the company to become a truly global maker. In essence, the completion of the 300,000-unit plant was an investment in the future and a strong expression of the will to further solidify its position as a global brand.

After experiencing the first and second oil shocks, the global automotive market saw a rise in the trend of front-wheel drive vehicles that offered better fuel efficiency and spacious interiors. German manufacturers such as Volkswagen and Japanese manufacturers were moving to adapt to this new trend. Hence, it was logical that Hyundai would develop an economical FWD model for the U.S. market. However, since FWD required sophisticated machining technologies, Hyundai, as a latecomer, had no choice but to form technical alliances with advanced companies to learn and develop FWD vehicles. Hyundai's initial choice for a partnership was Volkswagen, which at the time was searching for a production base in Asia to counter the Japanese brands. However, negotiations fell apart because Volkswagen insisted on a technical partnership based on capital participation. They strongly expressed their intention to participate in management and set conditions that infringed on Hyundai's sovereignty, such as refusing to establish a research center, similar to past discussions with Ford. Negotiations with other companies like Renault and Alfa Romeo ended in a similar manner. Ultimately, Hyundai reached out to Mitsubishi, with whom they had a friendly relationship through technical collaboration on developing the Pony. Mitsubishi agreed to a technology partnership on the condition that it

가지였다. 결국 현대자동차는 포니를 개발하면서 기술 제휴를 통해 우호적 관계를 맺어온 미쓰비시에 제휴 의사를 타진했고, 미쓰비시는 경영권 요구를 하지 않되 부분적 자본 참여와 기술료 수취, 그리고 긴밀한 협력 관계를 조건으로 기술 제휴를 수용했다. 미쓰비시 또한 치열한 미국 시장에서 살아남기 위해서는 자동차 회사 간 연합이 필요하다고 판단했고, 포니를 개발할 때처럼 현대자동차가 결국 언젠가는 전륜구동차를 만들 테니 이왕이면 기술료를 받고 제휴해 주자는 쪽으로 의견이 모였기 때문이다. 이처럼 현대자동차는 미쓰비시와 기술 제휴 및 합작 투자를 추진하면서 30만 대 공장 건설 및 국내 최초 전륜구동 차 개발 프로젝트인 'X카 프로젝트'를 공표할 수 있었다.

현대자동차는 이 야심 찬 계획을 현실화하기 위한 제반 준비를 착실히 실현해 나갔다. 전륜구동 기술 제휴 협상 과정에서 겪은 독자 기술이 없는 기업의 설움과 한계, 그리고 선진국의 엄격한 법규와 선진 테스트 시설에 대한 경험을 바탕으로 기술 자립의 기반을 다지기 위해 종합 주행 시험장 건설 및 제반 시험 설비 구축에 착수한 것이다. 이에 따라 1983년 12월, 당시 아시아 최고 수준인 총면적 약 79만3,388m²(24만 평)의 종합 주행 시험장을 완공했다. 그 결과 고속주회로, 크로스컨트리로, 벨지안로 등 약 19개의 시험로를 갖춘 종합 주행 시험장에서 내구성, 소음, 진동 등 다양한 성능 시험을 자체적으로 진행할 수 있었다.

1984년 11월에는 충돌 시험장과 제반 성능 평가가 가능한 다양한 시험 시설을 구축했다. 이로써 선진국의 자동차 시험 연구 기관과 동일한 수준의 안전성 평가는 물론, 영하 40°C부터 영상 60°C까지 극한의 온도에서 차의 성능을 평가하거나, 반복 작동으로 각 부품의 내구성을 테스트하는 것이 가능해졌다. 그동안 해외에서 진행하던 각종 테스트를 국

received some equity and technology licensing fees. They sought a close cooperative relationship, without demanding managerial control. Mitsubishi also believed that alliances among car companies were necessary to survive in the competitive U.S. market. They reasoned that since Hyundai would eventually develop a FWD vehicle as they did with the Pony, it was better to collaborate and receive royalties. Thus, through a technological partnership and joint investment with Mitsubishi, Hyundai was able to announce its plans to build a 300,000-unit plant as well as the "X-Car" project, Korea's first FWD vehicle.

Hyundai began working studiously to establish the basis for this ambitious plan. The company began constructing testing facilities and a comprehensive proving ground to establish a groundwork for technological independence. The foundation for this was its necessity of proprietary technology as well as its experiences in developed countries, such as trials in advanced testing facilities and dealing with strict regulations. Consequently, in December 1983, Hyundai completed what was then Asia's premier comprehensive proving ground, covering approximately a 79-ha land area. This facility featured around 19 different test tracks, including a high-speed circuit, cross-country track, and Belgian road, allowing for in-house testing of durability as well as NVH (noise, vibration, harshness) among other performance metrics.

In November 1984, Hyundai established new testing facilities for crash tests and various performance evaluations. These facilities enabled safety evaluations similar to those of auto-

30만 대 공장 건설 현장
Construction of the 300,000-unit plant

내에서 진행하게 된 만큼 독자 기술 개발, 외화 절약 및 원가 절감, 기술 인력 양성 효과를 모두 누릴 수 있게 되었다.

공작기계부가 추진하던 트랜스퍼 머신 개발에도 박차를 가해 설계에 들어간 지 1년 반 만에 국내 최초로 트랜스퍼 머신 제작에 성공, 1983년 6월부터 가동을 시작했다. 이로 인해 X카 양산에 소요되는 장비 521대 중 약 26%에 해당하는 135대를 자체 조달할 수 있었다. 이처럼 현대자동차는 트랜스퍼 머신 제작으로 해외 장비 수입을 줄임으로써 상당한 외화와 비용을 절감하게 되었을 뿐 아니라 기술 자립에도 한 발 더 다가갈 수 있었다. 더 나아가 현대자동차는 공작기계 제작 협력 업체를 양성하고 동반 성장을 모색하는 일에도 심혈을 기울였는데, 이는 자동차에 들어가는 수많은 부품을 제작하는 공작기계를 모두 자체 생산할 수는 없었기 때문이다. 이처럼 X카 프로젝트는 기술 자립과 국산화를 위한 다양하고 성실한 노력을 통해 차근차근 진척되어 나갔다.

motive testing institutions in advanced countries, including performance in extreme temperatures ranging from -40°C to 60°C and the durability of each component through repeated operations. As a result, Hyundai could conduct various tests domestically that were previously outsourced overseas. This led to benefits such as the development of proprietary technology, foreign currency savings, cost reduction, and the training of skilled technical personnel.

Hyundai's machine tool department also accelerated the development of transfer machines. It achieved a significant milestone by successfully manufacturing the first domestic transfer machine just 1.5 years after starting the design phase. This machine began operation in June 1983. This allowed the company to source 135 pieces of equipment, or 26% of the 521 pieces of equipment required for the mass production of "the X Car", from its own internal supply chain. By manufacturing the transfer machine in-house, Hyundai significantly reduced the need for importing similar equipment from abroad, saving a considerable amount of foreign currency and costs. This effort also moved Hyundai a step closer to technological independence. Furthermore, Hyundai devoted to nurturing collaborative partnerships with machine tool manufacturers, aiming for mutual growth. This was crucial because it was not feasible for Hyundai to produce all the machine tools necessary to make the myriad of components involved in a car. Like these, the X Car project advanced steadily through various earnest efforts towards technological independence and domestic production.

I. 개요

자동차 부품 및 완성차에 대한 자체 개발 능력의 배양과
선진 도입 기술의 토착화를 통해 당사 고유의 자동차를
개발할 수 있는 기본 능력을 갖추기 위한 기반을 마련 한다.

II. 기술 개발 계획

1. 정규 개발 계획

	PROJECT 내역	80	81	82	83	84	85
1)	PONY DIESEL 개발						
2)	ECE 1504 대책						
3)	PONY FACE LIFT (5DR, P/UP)						
4)	Y - CAR						
5)	X - CAR (5DR, 3DR, N/BACK)						
6)	FB 485 BUS						
7)	RB 485 BUS						
8)	HD 1000 NEW MODEL						
9)	현 차종 지원 PONY SERIES CORTINA GRANADA HD-1000 SERIES 8.5TON TRUCK SERIES 10.5TON TRUCK SERIES HD-170 BUS SERIES RB-585 BUS RB-635 BUS						

4. 배기 GAS 분석장치

순위	장 비 명	용 도	81
1	TORQUE MEASURMENT 외 측정장비	배출 가스 시험을 위한 HP 선정 및 엔진변수 측정	
2	DIRECT SAMPLING	엔진의 배출 가스 성분조사 (DIESEL 측정)	8
3'	EGR ANALYSIS SYSTEM	EGR RATE 측정	3
4	THROTTLE OPENING ANGLE METER 외 측정장비	TROTTLE 개도, 엔진온도 흡기부압 등 측정	4
5	CVS ANALYTIC EQUIPMENT	자동차 배출 가스 측정 (미국, 호주, 캐나다, 스웨덴)	
6	DILUTED SAMPLING SYSTEM	자동차 배출 가스 측정 (EEC 지역)	
7	보조 시설	VEHICLE LAMP, JACK 등	5
8	DISTRIBUTOR TESTER	배전기 진각 특성 조사	

제품개발연구소에서 작성한 기술 개발 계획서 일부(1981년 9월)
Excerpts from the 「Technology Development Plan」
prepared by the Product Development Research Center
(September 1981)

순위	설 비 명	용 도
1	기초 조사	○ KS, IEC, SAE 관련시험
2	담당자 교육 (과기처 시행 국비보조 기술 연수파견 81.9.24→	− 외부 소음 − 경보기 시험 − 배기계통 소음 시험 − 냉난방 계통 소음시험
3	소음 진동시험심 − 무향실 − 잔향실	○ 차량실내 소음 시험 ○ 차체구조의 소음진동 응답 시험
4	자동차 시험장치 − CHASSIS DYNO. − ENGINE DYNO,	○ 구동 계통 소음 진동시험 ○ ENGINE " ○ 흡 배기 계통 " ○ 재료의 소음, 진동, 특성시험
5	계측 및 분석 장치 − 측정장치	

8. 부품 시험 설비

순위	설 비 명	용 도	년 81
1	BALL JOINT 류 시험기	STEERING & SUSPENSION BALL JOINT 류의 피로시험	
2	WHEEL RIM ROLL TEST M/C	WHEEL RIM 의 ROLL 내구성 시험	
3	WHEEL BENDING FATIGUE TEST M/C	WHEEL 의 굽힘 내구성 시험	
4	PORTABLE POLARISCOPE	응력해석 및 강도개선	
5	CLUTCH FULL SIZE TESTER	CLUTCH SYSTEM 의 내구성능 시험	
6	BRAKE DYNAMOMETER (大)	BRAKE SYSTEM 의 성능 내구시험	
7	" " (小)	" "	
8	RADIATOR 시험기	RADIATOR 의 성능 내구시험	
9	FAN DYNAMOMETER	FAN 내구, 성능시험	
10	THERMOSTAT 내구 시험기	THERMOSTAT의 성능 내구시험	
11	VIBRATION TESTER	각종부품의 진동시험	
12	FRICTION TESTER	마찰 부품의 진동시험	
13	회전 가속 장비	FMVSS 206. DOOR LATCH 중 INERTIA LOAD TEST	

울산 공장에 건립한 종합 주행시험장 전경
The aerial view of the comprehensive proving ground site

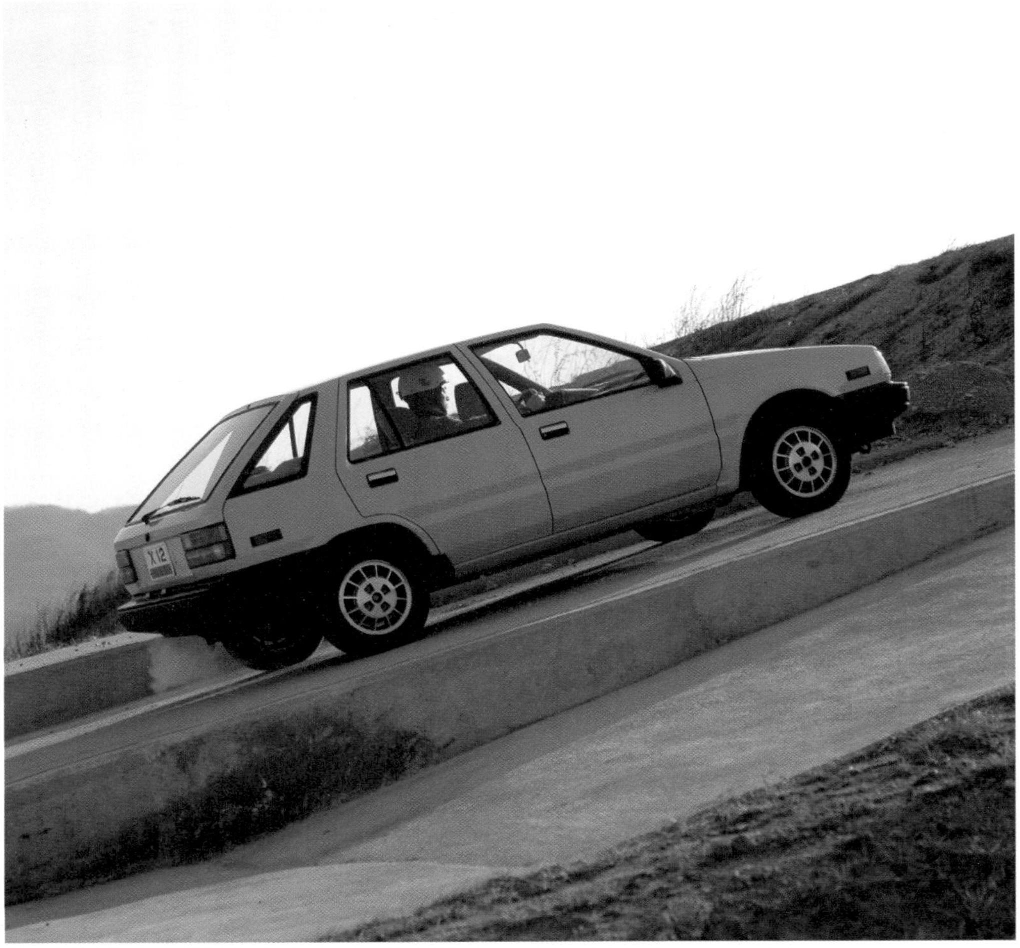

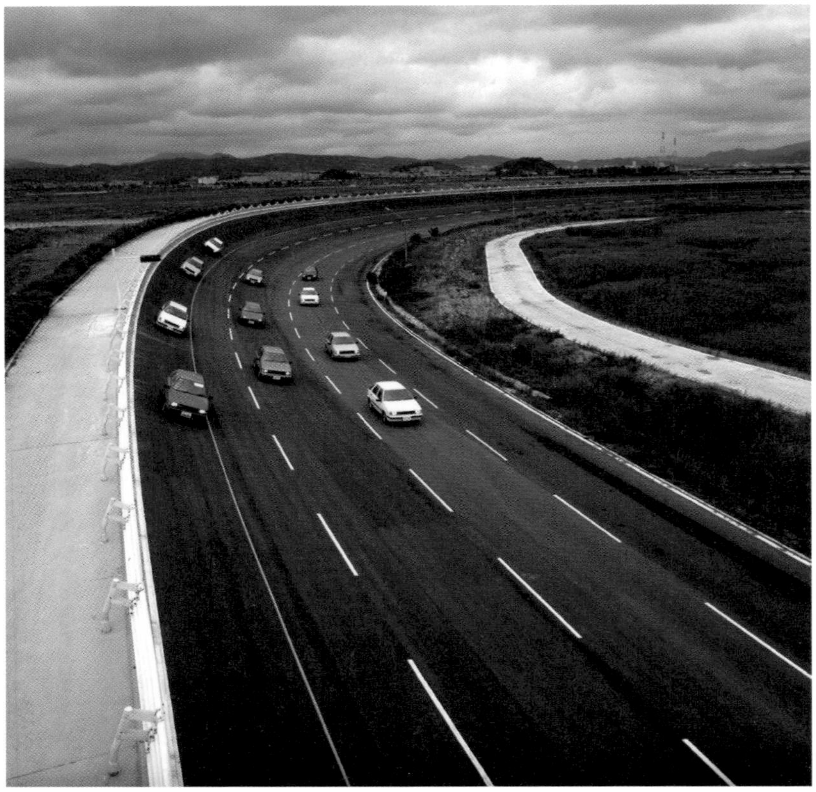

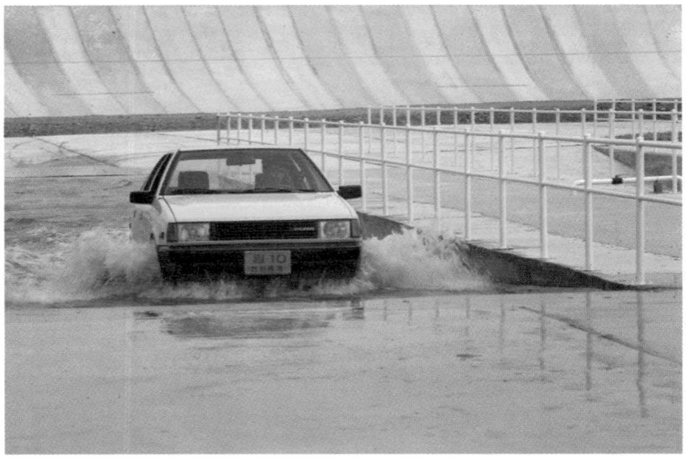

다양한 테스트를 진행 중인 미국 수출 전략 모델, X카
The "X Car", a strategic model for the U.S.
export, undergoing a range of tests

Chapter 3

다양한 테스트를 진행 중인 미국 수출 전략 모델, X카
The "X Car", a strategic model for the U.S.
export, undergoing a range of tests

캐나다 교통부 공인 테스트 기관인 미국 칼스팬사에서
CMVSS 테스트 중 안전도 테스트를 진행 중인 포니2
The Pony2 undergoing a safety test as a part of
the CMVSS testing process in Calspan,
an official testing institute recognized by the
Canadian Transportation Agency

포니2의 성공적인 캐나다 진출

현대자동차는 미국 진출을 위한 X카 프로젝트를 준비하는
동시에 북미 시장의 첫 번째 관문이라 할 수 있는 캐나다 시
장에 눈을 돌렸다. 1981년 말 시장 조사단을 캐나다에 파견
해 CMVSS(Canada Motor Vehicle Safety Standard, 캐
나다 자동차 안전 규제 기준) 등 현지 법규와 자동차 시장 전
반에 대해 면밀히 분석한 결과, 포니2의 사양 중 몇 가지만 변
경하면 캐나다 수출이 가능하다는 긍정적 결론을 내렸다. 이
에 따라 현지의 춥고 습한 기후에 꼭 필요한 서리 제거 장치
와 대용량 히터, 장거리 고속 주행이 빈번한 현지 운전자들
의 주행 습관에 적합한 5단 변속기, 현지에서 법규로 규정한
5-마일 범퍼* 등을 기존 모델에 장착해 수출형 모델로 개
선했다. 이때 장착된 5-마일 범퍼는 범퍼와 차체 사이 공간
을 고체 실리콘으로 채워 고무로 감싼 에너지 흡수형으로,
이 범퍼를 탑재한 캐나다 수출용 모델은 국내에서 포니2
CX(Canadian Export)로 시판되어 큰 인기를 누렸다.

The Pony2's successful foray into Canada

As Hyundai prepared to enter the U.S. market
through its "X Car" project, the company turned
to the Canadian market as the gateway to the
United States. In late 1981, Hyundai sent a market research team to Canada to analyze local
regulations, including Canada Motor Vehicle
Safety Standard (CMVSS), as well as the overall
automotive market. The analysis concluded that
with a few modifications, the Pony 2 could be
exported to Canada. As a result, Hyundai made
several changes to the existing model to create an
export version suitable for the Canadian market.
These changes included adding a defroster and
high-capacity heater essential for the cold and
humid climate, a 5-speed transmission to match
the driving habits of local drivers who often travel
long distances at high speeds, and a five-mph
bumper* to comply with local regulations. The
five-mph bumper developed for this purpose was
an Energy Absorbing Bumper, with a solid silicone
polymer wrapped in rubber used to fill the space
between the bumper and the chassis. The Pony2
with five-mph bumper, which was sold as the
Pony2 CX (Canadian Export) in Korea, also gained
significant popularity in the domestic market.

*
시속 5마일(8km/h)로 고정 벽에 충돌했을 때 범퍼가 충격을
흡수해 차량의 손상이 없어야 한다는 규정
The regulation states that a bumper must absorb
the impact when colliding with a fixed wall at 5
miles per hour (8 km/h), preventing any damage to
the vehicle.

1983년 2월에 설립된 캐나다 현지 법인 HACI
Hyundai Auto Canada Inc (HACI)
established in February 1983

당시 캐나다 정부의 보호무역 기조에 따른 수입 규제에 효과적으로 대응하기 위해 1983년 2월 현지법인 HACI(Hyundai Auto Canada Inc.)를 설립한 현대자동차는 법인 설립 전후로 몬트리올, 토론토, 밴쿠버, 퀘벡 등 캐나다 각지에서 열리는 현지 모터쇼에 참가해 포니를 알리는 데 매진했다. 덕분에 초창기 현대자동차의 딜러 모집에는 신청서가 1,500장이나 접수되는 등 30 대 1에 달하는 높은 경쟁률을 보였다. 현대자동차는 신생 브랜드로서 현지에 안착하기 위해 정비공 출신으로 자기 정비소를 가지고 있거나 현대 자동차만 판매하는 싱글 딜러를 자사 딜러로 선정했다.

이후에도 현대자동차는 '현대'와 '포니'의 인지도를 높이는 일에 많은 노력을 기울였다. 당시 캐나다에서 한국이라는 나라는 매우 생소했기 때문에 "현대 포니는 중동 사하라 사막을 거쳐 런던 피카딜리 광장을 지난 뒤, 중남미 안데스산맥을 넘어 지금 막 캐나다에 도착한 승용차다"라는 광고 문구를 내걸어 현대자동차가 전 세계 50여 개국에 자동차를 수출하는 글로벌 기업임을 강조했고, "First winter on sale,

Having established Hyundai Auto Canada Inc. (HACI) in February 1983 to respond to Canada's import regulations, Hyundai promoted the Pony in motor shows held across Canada, such as Montreal, Toronto, Vancouver, and Québec City. Thanks to these proactive efforts, the initial recruitment of Hyundai dealers saw an overwhelming response, with 1,500 applications, reflecting a high competition ratio of 30 to 1. In addition, to establish a strong foothold as a new brand in the local market, Hyundai selected dealers who were either former mechanics with their own repair shops or single dealers exclusively selling Hyundai vehicles.

Hyundai continued to put significant effort into raising the awareness of the names "Hyundai" and "Pony." Since Canadians were unfamiliar with Korea at the time, Hyundai emphasized that it was a global manufacturer that exports cars to more than 50 countries around world. The advertisement stated, "The Hyundai Pony has just arrived in Canada after traveling through the Sahara Desert in the Middle East, Piccadilly Circus in London, and the Andes Mountains in Latin America." Additionally, the slogan "First winter on sale, second winter in Canada" highlighted that the Pony had undergone rigorous testing in local harsh winter regions a year before its release. This left a strong impression on the locals. When sales began in January 1984, the Pony2 became a commercial success, selling 25,123 units alone — more than five times its first-year goal of 5,000 units. In 1985, the following year, 79,072 units of the Pony2 and the Stellar were sold in Canada, making Hyundai the number one import brand, sur-

포니2 캐나다 현지 인쇄 광고
The Canadian print advertisements
for the Pony2

second winter in Canada"라는 문구로 포니가 출시 1년 전부터 현지 혹한 지역에서 엄격한 테스트를 거쳤다는 점을 부각해 현지인에게 강한 인상을 남겼다. 1984년 1월 현지 판매가 시작되자마자 포니2는 날개 돋친 듯 팔려나갔고, 그해에만 수출 첫해 목표 물량이었던 5,000대의 5배가 넘는 2만 5,123대를 판매했다. 이듬해인 1985년에는 스텔라까지 포함해 약 7만9,072대를 판매해 일본 기업을 제치고 수입차 판매 1위를 기록했다.

이처럼 포니는 철저한 현지 진입 전략과 높은 상품성, 그리고 현대자동차에 호의적으로 변모한 시장 환경에 힘입어 캐나다에서 '포니 신화'를 써 내려갔다. 특히 높은 가성비는 포니의 가장 큰 인기 요인이었다. 당시 개발도상국이었던 한국은 관세에서 일본 차와 비교해 유리한 고지에 있었고, 상대적으로 인건비가 저렴해 생산 원가가 낮았기에 고급 옵션을 기본화해 판매해도 충분한 이윤을 확보할 수 있었다. 경쟁차 대비 월등한 포니의 가성비는 경제 불황을 겪고 난 현지인들에게 매력적인 소구점이 되었다. 또한 사후 관리와 정비가 편리하다는 것도 장점으로 작용했다. 딜러 대부분이 정비소를 운영한 경험이 있어 경쟁 차 대비 꼼꼼한 출고 전 검사와 사후 관리 서비스 제공이 가능했고, 자가 정비를 하던 많은 현지인에게 포니의 후륜구동 방식이 최신 트렌드인 전륜구동 방식보다 되레 친숙해 정비가 쉽다는 이유로 선호되었다. 게다가 당시 대외 환경 또한 현대자동차에 유리한 방향으로 조성되었다. 캐나다 정부의 수출 쿼터 제한으로 양보다 질을 중시하게 된 일본 기업들이 중형차 생산·판매에 주력함으로써

passing Japanese manufacturers.

The Pony achieved legendary status in Canada through thorough market entry strategies, high product quality, and favorable market dynamics. Its greatest appeal was its high cost-effectiveness. At that time, South Korea was still a developing country, thus had tariff advantages over Japanese cars. Additionally, lower labor costs resulted in lower production costs, allowing Hyundai to offer premium options as standard features while still securing sufficient profit. The Pony's superior cost-effectiveness compared to competitor vehicles attracted local consumers, especially during economic downturns. Another advantage was the ease of maintenance and repair. Most dealers had experience running repair shops, enabling them to provide meticulous pre-delivery inspections and after-sales services. Many locals found the Pony's rear-wheel-drive (RWD), considered outdated compared to the trends of the time, more familiar and easier to maintain than FWD vehicles. Moreover, external factors also favored Hyundai. The Canadian government's export quota restrictions led Japanese companies to focus on producing and selling mid-sized cars, creating a gap in the subcompact car market. As the Canadian economy began to recover from a recession, consumers who had postponed car purchases started buying new vehicles. This shift further boosted the success

소형차 시장에 공백이 생긴 데다, 그동안 경제 불황으로 차량 구매를 자제해 온 캐나다인들이 경제가 회복기에 접어들면서 신차 구매를 확대했기 때문이다.

그러나 순항이 지속될 것으로만 보이던 캐나다 시장에서 현대자동차는 예상치 못한 돌발 상황을 맞닥뜨리게 되었다. 현대자동차가 캐나다 시장에서 예상치 못한 대성공을 거두자 이를 경계한 경쟁사에서 반덤핑 혐의로 캐나다 정부에 제소를 한 것이다. 캐나다 정부의 덤핑 예비 판정을 받는 위기에 직면하기도 했지만, 현대자동차는 캐나다 관세청의 요구에 적극 협력하고 원칙에 따라 의연하게 대처하면서 이 소송을 승소로 이끌었다.

캐나다에서 포니2의 판매 흥행은 미국 진출의 탄탄한 발판이 되었다. 캐나다 진출 2년 만에 세계 유수의 기업을 제치고 당당히 수입차 판매 1위 자리에 오른 현대자동차의 스토리가 미국 딜러에게도 전해져 신생 브랜드인 현대자동차에 대한 관심을 불러모았기 때문이다. 또한 포니2의 캐나다 수출을 계기로 수출 물량이 대폭 증가하면서 1985년부터 현대자동차의 승용차 수출 물량이 내수 판매 물량을 앞지르게 되었고, 이로써 현대자동차는 본격적인 수출 주도형 기업으로 거듭날 수 있었다.

of the Pony.

However, just when it seemed like Hyundai was smoothly sailing in the Canadian market, the company encountered an unexpected challenge. Hyundai's unexpected success in Canada prompted competitors to accuse it of dumping, leading to a lawsuit with the Canadian government. Facing the risk of a preliminary dumping determination, Hyundai actively cooperated with the demands of the Canadian customs authorities. By handling the situation calmly and adhering to principles, Hyundai successfully won the lawsuit.

The success of the Pony2 in Canada laid a solid foundation for Hyundai's entry into the U.S. market. Within just two years of entering Canada, Hyundai overtook major global companies to become the top-selling import car brand. This story reached U.S. dealers, sparking interest in the Hyundai brand. Additionally, the surge in exports following the success of the Pony2 in Canada led to a significant increase in Hyundai's export volume. By 1985, Hyundai's passenger car exports surpassed domestic sales. This marked Hyundai's transformation into a truly export-driven company.

자동차의 본고장, 미국 상륙

30만 대 공장 건설과 미국 수출 전략 모델 개발 프로젝트, 이른바 'X카 프로젝트'는 현대자동차가 사활을 걸고 추진한 프로젝트였다. 국내 최초의 전륜구동 차였던 X카는 포니와 마찬가지로 이탈디자인이 디자인하고, 미쓰비시의 엔진과 섀시를 도입해 개발했다. 또한 미국 진출을 목표로 개발된 만큼 선진국의 안전 법규를 만족시키는 높은 안전성과 전륜구동차 특유의 높은 경제성, 넉넉한 실내 공간이 특징이었다.

미국 수출은 다년간 수출을 통해 축적한 경험과 노하우를 활용해 기존과 차원이 다른 규모로 오랜 기간 심혈을 기울여 준비했다. 1984년 1월부터는 시작차를 제작해 갓 완공된 울산의 종합 주행 시험장과 시험 시설에서 내구성, 배기가스, 충돌 등 각종 시험을 실시했다. 또한 양산에 앞서 파일럿 카를 제작해 국내뿐 아니라 북미 현지에 보내 테스트를 진행했다.

그리고 1985년 2월, 현대자동차는 공장 건설에 착수한 지 3년 5개월 만에 최신 설비를 갖춘 연간 30만 대 규모의 생산 공장을 완공했다. 이로써 현대자동차는 기존 15만 대 생산 능력에 30만 대를 더해 연간 총 45만 대의 생산 능력을 갖추게 되었고, 글로벌 시장에서 선진 기업들과 당당하게 겨룰 수 있는 글로벌 규모의 대량생산 능력을 확보했다. 공장 완공과 함께 본격적인 X카 양산에 돌입한 현대자동차는 미국 시장을 겨냥한 세 번째 고유 승용 모델 '포니 엑셀'*을 공개하고 국내 판매를 개시했다.

현대자동차의 미국 진출 준비는 1984년 1월 캐나다에 나가 있는 파견자를 통해 미국 현지 시장 조사에 착수하면서 본격화되었다. 당시 미국 시장은 제1·2차 오일쇼크로 인한 오랜 경기 침체에서 서서히 회복되는 단계였고, 그 여파로 유지비는 적게 들면서 연비 효율이 좋은 소형차 중심으로 자동차 시장이 재편되는 추세였다. 미국에서 일본 차의 수입 물량은

Making landfall in the United States, the birthplace of automobiles

The project to build a 300,000-unit plant and develop a U.S. export strategy model, known as the "X-Car" project, was a critical initiative for Hyundai. The "X-Car", the first FWD car in Korea, was designed by Italdesign and developed using Mitsubishi engines and chassis, similar to the Pony. However, since it was developed with the U.S. market in mind, the "X Car" boasted excellent safety in line with stringent safety regulations, excellent fuel economy from the FWD system, and a spacious interior.

The U.S. export strategy was meticulously prepared over a long period, utilizing years of accumulated experience and know-how. Starting in January 1984, Hyundai produced prototype cars and conducted various tests, including durability, emissions, and crash tests, at the newly completed proving ground and testing facilities in Ulsan. Before mass production, pilot cars were made and sent to Korea and the United States for field testing.

In February 1985, just three years and five months after breaking ground, Hyundai completed a state-of-the-art manufacturing plant with an annual capacity of 300,000 units. This achievement increased Hyundai's production capacity to a total of 450,000 units per year, enabling the company to compete confidently with leading global firms in mass production capabilities. With the completion of the plant, Hyundai began mass production of the "X-Car" and launched the Pony Excel*, its third unique passenger model aimed at the U.S. market, and began to sell it domestically.

30만 대 공장 준공식(1985년 2월)
The completion ceremony of a 300,000-unit plant (February 1985)

*
포니 5도어 모델의 국내 차명은 '포니 엑셀', 미국 현지 차명은 '엑셀', 포니 4도어 모델의 국내 차명은 '프레스토', 미국 현지 차명은 '엑셀 4도어'였다.
The 5-door model was called 'Pony Excel' in Korea and 'Excel' in the U.S., and the 4-door model was called 'Presto' in Korea and 'Excel 4-door' in the U.S.

현대자동차 최초의 전륜구동 모델인 포니 엑셀 신차 발표회
The launching show of the Pony Excel,
Hyundai's first front-wheel drive model

1981년부터 자율 규제에 묶여 있었기에, 당시 일본 기업은 부가가치가 높은 중형차 중심의 판매 전략을 펼치고 있었다. 이 같은 시장조사 결과를 기반으로 현대자동차는 미국 시장에서 충분히 승산이 있다고 판단했다. 현대자동차는 캐나다와 같은 방식으로 미국에서도 독자적인 현지법인을 운영하되 딜러가 현대자동차 단일 브랜드만 전담 판매하는 방식(single point dealership)을 채택하고, 경쟁 차의 70~80% 수준으로 가격을 책정해 경쟁력을 높이는 한편, 안정적 부품 공급을 위해 A/S망을 조기 구축한다는 현지 진출 전략을 수립했다.

이에 따라 현대자동차는 1985년 4월 미국 LA 근교에 현지법인 HMA(Hyundai Motor America)를 설립했다. 이어 자동차업계 경험이 풍부한 현지인을 채용하고, 딜러 모집을 위해 주요 자동차 잡지와 현지 딜러 협회인 NADA(National

Hyundai's preparations to enter the U.S. began in earnest in January 1984, with the start of local market research conducted through an emissary in Canada. At that time, the U.S. market was gradually recovering from a long economic downturn caused by the first and second oil shocks, with a shift towards small cars that were cost-effective and fuel-efficient. In addition, because imports had been capped under the Voluntary Restraint Agreement (VRA) since 1981, Japanese manufacturers were focusing on midsize cars for higher value-added in their sales strategies. Based on these market research findings, Hyundai concluded that it had a competitive chance in the U.S. market. Hyundai's strategy for the U.S. market was similar to its strategy for the Canadian market, which included operating its local subsidiary but with dealers specializing exclusively in Hyundai cars(single point dealership), pricing the models at about 70 to 80 percent of competitors' prices to increase price competitiveness, and establishing an early customer service network to guarantee a stable supply of components.

With these goals, Hyundai founded Hyundai Motor America (HMA) in Garden Grove, CA, in April 1985. They hired experienced local professionals and actively promoted dealer recruitment through major auto magazines and the National Automobile Dealer Association (NADA). Thanks to their success in Canada, U.S. dealers showed great interest in Hyundai. Despite stringent selection criteria, including the exclusive sale of Hyundai vehicles, a minimum capital of $1 million, and an independent building of at least 2 acres of total area, there

초기 미국법인 HMA 전경
HMA Headquarters in its early days

현대자동차 미국법인은 1985년 4월에 설립되었다.
Hyundai Motor America (HMA) was founded in
April 1985.

Automobile Dealer Association)를 통해 적극적으로 홍보
했다. 특히 캐나다에서의 판매 흥행으로 미국 딜러들은 현대자
동차에 높은 관심을 보였다. 그 결과 현대자동차만 취급해야 하
는 데다 자본금 100만 달러 이상에 건평 8,264m²(2,500평)
이상의 독립 건물을 확보해야한다는 까다로운 딜러 선발 조건을
덧붙였는데도 1986년 10 대 1, 1987년 26 대 1의 높은 경쟁률을
기록할 만큼 신청서가 대거 접수됨으로써 신생 자동차 회사임에
도 불구하고 경험이 풍부한 우수한 딜러를 선정할 수 있었다.

한편 현대자동차는 현지 판매 체계를 구축하면서 동시
에 미국 진출을 위한 필수 관문인 공해 규정과 안전 규정 통과
를 위한 테스트도 준비했다. 1985년 1월 디트로이트에 사무
소를 설립하고 공해 규정과 안전 규정 테스트를 진행했는데,
다행히 안전 테스트는 이미 울산 공장에서 주행 시험과 충돌
시험을 수차례 거쳐 무난히 합격했다. 그러나 공해 규정 테스
트는 통과하는 데 1년이 소요될 만큼 까다로웠다. 이는 미국
환경보호청(EPA, Environmental Protection Agency)이
관장하는 이산화탄소를 규제하는 연방 규정과 캘리포니아
대기환경청(CARB, California Air Resource Board)에서
관장하는 질소산화물을 규제하는 캘리포니아 규정을 모두
통과해야 했기 때문이다. 현대자동차는 미국 현지 환경보호
청에 19대, 교통연구센터에 12대 등 총 31대의 포니 엑셀을 시

was a high number of applications. In 1986,
the competition ratio was 10 to 1, and in 1987, it
soared to 26 to 1. This allowed Hyundai to select
experienced and excellent dealers, even as a new
entrant in the market.

Meanwhile, Hyundai prepared for essential
tests to comply with U.S. emission and safety
regulations while establishing its local sales network. In January 1985, they set up an office in
Detroit to conduct these tests. The safety tests
were straightforward, as they had already been
conducted multiple times at the Ulsan plant and
passed smoothly. However, passing the emission tests took a year due to their strict nature.
Hyundai had to meet both the federal regulations on carbon dioxide overseen by the Environmental Protection Agency (EPA) and the California regulations on nitrogen oxides managed
by the California Air Resources Board (CARB).
Hyundai sent a total of 31 Pony Excel cars for
testing: 19 to the EPA and 12 to the Transportation Research Center. The company then sent
10 more cars to conduct independent environmental tests in five states. These tests included
rigorous conditions in various U.S. regions, such
as the hot Arizona desert, the rugged Rocky

UNITED STATES ENVIRONMENTAL PROTECTION AGENCY

ANN ARBOR, MICHIGAN 48105

OFFICE OF
MOBILE SOURCES

1986 MODEL YEAR
CERTIFICATE OF CONFORMITY
WITH THE CLEAN AIR ACT OF 1970 ISSUED TO:

Robert E. Maxwell

HYUNDAI	HYNDA-LDV -01	JAN 7, 1986	
MANUFACTURER	CERTIFICATE NO.	DATE	OFFICE OF MOBILE SOURCES

Pursuant to section 206 of the Clean Air Act (42 U.S.C.7525) and 40 CFR Part 86, this certificate of conformity is hereby issued with respect to test vehicles which have been found to conform to the requirements of the regulations on Control of Air Pollution from New Motor Vehicles and New Motor Vehicle Engines (40 CFR Part 86) and which represent the following models of new motor vehicles, by engine family and evaporative emission family, more fully described in the application of the above named manufacturer:

HYUNDAI MOTOR COMPANY : PONY EXCEL .

Vehicles covered by this certificate have demonstrated compliance with the applicable emission standards at high and low altitudes as more fully described in the manufacturer's application.

This certificate covers engine family GHY1.5V2HFB0 /evaporative emission family GHY1.5FF , including 1.5-liter engines with pulse air injection , oxidation catalyst , three-way catalyst with oxygen sensor and feedback control of fuel/air ratio , exhaust gas recirculation , charcoal canister , and closed crankcase emission control systems, designed to meet emission standards specified in 40 CFR 86.085-8 at both high and low altitude as specified in the application. These vehicles are equipped with an emission control device which the Administrator has determined will be significantly impaired by the use of leaded gasoline. The certificate is issued subject to the conditions specified in 40 CFR 80.24.

This certificate of conformity covers only those new motor vehicles or new motor vehicle engines which conform, in all material respects, to the design specifications that applied to those vehicles or engines described in the documentation required by 40 CFR Part 86 and which are produced during the model year production period stated on this certificate of the said manufacturer, as defined in 40 CFR Part 86.

It is a term of this certificate that the manufacturer shall consent to all inspections described in 40 CFR 86.078-7(c), 86.606 and 86.1006-84 and authorized in a warrant or court order. Failure to comply with the requirements of such a warrant or court order may lead to a revocation or suspension of this certificate as specified in 40 CFR 86.085-30(c), (d) or (e). It is also a term of this certificate that this certificate may be revoked or suspended for the other reasons stated in 40 CFR 86.085-30(c), (d) or (e).

Catalyst-equipped vehicles, otherwise covered by this certificate, which are driven outside the United States, Canada, and Mexico will be presumed to have been operated on leaded gasoline resulting in deactivation of the catalysts. If these vehicles are imported or offered for importation without retrofit of the catalyst, they will be considered not to be within the coverage of this certificate unless included in a catalyst control program operated by a manufacturer or a United States Government Agency and approved by the Administrator.

미국 환경보호청(EPA)이 발행한 포니 엑셀 배기가스 테스트 합격 인증서(1986년 1월)
The certificate of conformity with the Clean Air Act for the Pony Excel, issued by the Environmental Protection Agency (EPA; January 1986)

미국 환경보호청의 배기가스 테스트 합격을 계기로 본격적인 미국 수출길이 열렸다.
Passing the EPA's emissions test was the starting point for Hyundai's entry into the U.S. market.

험용으로 보내 테스트를 진행했다. 이후에 10대를 별도로 보내 5개 주에서 자체적인 환경 테스트를 완료했고, 이에 무더운 애리조나사막, 로키산맥의 험준한 고갯길, 플로리다주의 고속도로 등 미주의 다양한 지역에서도 엄격한 현지 테스트가 이어졌다.

우여곡절 끝에 현대자동차는 1985년 12월 긴 테스트를 마무리하고, 마침내 EPA로부터 합격 통보를 받았다. 이어 1986년 1월 미국 환경보호청으로부터 배기가스 테스트 합격 인증서를 수령함으로써 본격적인 미국 수출길을 열게 되었다. 1986년 1월 울산 부두를 출발해 한 달 가까이 태평양을 건너온 포니 엑셀과 프레스토는 2월 플로리다주 잭슨빌항과 LA 롱비치항에 도착했다. 차가 도착하기 전 견본 하나 없는 상황에서도 500~3,000달러의 계약금을 낸 이들이 상당수였을 만큼 포니 엑셀에 대한 교민들의 관심은 열광적이었다. 자동차 산업의 종주국인 미국 시장에 국산차가 상륙했다는 사실만으로도 감격스러웠던 것이다. 당시 교민들은 미국인들에게 이구동성으로 "5,000년 역사를 지닌 한국인들이 그

Mountain passes, and the highways of Florida.

After various difficulties, Hyundai finally finished a long period of testing in December 1985 and received a passing notification from the EPA. Subsequently, in January 1986, they received certification for passing the emissions test from the EPA, opening the way for full-scale exports to the United States. The same month, a shipment of Pony Excels and Prestos departed from the Port of Ulsan. After a month-long voyage across the Pacific Ocean, the shipment of Pony Excels and Prestos arrived at the ports of Jacksonville, FL and Long Beach, CA, in February. The Korean-American community was waiting anxiously for the arrival of the Pony Excel, with many putting down $500-$3,000 to sign purchase agreements, even without having seen the car before. After all, how amazing is it to see a Korean car making landfall in the United States, the origin of the automotive industry? Members of the Korean-American community boasted to their ac-

옛날 신라 금관과 세계 최초 금속활자를 만들던 솜씨를 발휘해 차를 만들었다"라고 자랑했다.

포니 엑셀은 미국 수출 원년인 1986년에 목표한 10만 대 판매를 훨씬 상회하는 16만8,882대를 판매하며 화려한 신고식을 치렀다. 이 같은 성공적인 미국 진출은 포니 엑셀 자체의 우수한 상품성과 경쟁 차 대비 우수한 가격 경쟁력, 그리고 양질의 딜러 선정 등 치밀한 판매 전략이 조화를 이룬 결과였다. 캐나다 진출 상황과 마찬가지로 당사에 우호적이었던 대외 환경도 판매 호조에 긍정적으로 작용했다. 미국 언론은 포니 엑셀의 성공적인 현지 상륙에 대해 이렇게 평가했다. 매년 '미국의 올해 10대 상품'을 선정하는 〈포춘(Fortune)〉은 포니 엑셀을 "역사상 가장 빠른 매출 신장률을 보인 수입품"이라고 격찬했고, 자동차 전문지 〈오토모티브 뉴스(Automotive News)〉는 1986년 세계 자동차 산업에서 괄목할 만한 사건 중 하나로 '엑셀의 성공'을 지목했다.

전 세계에서 가장 큰 자동차 시장인 미국에서의 성공은 한국이 자동차 수출국으로서 대외적 공인을 받았다는 증거이자 한국의 기술력과 공업화 수준을 전 세계에 알리는 계기가 되었다. 또한 북미 수출을 기점으로 국내 자동차 생산량과 수출 물량이 대폭 늘어나면서 대한민국의 수출 산업은 섬유를 중심으로 한 경공업에서 기계공업 중심의 중화학공업으로 전환되었다. 현대자동차의 미국 진출은 글로벌 메이커로서 현대자동차의 브랜드 위상을 크게 제고한 것은 물론이고, 미국 내에서 자동차 외에도 가전제품 등 한국산 제품의 신뢰도를 높이는 데에도 중요한 역할을 했다.

현대자동차의 첫 번째 고유 모델인 포니가 출시된 시점부터 미국 수출 전략 모델인 포니 엑셀이 미국 시장에 안착하기까지 걸린 기간은 단 10년에 불과했다. 현대자동차에 이 과정은 수출이라는 새로운 길, 곧 험로를 개척하는 여정이었다.

quaintances, "We Koreans have a five-thousand-year history, and we came up with this car with the same expertise we used to create Silla's gold crown and the first metal printing blocks in the world."

In its first year of U.S. exports in 1986, the Pony Excel sold 168,882 units, far exceeding the target of 100,000. This impressive debut was due to the car's excellent quality, competitive pricing, and well-planned sales strategies, including the selection of high-quality dealers. Favorable external conditions, similar to those in Canada, also positively impacted sales. The Pony Excel's success was picked up by the U.S. media as well. *Fortune* which lists America's Top 10 Products of the Year, praised the Pony Excel as "the import with the fastest sales growth in history," and the *Automotive News* cited "the success of the Excel" as one of the most remarkable events in the global auto industry in 1986.

Hyundai's success in the U.S., the largest automotive market in the world, was proof that Korea had gained international recognition as an automobile exporter. It also showcased Korea's technological prowess and industrialization level to the world. Starting with exports to North America, domestic car production and exports significantly increased, shifting Korea's export industry from light industries like textiles to heavy and chemical industries focused on machinery. Hyundai's entry into the U.S. not only greatly enhanced its brand status as a global manufacturer but also played a crucial role in boosting the credibility of Korean products, including electronics, in the American market.

It merely took 10 years from the launch of

포니 엑셀의 미국 상륙을 보도한 국내 신문 기사들
Korean newspapers reporting on the Pony Excel's debut in the U.S. market

그 과정에서 현대자동차는 수출 관련 프로세스와 해외 영업 조직을 정비해 나가는 한편, 이미 닦은 수출길에 안주하지 않고 새로운 지역으로의 확장을 지속적으로 시도했다.

다양한 시행착오를 교훈 삼아 집요하게 스스로를 개선해 나가고, 장기적 시각에서 독창적 방식으로 위기를 극복해 나감으로써 현대자동차는 오늘날 한국을 대표하는 글로벌 기업으로 자리매김했다. 당시 개발도상국이었던 한국의 경제 여건을 고려할 때, 존재하지 않는 길을 새롭게 개척한 현대자동차의 도전은 대한민국 산업사와 수출사를 넘어 전 세계 자동차 산업사에서도 인상적인 사건이었다. 그리고 그 정신은 지금까지 이어져 미래 모빌리티로 향하는 현대자동차의 새로운 여정에 끊임없는 원동력이 되고 있다.

Hyundai's first original model Pony, to the successful establishment of the Pony Excel as an export strategy model in the U.S. market. For Hyundai, this period was an expedition into the uncharted territory of exports. During this journey, Hyundai refined its export-related processes and overseas sales organization. Moreover, the company continuously sought to expand into new regions, never resting on its existing achievements.

With unwavering determination and a creative approach when overcoming challenges, Hyundai established itself as a global leader representing Korea and has set an impressive example for the entire automotive industry worldwide. In an era when Korea was still considered a developing country, Hyundai blazed a trail where none existed before, surpassing expectations in the domestic market and conquering the global. The spirit of innovation and resilience that guided the company during its early years continues to propel Hyundai forward, inspiring its ongoing journey toward the future of mobility. As Hyundai sets its sights on new horizons and exciting opportunities, it remains an unstoppable force, leading the way for future generations.

염원하던 미국 수출을 위해 울산항 부두에서 선적 중인
포니 엑셀(1986년 1월)
The Pony Excel being loaded for export to the
United States in Ulsan, finally realizing the
company's dream (January 1986)

미국 플로리다주 잭슨빌항에 하역하는 포니 엑셀
(1986년 2월)
The Pony Excel being unloaded in the Port of
Jacksonville, FL (February 1986)

한 달 가까이 태평양을 가로질러 마침내 미국에 상륙했다.
The Pony Excel finally made its way to the
United States after a month-long voyage
across the Pacific.

서울 여의도 국회의사당 앞에 도열한 다양한 색상의 포니 라인업
Ponies with different colors lined up in front of the National
Assembly Building in Yeouido, Seoul

길에서 만난 각양각색 포니

The many Ponies on the road

대중의 다변화된 라이프스타일을 반영하다

포니가 출시된 1970년대 중반 이후부터 한국 경제가 초고
속 성장을 거듭하면서 대중 차 시장도 빠르게 성장했다. 또
한 자동차에 대한 대중의 요구와 취향이 다양해지면서 라인
업 확장의 필요성이 대두했는데, 현대자동차는 이러한 시대
변화에 맞춰 포니의 여러 파생 모델과 후속 차를 출시함으로
써 변화하는 트렌드와 대중의 다변화된 라이프스타일에 부
응해 나갔다.

**Adapting to the increasingly diverse lifestyles
of modern consumers**

From the mid-1970s when the Pony was first
launched, South Korea began to see a rapid
growth in the mass automobile market driven
by the country's fast-growing economy. During
this period, consumer needs and preferences
for cars became increasingly diverse, and there
was a growing demand to expand the car lineup. Keeping up with the changing consumer
tastes, Hyundai responded to these demands
by releasing various derivatives of the Pony and
subsequent models, tailoring to the evolving
trends and diverse lifestyles of the public.

포니   PONY

포니는 대한민국 최초의 대량 양산형 고유 모델이자 해외로 수출한 첫 번째 국산 승용차다. 미쓰비시 랜서 플랫폼에 조르제토 주지아로의 디자인을 입은 4도어 롱노즈 패스트백 모델로 국내에서 개발, 테스트, 생산 과정을 거친 만큼 비포장도로가 많았던 당시 국내 도로 환경과 한국인 체격에 적합했다. 또한 포니는 우수한 상품성과 경제성으로 출시 후 국내 승용차 시장을 석권하면서 대한민국의 대표 국민차로 자리매김했고, 동시에 여러 국가에 수출되면서 자동차를 대한민국의 대표 수출 산업으로 성장시키는 데 크게 기여했다.

The Pony represents a significant milestone in being Korea's first original model that was mass-produced and exported. It was a four-door fastback that was designed by Giorgetto Giugiaro based on the Mitsubishi Lancer's platform. It was developed, tested, and produced domestically, making it well-suited to the average physique of Koreans, as well as Korean roads — many of which were unpaved at the time. Upon its release, the Pony dominated the domestic passenger car market with its excellent performance, design, and affordability. It became a symbol of national pride and significantly contributed to establishing the automotive industry as a leading export sector for South Korea by being exported to several countries.

양산 개시 Start of production	1975년 12월 December 1975	
길이 Length (mm)	3,970	
너비 Width (mm)	1,558	
높이 Height (mm)	1,360	
휠베이스 Wheelbase (mm)	2,340	
구동 방식 Drive layout	후륜구동(FR) Front-engine, Rear-wheel drive (FR)	
엔진 Engine type	수냉식 직렬 4기통 가솔린 Water-cooled inline-four gasoline engine	
배기량 Displacement (cc)	1,238	1,439
최고 출력 Max. power (ps/rpm)	80/6,300	92/6,300
최대 토크 Max. torque (kg-m/rpm)	10.8/4,000	12.5/4,000
변속기 Transmission	4단 수동 4-speed manual	4단 수동 4-speed manual 3단 자동 3-speed automatic
공차 중량 Curb weight (kg)	870	900

포니 픽업

PONY Pickup

포니의 첫 파생 차인 포니 픽업은 포니 기본 차 개발 과정에서 내재화한 노하우를 기반으로 국내 기술진이 주도해 개발했다. 기본 차의 제반 장점을 그대로 계승한 포니 픽업은 승용차의 안락함과 화물차의 실용성을 겸비한 다용도 차로 국내외 시장에서 많은 사랑을 받았다. 특히 당시 국내에서 생산되던 픽업트럭 중 최소 회전 반경이 가장 작아 좁은 골목길에서도 자유로운 회전이 가능했고, 험로 주행에도 용이했다. 게다가 화물차로 분류돼 세금이 저렴했기 때문에 소형 화물 운반에 특화된 용달차나 자영업자를 위한 차량으로 큰 인기를 누렸다.

The Pony's first derivative model, the Pony Pickup was developed by Hyundai's engineers leveraging the expertise they had built during the development of the Pony 4-door base model. Inheriting most of the strengths of the base model, the Pony Pickup was widely loved both domestically and internationally for offering the comfort of a sedan and the practicality of a cargo vehicle. The Pony Pickup was particularly well-received in the market for its exceptionally low minimum turning radius, a feature that set it apart from other pickups in Korea at the time. This feature allowed for easy turning in small alleys and smooth off-road driving, making the Pony Pickup a popular choice. In addition, the tax rate was low on this model as it was classified as a cargo vehicle. Thus, it was beloved by drivers as a delivery truck for small goods and a reliable vehicle for small business owners.

양산 개시 Start of production	1976년 5월 May 1976	
길이 Length (mm)	3,958	
너비 Width (mm)	1,558	
높이 Height (mm)	1,368	
휠베이스 Wheelbase (mm)	2,340	
구동 방식 Drive layout	후륜구동(FR) Front-engine, Rear-wheel drive (FR)	
엔진 Engine type	수냉식 직렬 4기통 가솔린 Water-cooled inline-four gasoline engine	
배기량 Displacement (cc)	1,238	1,439
최고 출력 Max. power (ps/rpm)	80/6,300	92/6,300
최대 토크 Max. torque (kg-m/rpm)	10.8/4,000	12.5/4,000
변속기 Transmission	4단 수동 4-speed manual	
공차 중량 Curb weight(kg)	855	

포니 왜건

PONY Wagon

포니 왜건은 포니 기본 차를 기반으로 실내 공간을 확장해 화물 적재도 가능한 승용차로 출시되었다. 포니 픽업과 마찬가지로 국내 기술진이 주도해 개발했다. 왜건이라는 차형은 당시 국내 소비자에게 낯설었을 뿐 아니라 짐차 이미지가 있어 높은 판매고를 올리지는 못했다. 그러나 여행과 레저에 대한 관심이 증가하면서 넉넉한 트렁크 공간을 원하는 고객층의 사랑을 받았고, 수출 시장 확대에도 기여했다.

The Pony Wagon was developed based on the original Pony, with an expanded interior space to accommodate extra luggage. Similar to the pickup model, Hyundai's engineers played a key role in developing the derivative model. As the wagon type was unfamiliar to Korean consumers at the time and had a "freight vehicle" image, it did not achieve high sales initially. However as the interest in travel and outdoor activities grew, it became popular among consumers seeking a spacious trunk and eventually helped in driving up exports.

양산 개시 Start of production	1977년 4월 April 1977	
길이 Length (mm)	3,980	
너비 Width (mm)	1,560	
높이 Height (mm)	1,360	
휠베이스 Wheelbase (mm)	2,340	
구동 방식 Drive layout	후륜구동(FR) Front-engine, Rear-wheel drive (FR)	
엔진 Engine type	수냉식 직렬 4기통 가솔린 Water-cooled inline-four gasoline engine	
배기량 Displacement (cc)	1,238	1,439
최고 출력 Max. power (ps/rpm)	80/6,300	92/6,300
최대 토크 Max. torque (kg-m/rpm)	10.8/4,000	12.5/4,000
변속기 Transmission	4단 수동 4-speed manual	
공차 중량 Curb weight (kg)	940	

포니 3도어

PONY 3-Door

대중 차 보급이 확산되면서 자기 차를 직접 운전하는 오너 드라이버가 빠르게 늘어났다. 이런 추세를 따라 오너 드라이버를 위해 자동변속기를 장착한 '포니 오토매틱'을 1980년 1월 출시했고, 이어 4월에는 국내 최초 3도어 승용차 '포니 3도어'를 출시했다. 기본 차 대비 스포티한 디자인이 특징인 포니 3도어는 5인까지 승차가 가능했으며, 2인 승차 시에는 뒷좌석 등받이를 접어 뒷좌석에 더 많은 짐을 실을 수 있었다. 그 때문에 넓은 적재 공간이 필요한 오너 드라이버에게 인기를 끌었다.

As the distribution of mass-market cars expanded, the number of owner-drivers who drove their own vehicles rapidly increased. Economic growth increased the average wage of would-be drivers, and more people were able to own cars. To keep pace with this new trend, Hyundai released the Pony Automatic with an automatic transmission in January 1980. This was followed by the launch of the Pony 3-Door, Korea's first three-door passenger car, in April the same year. Sportier in design compared to the base model, the three-door hatchback could accommodate up to five people. When only two people were in the car, the backseats could be folded up to make more room for luggage. This feature made the interior more versatile, and thus made it popular among car owners who needed ample cargo space.

양산 개시 Start of production	1980년 3월 March 1980	
길이 Length (mm)	3,970	
너비 Width (mm)	1,560	
높이 Height (mm)	1,360	
휠베이스 Wheelbase (mm)	2,340	
구동 방식 Drive layout	후륜구동(FR) Front-engine, Rear-wheel drive (FR)	
엔진 Engine type	수냉식 직렬 4기통 가솔린 Water-cooled inline-four gasoline engine	
배기량 Displacement (cc)	1,238	1,439
최고 출력 Max. power (ps/rpm)	80/6,300	92/6,300
최대 토크 Max. torque (kg-m/rpm)	10.8/4,000	12.5/4,000
변속기 Transmission	4단 수동 4-speed manual	4단 수동 4-speed manual 3단 자동 3-speed automatic
공차 중량 Curb weight (kg)	870	900

포니2

PONY2

포니2는 5도어 해치백으로 재탄생한 포니의 페이스리프트 모델이다. 후속차는 아니었지만 디자인 변경 범위가 컸고, 상품성도 크게 향상되어 차명이 포니2로 결정되었다. 외장은 보닛과 도어를 제외하고 대폭 변경되었고, 내장 또한 대시보드와 스티어링 휠 등 주요 부분이 변경되었다. 이처럼 새로운 스타일의 포니2는 향상된 실용성과 성능으로 국내에서 폭발적 인기를 누렸을 뿐 아니라 북미 시장 진출의 전초기지인 캐나다에 수출되어 현지에서 베스트셀링 카로 등극했다. 1984년 5월 국내에서 캐나다 수출 사양인 에너지 흡수형 5-마일 범퍼를 장착해 안전성이 한층 강화된 포니2 CX(Canadian Export)를 출시하기도 했다.

The Pony 2 is a facelifted model of the Pony, redesigned as a 5-door hatchback. This was not a full model change, but the scope of the design changes and enhancements were extensive enough to warrant the name 'Pony2'. Significant changes were made to the exterior including new body panels, but the hood and doors remained unchanged. Major changes were also made to the interior including the dashboard and steering wheel, boosting practical functionality and performance. The Pony2 was not only a sensational hit in Korea, but also a bestseller in Canada — often considered the export gateway into the broader North American market. In May 1984, the Pony2 CX (Canadian Export) was launched in Korea, with enhanced vehicle safety thanks to the addition of an energy-absorbing five-mile bumper that was used for Canadian export vehicles.

양산 개시 Start of production	1982년 1월 January 1982	
길이 Length (mm)	4,029	
너비 Width (mm)	1,566	
높이 Height (mm)	1,367	
휠베이스 Wheelbase (mm)	2,340	
구동 방식 Drive layout	후륜구동(FR) Front-engine, Rear-wheel drive (FR)	
엔진 Engine type	수냉식 직렬 4기통 가솔린 Water-cooled inline-four gasoline engine	
배기량 Displacement (cc)	1,238	1,439
최고 출력 Max. power (ps/rpm)	80/6,300	92/6,300
최대 토크 Max. torque (kg-m/rpm)	10.8/4,000	12.5/4,000
변속기 Transmission	4단 수동 4-speed manual	4단 수동 4-speed manual 3단 자동 3-speed automatic
공차 중량 Curb weight (kg)	910	

포니2 픽업   PONY2 Pickup

포니2의 유일한 파생 차인 포니2 픽업은 승용 모델과 동일한 전면부 디자인에 400kg의 적재 용량을 갖춘 화물용 차였다. 포니 픽업과 비교해 B필러의 환기구, 리어 콤비네이션 램프 배열 등의 디자인이 변경되었고, 뛰어난 기동성과 정숙한 주행을 실현해 화물의 안전 수송과 승차감 향상을 동시에 이뤄냈다. 이 외에도 1984년 가변형 적재함 덮개를 장착한 포니2 픽업 컨버터블 탑(Convertible Top)을 출시해 소비자 선택의 폭을 넓혔다.

The only derivative of Pony2, the pickup model had the same front-end design as the Pony2 base model (which was a hatchback), but the pickup version offered a payload capacity of 400kg. The Pony2 Pickup included a number of design changes compared to the Pony Pickup, such as the air vent in the low end of the B pillar and the rear combination lamp arrangement. At the same time, it achieved excellent maneuverability and a quiet drive, offering both the safe delivery of cargo and upgraded driving comfort. Additionally, consumers were given a wider range of potential options with the launch of the Pony2 Pickup Convertible Top in 1984, offering an adjustable cover for the cargo bed.

양산 개시 Start of production	1982년 6월 June 1982	
길이 Length (mm)	3,998	
너비 Width (mm)	1,566	
높이 Height (mm)	1,367	
휠베이스 Wheelbase (mm)	2,340	
구동 방식 Drive layout	후륜구동(FR) Front-engine, Rear-wheel drive (FR)	
엔진 Engine type	수냉식 직렬 4기통 가솔린 Water-cooled inline-four gasoline engine	
배기량 Displacement (cc)	1,238	1,439
최고 출력 Max. power (ps/rpm)	80/6,300	92/6,300
최대 토크 Max. torque (kg-m/rpm)	10.8/4,000	12.5/4,000
변속기 Transmission	4단 수동 4-speed manual	
공차 중량 Curb weight (kg)	855	

소형차
포니 엑셀

PONY Excel

포니 엑셀(X카, Pony Excel)은 국내 최초의 전륜구동 승용차이자 미국에 수출된 최초의 국산차다. 현대자동차는 포니 엑셀을 통해 전 세계 최대 자동차 시장인 미국 진출에 성공하면서, 글로벌 브랜드로 비약적 성장을 한다. 포니 엑셀은 미쓰비시의 전륜구동 플랫폼을 탑재했으며, 스타일링은 조르제토 주지아로가 담당했다. 세계에서 가장 엄격한 북미 안전 및 배기가스 규정에 맞춰 개발한 만큼 안전성이 뛰어났고, 전륜구동 5도어 소형 해치백으로 높은 경제성과 실용성이 장점이었다. X카 프로젝트는 포니 엑셀에 이어 1985년 6월에 4도어 세단인 프레스토를, 1986년 9월에 3도어 해치백인 포니 엑셀 스포티(Sporty)를 출시하면서 마무리되었다. 특히 3도어 해치백 모델은 1987년 미쓰비시에서 리배징해 미국에서 프레시스(Precis)라는 차로 판매되기도 했다.

국내에서는 '뛰어난 포니'라는 의미로 포니 엑셀(Pony Excel)로 정했다. 포니 엑셀은 지역마다 차명이 달랐는데, 미국 시장에서는 엑셀(Excel), 유럽 시장에서는 포니(Pony)라는 이름을 사용했다.

The Pony Excel (X Car) is Korea's first front-wheel drive car and the first Korean car to be exported to the United States. Hyundai made a significant leap into the global market by entering the world's largest car market, the U.S., with the Pony Excel. The Pony Excel was equipped with Mitsubishi's front-wheel drive platform and was styled by Giugiaro. Developed to meet the stringent North American safety and emissions standards, the Pony Excel was distinguished by its safety. Being a front-wheel drive, five-door compact hatchback, the model was both affordable and practical. The "X Car" project included the four-door sedan Presto (launched in June 1985) and the three-door hatchback Pony Excel Sporty (launched in September 1986). The three-door hatchback model, in particular, was rebadged by Mitsubishi in 1987 to be sold under the name Precis in the U.S. market.

It was named the Pony Excel in Korea, meaning "excellent Pony." The Pony Excel had different names depending on the region: it was called "Excel" in the U.S. and "Pony" in Europe.

양산 개시 Start of production	1985년 2월 February 1985		
유형 Type	1.3 기본형 1.3 Basic	1.5 고급형 1.5 Premium	AMX
길이 Length (mm)	3,985		4,088
너비 Width (mm)	1,595		
높이 Height (mm)	1,380		
휠베이스 Wheelbase (mm)	2,380		
구동 방식 Drive layout	전륜구동 (FF) Front-engine, Front-wheel drive (FF)		
엔진 Engine type	수냉식 직렬 4기통 가솔린 Water-cooled inline-four gasoline engine		
배기량 Displacement (cc)	1,298	1,468	1,468
최고 출력 Max. power (ps/rpm)	77/5,500	87/5,500	87/5,500
최대 토크 Max. torque (kg-m/rpm)	11/3,500	12.5/3,500	12.5/3,500
변속기 Transmission	4단 수동 4-speed manual	5단 수동 5-speed manual 3단 자동 3-speed automatic	5단 수동 5-speed manual 3단 자동 3-speed automatic
공차 중량 Curb weight (kg)	860	880	930

소형차

엑셀

Sub-compact car

EXCEL

엑셀(X-2카, Excel)은 1세대 포니, 2세대 포니 엑셀(X카)에 이은 3세대 소형차로 자동차 대중화로 고객의 눈높이가 높아지면서 '소형차는 저렴해서 성능이 좋지 않다'는 인식을 극복하기 위해 차급을 뛰어넘는 혁신적 상품성을 적용했다. 이에 출시 당시 광고 카피도 차원이 다른 차를 의미하는 '제3세대 승용차'였다. 엑셀은 당시 최신 트렌드인 에어로다이내믹 스타일을 적용한 4도어 세단으로 현대자동차 내부 인력이 디자인하고, 다중 제어 연료 분사 방식인 MPI(Multi Point Injection) 엔진 등 최첨단 기술을 대거 적용해 안전성과 편의성을 강화했다. 이로써 엑셀은 국내외 시장에서 포니 엑셀이 세운 '엑셀 신화'를 계속 이어갔으며, 1991년 7월 단일 차종으로는 국내 최초로 200만 대 생산을 돌파하는 기록을 세웠다.

Excel (X-2 car) was Hyundai's third generation sub-compact car followed by the Pony and the Pony Excel (X Car). It was the result of ambitious innovations designed to create a product that transcended the sub-compact car market. The goal was to dispel the growing perception that small cars were cheap and lacked performance, as consumer expectations rose with the growing availability of cars. In that spirit, the advertising slogan for the model was "the third-generation sedan," designed to put the Excel on a whole new level. It was a four-door sedan, designed by Hyundai engineers, which boasted an aerodynamic design — a leading trend at the time. Safety and convenience were bolstered through the application of a series of cutting-edge technologies including the multi-point injection (MPI) engine. Excel continued the record-breaking legacy of the Pony Excel, and in July 1991, became the first Korean model to produce over 2 million vehicles.

양산 개시 Start of production	1989년 4월 April 1989		
유형 Type	1.3	1.5 FBC	1.5 MPI
길이 Length (mm)	4,100(3도어, 5도어), 4,275(4도어) 4,100 (3-door, 5-door), 4,275 (4-door)		
너비 Width (mm)	1,605		
높이 Height (mm)	1,385		
휠베이스 Wheelbase (mm)	2,385		
구동 방식 Drive layout	전륜구동 (FF) Front-engine, Front-wheel drive (FF)		
엔진 Engine type	수냉식 직렬 4기통 가솔린 Water-cooled inline-four gasoline engine		
배기량 Displacement (cc)	1,298	1,468	1,468
최고 출력 Max. power (ps/rpm)	82/5,500	86/5,000	97/5,500
최대 토크 Max. torque (kg-m/rpm)	12.1/3,500	13.9/2,500	14.3/3,000
변속기 Transmission	4단 수동 4-speed manual	4단 수동 4-speed manual 5단 수동 5-speed manual 3단 자동 3-speed automatic	5단 수동 5-speed manual 4단 자동 4-speed automatic
공차 중량 Curb weight (kg)	955	961	989

소형차

엑센트

엑센트(X-3카, Accent)는 엑셀의 후속 모델로 국내 최초 100% 독자 기술로 개발한 국내 자동차 산업의 새로운 이정표를 세운 차다. 현대자동차가 독자 개발한 뉴 알파엔진과 알파 트랜스미션을 장착했으며, 기존 소형차의 보수적인 이미지를 탈피하기 위해 최신 감각의 올라운드 클린 보디 스타일과 젊은 세대가 선호하는 빨강, 진보라, 연녹색 등 강렬한 외장 컬러를 적용해 국내에서 선풍적 인기를 끌었다. 또한 엑센트는 전 부품의 85% 이상을 재활용할 수 있는 리사이클링 기술을 적용해 친환경성을 강화했고, 고장력 강판 등 경량화 소재를 사용함으로써 연비와 안정성을 높였다. 차명 'Accent'는 '신기술로 자동차의 신기원을 창조하는 신세계 자동차(Advanced Compact Car of Epoch-making New Technology)'라는 의미를 담은 축약어로 '강조'를 뜻하는 음악 용어에서 영감을 얻었다.

Sub-compact car

ACCENT

The Accent (X-3 car) is the successor to the Excel and marks a new milestone in the domestic automotive industry as the first car developed entirely with Hyundai's indigenous technologies. It was equipped with the new Alpha engine and transmission, both of which had been independently developed by Hyundai. In order to break away from the conservative image often associated with small cars at the time, the Accent was designed in an all-round clean body with vivid exterior colors that appealed to young consumers such as red, purple, and light green, becoming a sensational hit in Korea. In addition, the model was eco-friendly as more than 85% of its parts were recyclable. Fuel efficiency and safety had also undergone an upgrade with the use of light-weight materials such as high strength steel. Short for "Advanced Compact Car of Epoch-making New Technology," the name Accent was also inspired by the musical term that means "to stress."

양산 개시 Start of production	1994년 4월 April 1994	
유형 Type	1.3	1.5
길이 Length (mm)	4,105(3도어, 5도어), 4,115(4도어) 4,105 (3-door, 5-door), 4,115 (4-door)	
너비 Width (mm)	1,620	
높이 Height (mm)	1,395	
휠베이스 Wheelbase (mm)	2,400	
구동 방식 Drive layout	전륜구동 (FF) Front-engine, Front-wheel drive (FF)	
엔진 Engine type	수냉식 직렬 4기통 가솔린 Water-cooled inline-four gasoline engine	
배기량 Displacement (cc)	1,341	1,495
최고 출력 Max. power (ps/rpm)	86/5,500	96/5,500
최대 토크 Max. torque (kg-m/rpm)	12.5/3,000	13.9/3,000
변속기 Transmission	5단 수동 5-speed manual 4단 자동 4-speed automatic	5단 수동 5-speed manual 4단 자동 4-speed automatic
공차 중량 Curb weight (kg)	950	960

울산 현대 조선소에서 촬영한 포니
The Pony photographed at the Hyundai
shipyard in Ulsan

길 위의 포니, 길 밖의 포니: 키워드로 보는 포니 외전 그동안 잘 알려지지 않았던 포니의 이야기

Highlights of the Pony off the road: discovering the untold stories of Hyundai's Pony

현대 조선소

과거에 촬영된 포니 화보집에는 유독 울산의 현대 조선소를 배경으로 찍은 사진이 많다. 이는 현대가 수출보국(輸出報國)을 위해 척박한 환경에서 조선 산업과 자동차 산업을 독자적으로 일궈내고, 조선소와 자동차가 개발도상국이었던 한국의 잠재력과 현대의 추진력을 입증하는 중요한 상징이었기 때문이다. 당시 현대는 조선소와 초대형 선박을 2년 3개월 만에 초단기로 완공해 바다에 띄우는 저력을 보여주었다.

조선 사업 추진을 위해 영국을 방문한 정주영 선대회장이 거북선이 그려진 500원짜리 지폐를 보여주며 "한국은 영국보다 300년 앞서 조선의 역사를 쓴 나라다"라고 설득해 영국으로부터 차관을 받아낸 일화는 유명하다. 현대 조선소의 대형 선박 건조 현장은 한국을 찾은 해외 경제 사절단에게 깊은 인상을 남겼고, 포니 프로젝트의 실현 가능성에 반신반의하던 조르제토 주지아로와 조지 턴불에게도 프로젝트 성공에 대한 확신을 심어주었다. 이처럼 현대 조선소는 포니 프로젝트의 다국적 드림팀 결성을 가능하게 한 실질적 매개체였다.

Hyundai Shipyard

In past photo collections of the Pony, many images were notably set against the backdrop of Hyundai's Ulsan shipyard. Committed to driving up exports as part of its contribution to the national economic development, Hyundai pioneered the development of the shipbuilding and automotive industries from the ground up. The shipyard and cars symbolized the potential of Korea, which was still a developing country at the time, as well as Hyundai's strong drive for industrial development. In an unprecedented success, Hyundai constructed a shipyard and a fully operational oil tanker in just two years and three months.

A famous anecdote involves Hyundai's Founding Chairman Ju-yung Chung persuading British financiers. He showed them an image of the Turtle Ship — the famous Korean warship from the 1500s — printed on the Korean 500-won bill and claimed, "Korea has a history of the Joseon Dynasty dating back 300 years before England." This helped secure a loan for Hyundai's shipbuilding venture. The sight of large ships being constructed at the Hyundai shipyard left a lasting impression on foreign economic delegations visiting Korea. It also convinced Giorgetto Giugiaro and George Turnbull, who were initially skeptical about the feasibility of the Pony project, of its potential success. Ultimately, the shipyard played a crucial role in forming the multinational dream team for the project.

한국의 문화유산

현대자동차가 포니와 포니 엑셀을 개발할 당시 미쓰비시와
기술 협력 계약을 체결할 수 있었던 것은 우리 옛 선조들이 남
긴 문화유산에 힘입은 바가 컸다. 미쓰비시의 구보 도미오 회
장은 평소 자신을 '백제의 후예'라고 할 만큼 한국의 문화와
역사에 관심이 많았다. 언젠가 그가 현대자동차 울산 공장을
방문했을 때, 3일간의 짧은 방문 일정에도 불구하고 반드시
부여를 둘러볼 수 있게 해달라고 부탁한 건 이 때문이다. 미쓰
비시 교토 제작소의 아라이 소장 역시 경주의 유적을 둘러본
후 현대자동차와의 기술 제휴에 긍정적 의견을 피력했고, 이
는 계약이 성사되는 데 결정적 역할을 했다.

　　이후 엔진 연수를 위해 온 현대자동차 직원들에게 아라
이 소장은 "경주에 가보니 옛날 유적이 많아 참으로 좋았습니
다. 예전에는 당신들이 우리 선생이었던 거지요. 이번에는 우
리가 가르쳐줄 테니 무엇이든 물어보십시오"[12]라는 말을 남
겼다. 이 같은 경험을 바탕으로 당시 울산 공장 직원들은 외국
인 기술자들이 한국에 처음 방문할 때면 꼭 경주에 들러 에밀
레종 같은 문화유산에 대해 설명해 주었는데, 이는 우리 선조
들이 뛰어난 금속 기술을 가지고 있었다는 점을 널리 알리고,
그 후손인 한국인 기술자들 또한 잠재력이 풍부한 파트너라
는 점을 각인시킨 것이다.

Cultural Heritage of Korea

The technical collaboration between Hyundai
and Mitsubishi when developing the Pony and
the Pony Excel was largely owed to the cultural
heritage of the Korean ancestors. Mitsubishi's
Chairman, Kubo Tomio, had a great interest in
Korean culture and history, often referring to
himself as a descendant of the Baekje Dynasty.
He requested a tour of Buyeo, once the capital
of Baekje, during his three-day visit to the Ulsan
plant of Hyundai. Director Seiyu Arai of Mitsubishi Kyoto plant also expressed a positive opinion
on the technology partnership with Hyundai
after visiting historical sites in Gyeongju. This
played a crucial role in finalizing the contract.

　　Later, when Hyundai employees came for
engineering training, Director Arai remarked,
"Visiting Gyeongju and seeing the ancient sites
was truly wonderful. In the past, you were our
teachers. Now, it's our turn to teach you, so feel
free to ask anything."[12] Based on these experiences, Hyundai's employees at the Ulsan plant
made it a point to introduce foreign technicians
to cultural heritage sites like the Emille Bell in
Gyeongju during their first visit to Korea. This was
to highlight the advanced metalworking skills of
their Korean ancestors and to emphasize that
Hyundai technicians, who inherited this DNA,
would be great partners with much to offer.

경주박물관을 둘러보는 미쓰비시 구보 도미오 회장 일행
(1982년 4월)
Chairman Kubo of Mitsubishi and his entourage
visiting the Gyeongju National Museum
(April 1982)

서울 광화문에서 진행된 '20년 이상 무사고 운전자의 날'
기념식 (1981년 11월)
The "Accident-Free Drivers for more than
20 Years Day" ceremony at Gwanghwamun,
Seoul (November 1981)

포니가 만든 택시 문화

포니 출시를 기점으로 택시가 빠르게 보급됨에 따라 택시와 관련한 다양한 행사가 열렸다. 1975년 말, 서울시 기준 554대에 불과하던 개인택시가 1978년 8월 1만 대를 넘어섰고, 일반 택시와 합하면 총 2만4,650대의 택시가 서울 시내를 누비게 되면서 택시가 수송하는 교통 인구 역시 하루 200만 명 수준으로 늘어났다.[13]

당시 도심을 활보한 택시 대부분이 포니였던 만큼 포니가 새로운 교통 문화 조성에 기여했다고 해도 과언이 아니다. 서울 여의도광장이나 서울시청 등지에서 개인택시 발대식이 열리기 시작했고, 안전 운전과 교통 법칙 준수를 독려하기 위한 '무사고 운전자의 날'도 제정되었다. 특히 1981년 11월 12일 처음 열린 '무사고 운전자의 날' 기념식에서는 20년 이상 무사고 운전사 26명에게 노란색 포니 택시를 부상으로 제공해 관심을 모았다. 여성 개인택시 운전사 발대식도 개최되었다. 포니 출시 후 오너 드라이버를 지향하는 여성 운전자들이 급증하면서 택시 기사의 여성 비중이 높아진 것이다. 이 외에도 공항 택시, 터미널 택시, 호텔 전용 택시 등 다양한 전용 택시가 등장했다.

Taxi culture kickstarted by the Pony

The launch of the Pony kickstarted the spread of taxis and a variety of taxi-related events. By the end of 1975, there were only 554 private taxis in Seoul, but this number exceeded 10,000 by August 1978. Including regular taxis, there were a total of 24,650 taxis navigating the streets of Seoul, increasing the daily transport population to approximately 2 million people.[13]

Given that most taxis in the city were Ponies, it's fair to say the Pony contributed to creating a new transportation culture. License-awarding ceremonies for private taxis began in places like Yeouido Plaza and Seoul City Hall, and the "Accident-Free Driver's Day" was established to encourage safe driving and adherence to traffic laws. Particularly noteworthy was the first "Accident-Free Driver's Day" ceremony on November 12, 1981, where 26 drivers with over 20 years of accident-free driving were awarded a yellow Pony taxi, garnering significant attention. There was also a license-awarding ceremony for female private taxi drivers. After the release of the Pony, there was a surge in female drivers aiming to be owner-operators, increasing the proportion of women taxi drivers. Additionally, various specialized taxis emerged, including airport taxis, terminal taxis, and hotel-exclusive taxis.

서울시청 앞에서 진행된 개인택시 발대식(1976년 9월)
The license awarding ceremony for owner-
operated taxi in front of Seoul City Hall
(September 1976)

Chapter 3

발대식에 참가한 차량 대부분이 포니 택시다.
Most of the vehicles that participated in
the license-awarding ceremony were Pony
taxis.

한국과 에콰도르 간 수출 증대 방안을 협의한 내용을 다룬
당시 신문 기사(1977년 10월)[14]
A newspaper article covering the agreement for
expanding mutual export between Korea and
Ecuador (October 1977)[14]

포니와 바나나

포니의 공식적인 첫 해외 수출국인 에콰도르와의 거래는 구상무역 형태로 이루어졌다. 구상무역은 '수출자에 대한 수입대금의 전부 또는 일부를 수입자가 제품으로 지급하는 거래'를 의미하는 것으로, 당시 에콰도르의 주산물이 석유와 바나나였던 만큼 포니와 바나나를 맞바꾸는 형태의 거래가 이루어진 것이다. 덕분에 당시 한국 국민은 쉽게 접하기 어려웠던 고급 과일인 바나나를 알게 모르게 많이 먹을 수 있었다는 후문이다.

그러나 당시 한국 농수산부는 바나나 농사를 특화 사업으로 여겨 쉽사리 수입 허가를 내주려고 하지 않았다. 이에 현대자동차는 이제 막 걸음마를 시작한 자동차 수출을 위해 바나나 수입을 허가해 주어야 한다는 공문을 상공부와 농수산부에 여러 차례 보내 가까스로 설득하는 데 성공했다. 또한 에콰도르로 향하는 자동차 수출은 과야킬(Guayaquil)항에서 바나나를 실은 전용 냉동선이 부산항에 들어오면 그 배에 포니를 실어 보내는 방식으로 진행되었는데, 냉동선은 자동차 전용선이 아니었기에 큰 줄로 차를 들어 올려 선적해야 했다. 이처럼 '포니와 바나나' 일화는 해외 수출길을 열기 위해 당시 임직원들이 얼마나 고군분투하며 방법을 강구해 나갔는지를 보여주는 사례라 할 수 있다.

The Pony and bananas

The trade with Ecuador, the first official export destination for the Pony, was conducted through countertrade. Countertrade refers to when the importer pays the exporter entirely or partially with goods instead of money. The payment for the Pony was made in bananas, which was a key export item for Ecuador along with petroleum. It is said that this trade led to Korean people having greater access to bananas, which were still considered a luxury fruit at the time.

However, the Ministry for Food, Agriculture, Forestry and Fisheries at the time saw bananas as a priority agricultural project for Korea and would not issue a permit for importing the fruit. After submitting multiple appeal letters to the Ministry of Industry and Commerce as well as the Ministry for Food, Agriculture, Forestry and Fisheries to request for the approval of banana import to promote the export of Korean automobiles, which was still in a nascent stage, Hyundai finally managed to persuade the government agencies to allow the import of bananas. The export of cars to Ecuador proceeded by loading Ponies onto the refrigerated ships that brought bananas from Guayaquil to Busan Port. Since these ships were not designed for cars, the vehicles had to be hoisted aboard with large belts. The "Pony and bananas" story illustrates the struggle and efforts of Hyundai employees at the time to create opportunities to export the Pony.

에콰도르에서 20년간 택시로 운행된 포니
The reimported Pony that had operated as a
taxi for 20 years in Ecuador

포니 택시의 금의환향

1996년 7월, 현대자동차는 에콰도르 현지에서 20년간 택시로 운행한 포니를 국내에 역수입했다. 다시 한국 땅을 밟게 된 포니 택시는 현대자동차가 1976년 에콰도르에 수출한 초창기 모델로, 150만km라는 장거리 주행 이력에도 차량 상태와 성능이 양호해 포니의 탄탄한 내구성을 입증했다. 이 택시는 반입당시 한국기네스협회에 최장 주행 차량으로 등록됐으며, 현재는 현대자동차 남양연구소에 보관돼 있다.

해외에 수출된 포니를 국내에 들여온 사례는 또 있다. 1980년대 초반에 이집트로 수출한 포니를 광주민주화운동을 다룬 영화 〈화려한 휴가〉의 소품으로 다시 들여온 것이다. 이 영화 속 주인공의 직업이 택시 기사였기에 1980년대 시대상을 구현하기 위해서는 당대를 상징하는 포니 택시가 반드시 필요했다. 그러나 국내에서는 포니 중고차를 좀처럼 구할 수 없어 고민하던 제작진이 이집트에서는 포니가 여전히 택시로 운행되고 있다는 소식을 듣고 총 5대의 포니 택시를 공수해 와 촬영을 마쳤다.

The honorable return of Pony taxis

In July 1996, Hyundai re-imported the Pony that had been used as a taxi in Ecuador for 20 years. The taxi that was imported back to Korea was an early model that was exported to Ecuador in 1976. Despite the high mileage of 1.5 million kilometers, the car was in good shape and demonstrated solid performance, proving the durability of the Pony. Upon its return, it was registered with the Korea Guinness Association as the vehicle with the longest driving record and is now kept at Hyundai's Namyang R&D Center.

In another similar case, a few Ponies were imported back into Korea after they were exported to Egypt during the early 1980s. The Ponies were re-imported to be used as props for the film "May 18", which depicted the Gwangju Uprising. The film's protagonist being a taxi driver necessitated the inclusion of a Pony taxi to accurately reflect the era of the 1980s. The production team was struggling to find any used Pony model in Korea when they learned that the early Pony models were still being used as taxis in Egypt. A total of five Pony taxis were imported back to Korea for the production of the film.

텔렉스

이메일, 화상통화, 스마트폰 메신저 등이 일상화된 오늘날
과 달리 1970~1980년대에는 국제통신 환경이 열악하기 그
지없었다. 국제우편은 분실 위험이 높았을 뿐 아니라 주고
받는 데 오랜 기간이 소요돼 비즈니스에 활용하기는 적합하
지 않았고, 그나마 텔렉스가 가장 나은 통신수단이었지만 그
마저도 원활하지 않아 애를 먹었다. 텔렉스는 '텔레타이프
(teletype, 인쇄전신기)'와 '익스체인지(exchange, 교환
기)'의 합성어로 1970~1980년대 가장 보편화된 국제통신
수단이었으며, 현대자동차도 포드와 합작사 설립을 위해 공
문서를 주고받을 때나 포니 개발 과정에서 이탈리아와 설계
도면을 주고받을 때, 영국·프랑스·일본 등 해외 각지의 협력
업체와 설비 구매를 협의할 때 텔렉스로 소통을 했다.

하지만 대개의 경우 국제통신 환경이 불안정하고 수신
문서의 인쇄 속도가 느려 빠른 소통이 어려웠을 뿐 아니라 접
속 시간에 따라 요금이 부과돼 비용 부담을 줄이고자 약어를
이용하는 경우도 많았다. 그 때문에 해외에서의 다양한 이슈
를 한국 본사에 전달하고 의사 결정을 받는 과정이 오늘날처
럼 기민하지는 못했다. 그런 사정을 고려했을 때 당시 열악한
국제통신 환경에서 현대자동차가 전 세계 다양한 국가와 수
많은 사안을 끊임없이 소통하며 포니를 단기간에 개발·생산·
수출했다는 것은 놀라운 일이 아닐 수 없다.

Telex

Unlike today, where emails, video calls, and
smartphone messengers are commonplace,
the international communication environment
during the 1970s and 1980s was extremely poor.
International postal service was not only risky
due to the high chance of loss but also took a
long time to send and receive, making it unsuit-
able for business use. Telex was considered the
best means of communication at the time, but
even that was not without its challenges. Telex, a
portmanteau of "teletype" and "exchange," was
the most common international communication
method during the 1970s and 80s. Hyundai used
telex to exchange official documents with Ford
for a joint venture, share design blueprints with
Italy during the Pony's development, and discuss equipment purchases with collaborators in
the UK, France, Japan, and other countries.

However, the international communication
environment was often unstable, and the slow
printing speed of received documents made
fast communication difficult. Additionally, communication costs were charged based on connection time, leading many to use abbreviations
to reduce expenses. For these reasons, reporting various issues to the headquarters in Korea
and sharing the decisions made was rarely as
efficient as today. It is remarkable that Hyundai
continued to communicate with its partners in
various countries under such challenging circumstances and successfully developed, produced, and exported the Pony in such a short
period of time.

                                          YOURS RESPECTFULLY
                              FORDMOTOR COMPANY
                              BY   _ _ _ _ _ _ _ _ _ _ _ _ _

CONCUR
KOREA GROUP
BY
    _ _ _ _ _ _ _ _ _ _ _ _ _ _ _ _

        BEFORE AGREEING TO THE CHANGE IN THE APPLICABLE LAW PRO-

VISION WE SHOULD APPRECIATE RECEIVING YOUR OPINION THAT AFTER

EXECUTION THE PAYMENT PROVISIONS AND THE TERMINATION PROVISIONS

OF THE T/A AGREEMENT WOULD BE ENFORCEABLE UNDER KOREAN LAW AND

WOULD BE ENFORCED BY KOREAN COURTS STOP PARA

     PLEASE REVIEW THE DRAFT LETTER FIRCE WITH CHUNG SE AND THEN

WITH YANG STOP IF ALLL SATISFACTORY SO SIVISE US BY TELEXY

NOT CABLE / AND WE WILL DISPATCH SIGNED LETTER TO YOU FOR SIG-

NATURE BY KOREA GROUP AND FILING WITH   STOP BEST REGARDS

     DUNCAN/TOTTEN FORDMOTOR CO AMERICAN   DEARBORN MICH

CHOSUN 2399S
FORDMTR DRBN C

• • • • • =

다- 97E

국내 최초의 모터쇼

현대자동차는 창립 10주년을 맞아 1977년 9월 16일부터 26일까지 11일간 여의도 한국기계산업진흥회 전시관에서 자동차 전시회를 개최했다. 창립 행사의 일환으로 열린 자동차 전시회는 국내 최초의 대규모 자동차 전시회로 포니와 포니 쿠페 등 승용차와 버스, 트럭, 특장차 등 21개 차종과 70개 관련 부품을 볼 수 있었다. 특히 부품 전시관에는 부품 국산화의 성과를 한눈에 확인할 수 있도록 엔진, 내·외장 부품, 전장품 등 자동차 부품은 물론 현대자동차가 자체 제작한 주·단조품, 프레스 부품, 엔진 조립품 등도 함께 전시되었다.

9월 16일 전시회 개막일에는 각국 외교 사절과 정부 관계 인사, 그룹사 임직원, 부품업체 관계자, 해외 딜러, 취재 기자 등 모두 700여 명이 참석했으며, 전시회 기간에 총 17만 명의 관람객이 다녀가 대성황을 이뤘다. 이는 전례 없던 규모의 자동차 관련 전시회로 사실상 국내 첫 모터쇼라 할 수 있다. 특히 이 전시회는 일반 시민이 한국 자동차 공업의 발전상을 직접 눈으로 확인할 수 있게 했다는 점에서 국민적 자부심을 고취시킨 행사였다.

Korea's first Motor Show

In celebration of the 10th founding anniversary, Hyundai organized an auto show at the exhibition hall of the Association of Machinery Industry in Yeouido between September 16 and September 26, 1977. As the first large-scale motor show that was held as part of Hyundai's anniversary celebrations, it showcased 21 models, including passenger cars such as the Pony and the Pony Coupe, buses, trucks, and special vehicles, along with 70 types of auto parts. The parts exhibition area showcased the achievements in parts localization, displaying engines, interior and exterior parts, electrical components, and Hyundai's own forged, casted, and pressed parts as well as engine assemblies.

On the opening day, September 16, about 700 people attended, including foreign diplomats, government officials, group company employees, parts suppliers, overseas dealers, and journalists. The exhibition attracted a total of 170,000 visitors, making it a huge success. This unprecedented scale of automotive exhibition could be considered the country's first motor show. It was particularly inspiring as it was open to the general public, who could witness firsthand the growth of Korea's automotive industry.

현대자동차 창립 10주년 기념 자동차 전시회 (1977년 9월)
The automobile exhibition celebrating the 10th anniversary
of Hyundai Motor Company's founding (September 1977)

국내 최초 모터쇼라 할 수 있는 현대자동차
창립 10주년 자동차 전시회
Hyundai Motor's 10th anniversary exhibition,
which can be called Korea's first motor show

Chapter 3

창립 10주년 행사의 일환으로 열린 국내 최초의 대규모 자동차 전시회로 포니와 포니
쿠페 등 21개 차종과 70개 관련 부품이 전시됐다.
This was the first large-scale automobile exhibition in Korea
implemented as a part of the anniversary events. It featured 21 models,
including the Pony and Pony Coupe, and 70 components.

국가등록문화재 제553호

국가등록문화재는 근현대 건축물과 시설, 유물 중 역사적·예술적·사회적·학술적으로 보전할 가치가 있는 유산을 대상으로 선정한다. 포니는 한국 자동차 공업의 자립과 도약의 발판이 된 차종으로 자동차 산업과 기술 발전에 획기적 역할을 했다는 점을 인정받아 2013년 8월 27일 국가등록문화재로 지정되었다. 국가등록문화재 제553호로 등록된 포니는 1975년 12월에 생산된 4도어 모델로 지금은 시중에 거의 남아 있지 않은 귀한 모델이다. 포니는 이외에도 2016년 국립중앙과학관이 선정한 '보존 가치 높은 10대 제품'에 이름을 올린 데 이어, 2022년에는 국가중요과학기술자료로 등록되는 등 시간이 흘러도 변함없이 가치를 인정받고 있다.

National Registered Cultural Heritage No. 553

The National Registered Cultural Heritage is selected among historical buildings, facilities, and artifacts from the pre-modern and contemporary periods that are deemed valuable for their historical, artistic, social, and academic significance. On August 27, 2013, the Pony was registered as a National Cultural Heritage for its groundbreaking role in the development of Korea's automotive industry and technology as well as its contribution to the independence and progress of the industry. The Pony model that was registered as National Cultural Heritage No. 553 was the four-door model produced in December 1975, which is rarely found in the market today. In further recognition of its enduring value, the Pony was also included in the list of "10 products most worthy of conservation" in 2016 and registered as a key national scientific and technological material in 2022 by the National Science Museum of Korea.

1984년 LA 올림픽 선수단 귀국 환영 카퍼레이드
(1984년 8월)[15]
A car parade dedicated to Korean athletes
returning from the 1984 LA Olympics
(August 1984)[15]

©e영상역사관
©ehistory.go.kr

포니 퍼레이드 오픈카

1970~1980년대 해외에서 국위를 선양한 스포츠 선수나 예술가, 한국을 방문한 해외 정상을 환영한 의미로 실시한 카퍼레이드는 서울시의 정례화된 행사 중 하나였다. 카퍼레이드는 주로 김포공항에서 서울시청까지 펼쳐졌는데, 당시 서울시는 각종 행사에 사용할 퍼레이드용 오픈카가 없어 택시를 빌려 행사를 치르는 등 곤란을 겪고 있었다. 이를 본 현대자동차는 1979년 4월 포니를 개조한 퍼레이드용 오픈카 10대를 제작해 서울시에 기증했다. 1979년 3월 형식 승인도 받았다.

이후 포니 오픈카는 아시안게임, 올림픽, 기능올림픽 등 메달리스트 환영식 등 다양한 국가 행사에서 퍼레이드 카로 활약했다. 포니 오픈카는 퍼레이드 목적에 맞게 스탠딩 롤바를 설치해 행사의 주역들이 안정감 있게 서서 이동할 수 있도록 제작되었고, 1988년 서울올림픽대회 카퍼레이드 행사에도 투입되어 선수단과 올림픽 마스코트인 호돌이를 태우기도 했다.

The Pony as an open-top car for parades

During the 1970s and 80s, it was customary to organize car parades in Seoul to welcome athletes and artists who promoted the national image overseas as well as foreign heads of state visiting Korea. The car parades usually started at Gimpo International Airport and continued to Seoul City Hall. The Seoul city government, however, struggled to source open-top cars for these parades and had to rely on leased taxis. To respond to this challenge, Hyundai remodeled the Pony vehicles to manufacture and donate 10 open-top cars to the city government in April 1979. The modified vehicles were homologated in March of the same year.

From then on, the Pony open-top cars were used in parades for various national events such as the Asian Games, Olympics, and Skill Olympics to welcome medalists. To serve their purpose as a parade car, the open-top vehicles were each equipped with a standing roll bar to provide stable support to the stars of parades while they were standing in the vehicles. The cars were also used in the 1988 Seoul Olympic parade, carrying athletes and the Olympic mascot, Hodori.

길 위의 포니, 길 밖의 포니: 키워드로 보는 포니 외전
그동안 잘 알려지지 않았던 포니의 이야기

Highlights of the Pony off the road:
discovering the untold stories of Hyundai's Pony

서울시에 기증한 포니 퍼레이드용 오픈카(1979년 4월)
The Pony open-top cars donated to the City of
Seoul for parades (April 1979)

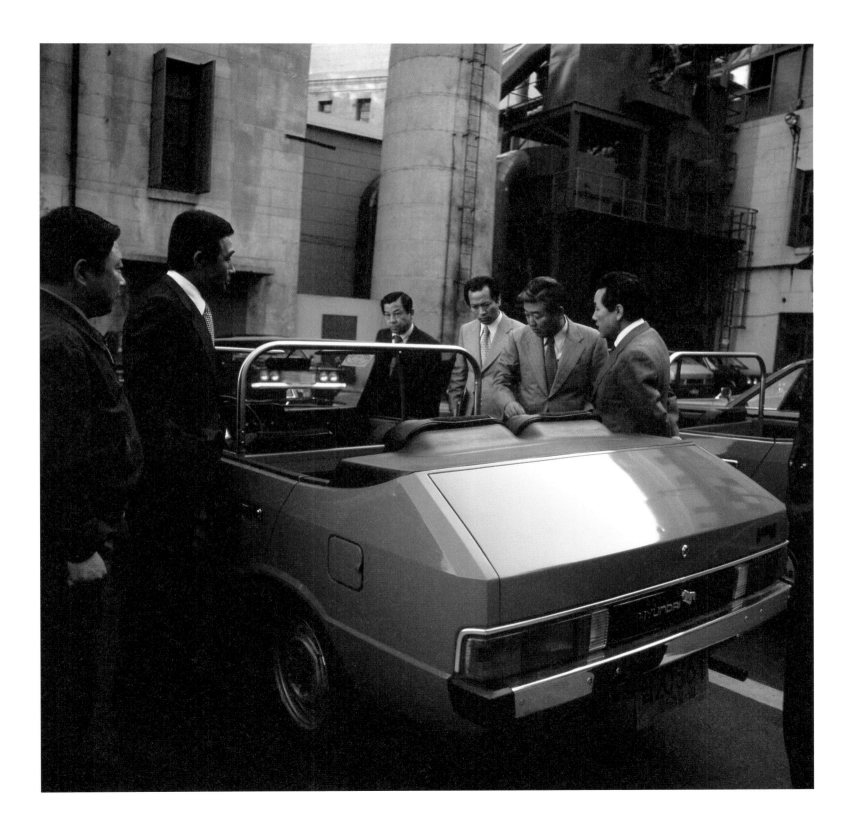

포니 쿠페 양산 프로젝트

1974년 10월 토리노 모터쇼에서 포니와 함께 공개된 포니 쿠페는 당시 혁신적이면서도 미래지향적인 디자인으로 전 세계의 이목이 집중되었다. 오늘날 대한민국 최초의 콘셉트 카로 알려져 있는 포니 쿠페는 현대자동차가 독자 모델 개발을 결심했을 때부터 미국과 유럽 등 선진 시장을 공략하겠다는 담대한 꿈을 품고 기획되었다. 포니 쿠페는 토리노 모터쇼 공개 당시 실제 구동이 가능한 프로토타입으로 제작되었다는 점에서 오늘날 쇼 카 형식의 콘셉트 카와는 차별화된다.

현대자동차는 포니가 출시된 1976년 2월, 이탈디자인이 리스타일링 작업을 제의해 온 것을 계기로 포니 쿠페 양산 프로젝트에 본격 착수했다. 1977년에는 현대자동차 실무자들이 이탈리아에서 포니 쿠페의 설계 작업을 진행한 후 완성된 도면을 가지고 귀국했다. 이후 국내 기술자의 손으로 프로토타입 카와 보디 인 화이트(BIW, Body In White)를 제작하고, 금형 제작과 세부 부품 개발까지 이루어지는 등 양산 준비를 상당한 수준까지 진행했으나, 1979년 예상치 못한 난관에 봉착한다. 전 세계를 강타한 제2차 오일쇼크와 이로 인한 경제 불황의 여파가 현대자동차에도 미친 것이다.

현대자동차는 당시 포니 연간 생산 10만 대 체제 구축을 위해 대규모 차관을 얻어 설비투자를 진행하던 중이었던 만큼 상당한 타격을 입었다. 고금리와 환율 급등으로 인한 자금난이 심화했기 때문이다. 포니 쿠페 양산화 프로젝트에는 당시로서는 천문학적 예산인 95억 원이 투입되었으나, 생존을 위해 감량 경영 체제에 돌입한 현대자동차는 1981년 상대적으로 시장성이 낮다고 판단한 포니 쿠페 양산 계획을 전면 백지화했다.

이처럼 포니 쿠페는 양산에 이르지는 못했으나 현대자

The Pony Coupe mass production project

First unveiled to the world at the Turin Motor Show in October 1974 alongside the Pony, the Pony Coupe drew worldwide attention with its innovative and futuristic design. Known today as Korea's first concept car, the Pony Coupe was conceived with the bold ambition of targeting advanced markets in the U.S. and Europe, marking Hyundai's determination to develop its own model. Distinguished from today's concept cars, the Pony Coupe was presented as a drivable prototype at the Turin Motor Show.

In February 1976, following the launch of the Pony, Hyundai embarked on the Pony Coupe mass production project after Italdesign proposed a restyling initiative. By 1977, Hyundai's team had completed the design work in Italy and returned home with the finished blueprints. Subsequently, the prototype car and the Body-In-White (BIW) were crafted by domestic engineers, progressing significantly in mold creation and component development for mass production. However, in 1979, unforeseen challenges arose due to the second oil shock and the resulting economic recession, which also impacted the company as well.

At the time, Hyundai was heavily affected as it was securing a large loan to invest in facilities and equipments for reaching an annual production of 100,000 units for the Pony. The company faced significant challenges due to high interest rates and a sharp increase in exchange rates, which exacerbated its financial difficulties. The Pony Coupe's mass production project, which had an astronomical budget of 9.5 billion KRW at the time, was ultimately scrapped in 1981. Hyun-

토리노 모터쇼에서 공개한 포니 쿠페 프로토카
The Pony Coupe prototype unveiled at the
Turin Motor Show

동차의 담대한 도전 정신이 깃든 모델로 오늘날 현대자동차
의 라인업에 지속적 영감을 주고 있다.

dai, prioritizing survival, entered a lean management system and decided to cancel the relatively
less marketable Pony Coupe production plan.

Although the Pony Coupe never reached
mass production, it remains as a symbol of
Hyundai's bold ambitions and provide inspiration for its current product line-ups.

길 위의 포니, 길 밖의 포니: 키워드로 보는 포니 외전
그동안 잘 알려지지 않았던 포니의 이야기

Highlights of the Pony off the road:
discovering the untold stories of Hyundai's Pony

포니 쿠페 클레이 모델 제작 과정
Making of a Pony Coupe clay model

국내 기술자의 손으로 클레이 모델을 제작하고 목형 모델을 계측하는 등 일련의 과정을
직접 수행하면서 사내 디자인 역량이 축적되고 프로세스가 정립되기 시작했다.
Having Korean engineers make a clay model and take measurements
with a wooden model helped the company build its design capabilities
and establish a standard process.

포니 쿠페 프로토타입 실내 계측 모습
Interior measurement with the prototype body
of the Pony Coupe

Chapter 3

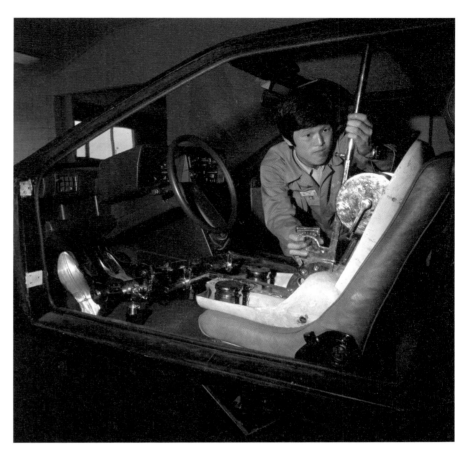

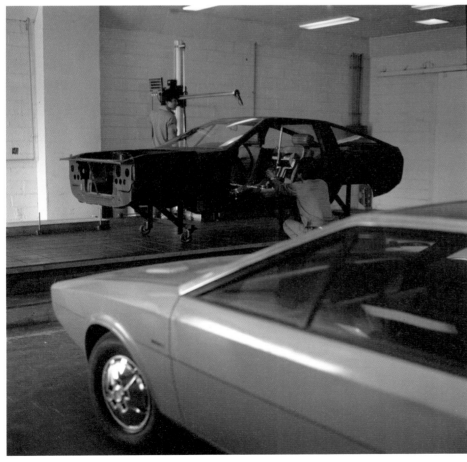

포니 쿠페 프로토타입 실내 계측 모습
Interior measurement with the prototype body
of the Pony Coupe

포니 쿠페 양산 준비 과정에서 제작한 스타일링 모델 및
프로토타입(초기형)
The styling model and prototype constructed
in the preparatory stage for the Pony Coupe's
mass production (early model)

Chapter 3

길 위의 포니, 길 밖의 포니: 키워드로 보는 포니 외전
그동안 잘 알려지지 않았던 포니의 이야기

Highlights of the Pony off the road:
discovering the untold stories of Hyundai's Pony

포니 쿠페 양산 준비 과정에서 제작한 프로토타입(후기형)
The prototype constructed in the preparatory
stage for the Pony Coupe's mass production
(late model)

Chapter 3

선진국으로 수출을 꿈꿨던 현대자동차의 담대한
도전 정신이 깃든 모델이다.

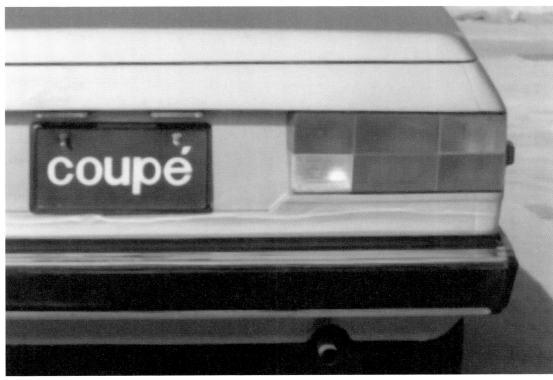

선진국으로 수출을 꿈꿨던 현대자동차의 담대한
도전 정신이 깃든 모델이다.
This model captures Hyundai's audacious
dream of exporting to advanced markets.

프레스 금형으로 만든 패널을 탈부착하면서 외관의 치수 품질 점검을
진행하는 모습이다. 이처럼 포니 쿠페 양산화 프로젝트는 금형 제작과 세부
부품 개발까지 상당 수준 진행되었다.

This process involved attaching and removing panels made
through press die to check the quality of the exterior and
the measurements. With the molding and component
design out of the way, the Pony Coupe's mass production
project was getting closer to completion.

포니 쿠페 양산 프로젝트를 기록한 필름 모음
A collection of films recording the Pony Coupe
mass production project

길은 또 다른 길로 이어져
역사가 되고

Blazing new trails to
make history

일상 풍경을 바꾼 마이카

포니가 길 위를 달리기 시작하자 새로운 풍경이 펼쳐졌다. 한국에 '마이카 시대'가 열린 것이다. 포니의 보급으로 이전에 없던 교통 문화가 만들어지고, 관련 산업이 확장되면서 대중은 더 나은 일상을 누릴 수 있게 되었다. 자가용이 본격적으로 보급되기 이전인 1970년대 초까지만 해도 자동차는 부유층의 전유물이었기 때문에 당시 자가용 보유자는 대부분 운전기사를 고용했다. 하지만 보유 경제성이 높은 소형차 포니가 출시되면서 상황이 크게 달라졌다. 마이카를 갖게 된 대중은 자가용을 직접 운전하는 오너 드라이버로서 운전면허를 따고 운전을 배우는 경우가 급격히 늘었다. 이에 따라 곳곳에 운전면허 학원과 시험장이 들어서고, 중고 자동차 매매 업소와 렌터카업체, 민간 주차장, 경정비업체도 빠르게 증가했으며, 자동차 할부 금융과 보험 등 연관 산업도 크게 확장했다. 더불어 차량의 폭발적 증가로 도로 정체와 주차난 등 사회문제가 대두했는데, 이는 대한민국에서 도시화와 산업화가 본격화되기 시작했음을 의미했다.

　한편 마이카 소유로 인한 생활 반경의 확장은 고도성장으로 중산층이 된 시민들의 삶의 질을 향상시켰다. 출퇴근 시 자가 차량을 이용해 '도어 투 도어(door to door)'의 편의성을 도모하는 이가 많아지고, 도시 간 이동이 보다 자유로워지자 여행과 레저, 외식, 쇼핑 등 다양한 여가 문화가 급속도로 발전했다. 또한 시공간적 제약에서 벗어나면서 개인이 자기 시간을 운영·관리하기가 수월해졌고, 집이나 일터를 선택할 때도 이동 거리와 대중교통 수단을 크게 염두에 두지 않을 수 있게 되었다. 또 마이카는 다목적 용도로 활용되었는데, 예를 들면 포니 픽업은 평소에는 물품 배달이나 개인 용달 등 생계 수단으로 이용하다 주말에는 나들이용으로 활용했다. 포니로 인한 자동차의 대중화는 자동차 보유 여부가 중산층 진입

Car ownership transforming daily life

Once the Pony hit the road, it set in motion a cascade of changes along its journey. The era of car ownership, often called the era of "my car," created new transportation trends, expanded related industries, and improved the everyday experiences of people. Until the early 1970s, when car ownership was not common, cars were considered a luxury reserved only for the wealthy with chauffeurs. It was the arrival of the small and affordable Pony that changed this trend. General consumers could now own a car as well, resulting in a surge of people getting a driver's license to drive their own vehicle. This led to an increasing number of driving schools and driver's license offices as well as car rental companies, private parking lot operators, and repair service providers. The rise in the number of drivers also played a crucial role in the substantial expansion of automobile-related industries such as auto financing and car insurance. In addition, the explosive growth in the number of vehicles caused a rapid rise in traffic jams and parking issues, signaling the beginning of urbanization and industrialization in Korea.

　Car ownership also extended the daily travel distance for the growing middle class that formed during the rapid economic development — ultimately improving their quality of life. Many people sought the convenience of 'door to door' commutes using their own cars. As travel between cities became easier, various leisure cultures such as travel, dining out, shopping, and leisure activities rapidly developed. Additionally, escaping the constraints of time and space made it easier for individuals to manage their time and

한국인의 일상 풍경을 바꾼 포니
The Pony brought changes to Koreans' daily lives

포니는 많은 중산층 가정의 생애 첫 차로 집안의 대소사를
함께했다.
As the first car owned by many middle-class
families, the Pony accompanied many Korean
families through the ups and downs of life.

의 전제 조건처럼 인식되는 사회 통념으로 이어져, 생애 첫 차
를 장만한 가정에서는 마이카 앞에서 온 가족이 함께 사진 촬
영을 하는 것이 풍속으로 자리매김하기도 했다.

　이처럼 포니는 1970~1980년대에 사회·경제적 활동
의 중추를 담당하며 가정을 꾸린 세대에게 첫 번째 마이카로
서 특별한 의미를 지녔다. 포니는 가족의 생계 수단이자 집안
대소사를 함께하는 동반자였으며, 가족이나 연인 등 사랑하
는 사람과 함께 떠나는 여행길의 파트너였다. 그런 의미에서
1980년대를 배경으로 한 영화와 드라마에 포니가 시대적 상
징으로서 향수 가득한 추억의 아이템으로 등장하는 것은 어
찌 보면 당연한 일이라 할 수 있다.

choose homes or workplaces without worrying
much about commuting distances or public
transportation. Car ownership also meant access
to a vehicle for multiple purposes. For instance,
the Pony Pickup was used for deliveries or as a
personal courier during the week and for outings
on weekends. The popularization of cars through
the Pony led to a societal notion where owning
a car became almost a prerequisite for being
considered middle class. Taking a family photo
in front of one's first car became a social custom
for households purchasing their first vehicle.

　For the generation of people who played
a central role in driving social and economic
activities in Korea during the 1970s and 80s,
the Pony held a special place as their very first
family car. To this generation of consumers, the
Pony was not only an effective means to make
a living but also a companion that served them
through important family events and travels
with their loved ones. It is natural for the Pony to
appear in movies and dramas set in the 1980s as
a nostalgic symbol, evoking fond memories of
that era.

포니 앞에서 촬영한 가족사진
Family photographs taken with Pony

자동차가 급속히 보급되던 1970~1980년대 생애 첫 차를 구매한 가정에서 차와 함께
가족사진을 찍는 것이 유행했다.

As automobiles began to be widely used in the 70s and 80s,
taking family photographs with their first car became a trend.

가족 여행의 동반자였던 포니
The Pony, a companion for family trips

평일에는 생계용으로, 주말에는 레저용으로 활용된 포니 픽업
The Pony Pickup, used for work during the week and leisure on weekends.

가변형 적재함 덮개를 장착한 포니2 픽업 컨버터블 탑
The Pony2 Pickup with a convertible top for the cargo bed

400kg의 적재 용량을 갖춘 화물용 차로 각광받았다.
This model gained popularity as a cargo vehicle with a loading
capacity of 400kg.

넉넉한 트렁크 공간으로 각광받은 포니 왜건
The Pony Wagon, which featured ample trunk space

레저 용으로도 활용된 포니 왜건
The Pony Wagon, utilized also for leisure activities

또 다른 길로 이어지는 길

포니는 한국인의 일상뿐 아니라 대한민국 자동차 산업에도 큰 영향을 미쳤다. 부품 국산화로 자동차 부품 산업의 성장·발전을 견인하고, 꾸준한 수출 물량 확대로 자동차 산업이 대한민국 수출 산업의 핵심으로 자리 잡는 데 기여했다.

자동차 산업에서 완성차업계와 자동차 부품업계는 상호 보완적 동반자 관계로, 국산차 포니의 양산은 자동차 산업 불모지에서 대한민국 자동차 부품 공업 발전의 초석이 되었다. 포니를 통해 달성한 높은 부품 국산화율과 이후에도 지속된 현대자동차의 부품 국산화에 대한 집요한 노력은 국내 자동차 부품 산업의 양적 확대와 질적 성장으로 이어졌다. 또한 포니를 통해 개척한 전 세계의 수출길은 포니 이후 쏘나타, 엑센트, 싼타페 등 다양한 신규 라인업을 수출하는 기반이 되었다. 오늘날 자동차 산업은 수출 주도형 국가로 성장한 대한민국의 핵심 수출 산업으로 자리매김해 2021년 대한민국 10대 수출 품목 중 자동차와 자동차 부품이 각각 2위와 6위를 차지했다.[16]

특기할 만한 점은 현대자동차가 글로벌 브랜드로 성장하고 수출 물량이 증대되면서 국내 자동차 부품업계의 수출 물량 역시 대폭 늘었을뿐더러 현대자동차의 해외 생산 기지 설립에 맞춰 국내 부품업체가 해외에 동반 진출하는 경우도 크게 증가했다는 사실이다. 1997년 34개 사에 불과하던 해외 동반 진출 1·2차 협력사가 2020년에는 748개 사로 20배 이상 증가했을 정도다.[17] 이 같은 현대자동차의 해외 동반 진출 노력은 국내 부품업체가 글로벌 기업으로 성장하는 데도 한몫을 담당했다.

이처럼 포니는 현대자동차가 오늘날 세계 자동차 시장에서 남다른 위상을 차지하게 된 시작점이었다. 세계 자동차 산업사에서 후발 주자인 개발도상국이 대량 양산형 고유 모델을 개발한 사례는 찾아보기 어려울 정도로 대단한 일이었

Paving new paths

The Pony not only reshaped the daily lives of general consumers in Korea but also had a significant impact on the country's automotive industry. It led to the growth and development of the auto parts industry through the localization of components and contributed to making the automotive industry a key part of Korea's export sector through consistent expansion of export volumes.

Given that automakers and auto parts manufacturers are close partners within the automotive industry ecosystem, the mass domestic production of the Pony laid the foundation for the development of South Korea's auto parts industry in what was almost non-existant at the time. Even after achieving a high localization rate of auto parts, Hyundai maintained its razor focus on enhancing domestic production of components — contributing to the growth of the auto parts sector both in quality and quantity. Moreover, the export paths pioneered through the Pony became the basis for exporting a variety of new lineups such as the Accent and Santa Fe. Today, the automotive industry is a core export industry for South Korea, which has grown into an export-driven country, with automobiles and auto parts ranking second and sixth, respectively, among South Korea's top 10 export items in 2021.[16]

Notably, as Hyundai became a global brand and saw an increase in export volumes, the export volumes of the domestic auto parts industry also significantly increased. Furthermore, the establishment of Hyundai's overseas production bases led to a substantial increase in domestic parts

다. 게다가 포니는 산업적 기반이 약한 불모의 환경에서 한 자동차 회사가 설립된 지 10년도 안 되는 기간에 양산한 고유 모델이었다. 그러나 현대자동차는 이 같은 저력을 바탕으로 지속적 연구 개발과 시장 확대를 추진했고, 자동차 산업의 후발 주자에서 추격자를 거쳐 마침내 선도 기업으로 자리매김했다. 현대자동차그룹이 2022년 전 세계에 684만 대의 완성차를 판매함으로써 자동차업계 글로벌 판매 순위 3위 기업으로 발돋움[18]한 것은 이러한 성장에 대한 공식적 입증이라 할 수 있다. 화석연료 시대 인류 최고의 발명품 중 하나이자 국가 산업 발전과 기술력의 상징인 자동차 산업을 선도하는 기업으로 우뚝 선 것이다.

　　이 같은 결과가 내연기관 시대의 정점이자 종말을 눈앞에 둔 시점에 이루어졌다는 것은 남다른 의미가 있다. 포니에서 비롯된 현대자동차의 도전적 여정은 빈약한 물리적 토대에서 시작된 약자의 도전이 그 시대의 정점에서 놀라운 결실을 본 감동적 사건이기 때문이다. 이는 전혀 다른 시대의 문이 열리는 분기점에서 현대자동차가 이제 새 시대를 선도하는

companies expanding abroad alongside Hyundai. From only 34 companies in 1997, the number of first and second-tier suppliers participating in overseas expansion increased to 748 companies by 2020, recording a remarkable 20-fold increase.[17] Hyundai's efforts in overseas co-expansion also played a role in helping domestic parts companies grow into global enterprises.

　　As illustrated, the Pony served as the starting point for Hyundai to gain the prestige it now holds in the global automotive market. Throughout its history, the global automotive industry has rarely seen a company from a developing country that developed its own mass-production model. What is even more impressive about the Pony is that it was launched less than 10 years after the company was founded in a country with barely any industrial infrastructure. Instead of staying complacent with this achievement, Hyundai continued its research and development to expand its market, suc-

"우리에게는 세계 제일의 무기가 있는데, 그 무기란 바로 '세계에서 가장 우수한 기능공'들이다. 이 훌륭하고 우수한 이들의 능력과 헌신에 힘입어 머지않아 한국의 자동차, 우리의 자동차 부품이 세계시장을 휩쓰는 날이 온다고 나는 확신한다."

"We had, and still have, the most powerful weapon in the world: the most tenacious and resilient workers. Thanks to the outstanding workers and their dedication, I am confident that Korean cars and auto parts will dominate the world one day."

정주영 선대회장 Founding Chairman Ju-yung Chung

기업으로서 새로운 위치에 서게 됐음을 의미한다. 잘사는 나라에 대한 열망, 한국인의 잠재성에 대한 창업주의 믿음에 기초해 세상에 출현한 포니의 여정은 한국인이라면 누구나 기억하는 역사가 되었고, 현대자동차가 글로벌 기업으로 발돋움할 수 있게 한 원동력이 되었다. 문명 대변혁의 출발선에 선 지금, 포니의 유산은 현대자동차의 정신에 깃들어 인류의 진보를 위한 새 신화를 써 내려갈 준비를 하고 있다.

cessfully evolving from a late starter into a fast follower and eventually a leader. The fact that Hyundai Motor Group sold 6.84 million vehicles worldwide in 2022, becoming the third-largest company in global car sales, officially proves the company's rapid growth.[18] It has risen to become a leading company in the automotive industry — one of the greatest inventions of the fossil fuel era and a symbol of national industrial development and technological prowess.

The fact that this result was achieved at the pinnacle and the end of the internal combustion engine era holds special significance. It encapsulates the significance of Hyundai's ambitious journey — the late starter that began its journey without any proper foundation has remarkably come out on top at the peak of an era. This positions Hyundai to lead an entirely new era that is about to begin. The Pony's journey started with Korea's national aspiration for economic growth and the Founding Chairman's faith in the potential of the Korean people. This journey has now become a history that every Korean remembers, that catapulted Hyundai onto the global stage. As a revolutionary shift in civilization is underway, the legacy of the Pony, instilled in Hyundai's DNA, is preparing the company for yet another chapter in the progress of humanity.

새로운 이정표
앞에 서다

Standing at the
forefront of a
new milestone

대한민국 길에 대한 새 역사를 써온
현대자동차는 오늘날 스마트 모빌리티
기업으로서 '인류를 위한 진보'를 거듭하며
미래의 길을 새롭게 개척해 나가고 있다.
그 여정에서 포니는 현대자동차의 원형으로서
자기다움의 기준과 함께 창의적 영감을
제공하고 있다.

Having written the modern history
of Korea's road and automotive
industry, Hyundai is now pioneering
a new path for humanity with smart
mobility solutions.
And on this path, the Pony stands
as a significant symbol of Hyundai's
origin story — setting the standards
for the brand's identity while
continuously providing the creative
inspiration needed to bring new and
innovative solutions to the world.

포니는 멈추지 않는다: 포니의 계승자들

The immortal Pony: the Pony's successors

포니가 달려온 시대는 화석연료를 통한 현대 문명의 양적 성장이 정점을 이루던 시기이자 개발도상국이던 대한민국이 산업화를 통해 국가 경제의 토대를 마련하기 위해 전력을 다하던 때다. 이 시대를 달린 포니는 대한민국 역사에서 자신의 역할을 충실히 완수했다.

　　포니 출시를 기점으로 자동차 산업은 한국의 경제성장을 주도하는 주요 굴뚝 산업이 되었고, 자동차를 '달리는 국기'라고 지칭한 창업주의 생각처럼 자동차 산업은 대한민국의 대표적 수출 산업으로 성장했다. 그리고 자동차 산업 강국이 된 대한민국은 현재 선진국 대열에 합류했다.

The Pony was a car for a different era, as it was a period in which extensive growth premised on fossil fuels had peaked, and South Korea - a developing country at the time - was single-mindedly seeking to create a strong economic base through industrialization. The Pony faithfully fulfilled its purpose in this period of South Korean history.

　　The Pony's release led to the car industry becoming a key motor of growth in Korea's economy. The founder of Hyundai thought of cars as a symbol of the nation like the national flag, and his vision helped to grow the automotive sector into one of the country's principal export industries. South Korea has become a car manufacturing powerhouse and joined the ranks of the world's developed nations.

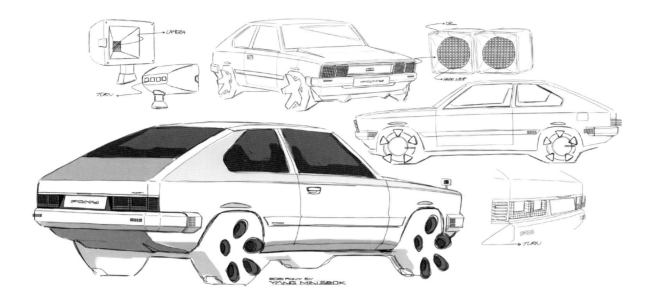

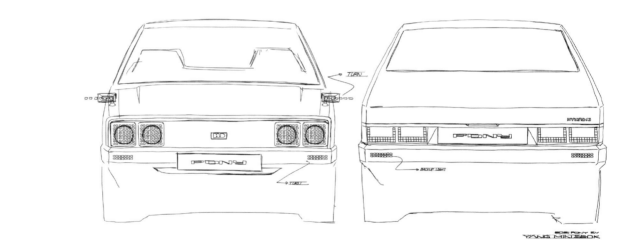

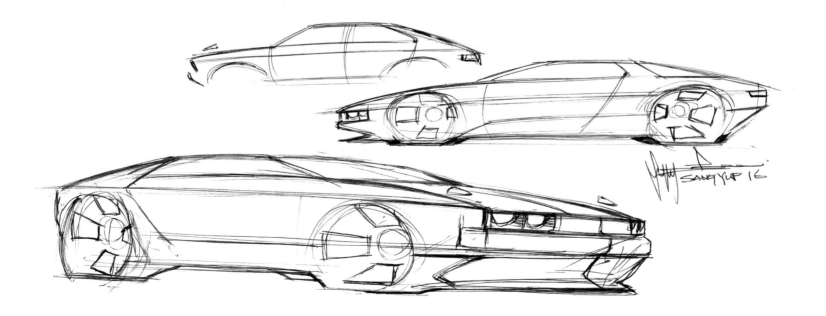

그러나 역사는 늘 새로운 도전을 요구한다. 고도의 지능형 정보 네트워크 기술 발달과 기후 재난으로 상징되는 현재의 지구촌은 문명의 진화와 인류의 생존이라는 두 가지 도전에 직면해 있다. 이 도전적 환경 변화는 인류로 하여금 화석연료 시대의 종말이 임박했음을 강력하게 환기하고 있는데, 이는 자동차 산업에 있어서는 내연기관 시대에서 전동화 시대로 전환하는 것을 뜻한다.

20세기에 꽃피웠던 자동차 기업들이 전동화 기업으로 탈바꿈하는 데 사활을 걸고 있으며, 이에 따라 글로벌 자동차 업계는 지각변동이 일어날 수밖에 없다. 이러한 변화 속에서 현대자동차는 지속 가능한 스마트 모빌리티 분야로 업을 확장하면서도 자기다움을 공고히 하려는 노력을 지속하고 있다. 내연기관차와 전혀 다른 장르인 전기차의 디자인 방향성을 수립하는 데 포니에서 영감을 얻은 것이 그 예다.

포니는 과거 불모지나 다름없는 산업 환경 속에서 독자적 디자인을 만든 한국 자동차 산업사 최초의 시도인 동시에, 지속 가능한 미래를 지향하는 오늘날의 현대자동차처럼 더 나은 내일을 꿈꾼 창업주의 염원이 깃든 현대자동차의 원형(originality)이기 때문이다. 전동화 전환기에 포니의 디자인적 유산을 계승함으로써 다시 한번 자기다움을 다지고 있는 대표적 전동화 모델을 소개한다.

But history always poses fresh challenges. The development of advanced intelligent information networks and climate disasters symbolize the global village we live in today, which faces the twin challenges of civilization-level progress and the very survival of humanity. These challenges mean the fossil fuel era is drawing to a close. In the car industry, they have augured a transition from the internal combustion engine to the electric car.

The tectonic plates of the industry are unavoidably shifting. Today, the automotive giants of the twentieth century are facing the existential challenge of reinventing themselves as electric car manufacturers. The entire industry is undergoing a seismic. Against this backdrop, Hyundai has made strides in both sustainable and smart mobility, while also striving to maintain its distinctive position. As electric cars differ significantly from internal combustion engine-powered cars, Hyundai has drawn inspiration from the Pony's design to guide its direction in this rapidly evolving field.

The Pony had a unique design. It was the first South Korean car developed by a South Korean company, emerging from a barren and forbidding industrial environment. It exemplified the originality of the Hyundai Motor Company, a firm imbued with the hopes of the Founding Chairman dreaming of a better tomorrow. Today Hyundai still seeks to build a sustainable future. As is it transitions to electric cars, Hyundai is taking inspiration from the Pony, introducing its distinctive features through its major electric cars.

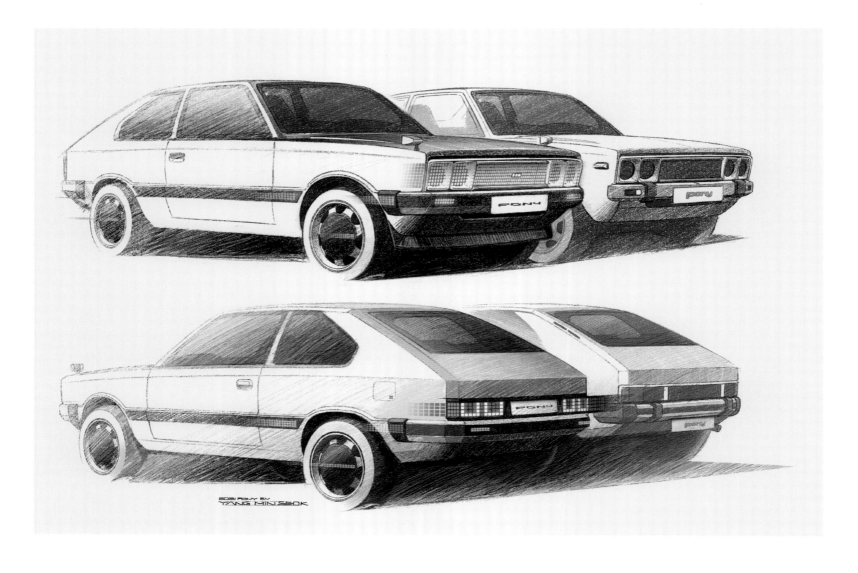

포니를 오마주한 헤리티지 시리즈 포니의 스케치
Sketches for the Heritage Series Pony,
a homage to the Pony

헤리티지 시리즈 포니

현대자동차는 미래 디자인에 대한 영감을 얻기 위해 자사의 과거 모델을 전동화 시대 모델로 재해석하는 '헤리티지 시리즈' 프로젝트를 진행하고 있다. 이 프로젝트의 첫 번째 산물인 '헤리티지 시리즈 포니'는 오리지널 포니를 오마주한 모델로 파나마에서 공수한 포니 3도어 모델을 분해해 오리지널 모델 고유의 클래식한 외관에 전기차에 적용할 여러 가지 신기술과 디자인 요소를 추가하고 다시 조립하는 과정을 거쳐 과거와 미래가 공존하는 특별한 자동차를 탄생시켰다.

　헤드라이트와 리어 램프는 기존 포니의 각진 사각 램프 형상을 유지하되 1970년대와 1980년대의 8비트 픽셀 그래픽을 오마주한 '파라메트릭 픽셀(parametric pixels)'을 적용했다. 이미지를 구성하는 최소 단위인 픽셀을 디지털 시대의 핵심 디자인 요소로 활용함으로써 아날로그와 디지털 세대를 관통한다는 의미를 담았다. 이와 더불어 1970년도에 주로 사용한 닉시 튜브(Nixie Tube, 진공관) 스타일의 계기판을 적용해 포니가 출시되었을 당시의 감성을 더했으며, 오리

Heritage Series Pony

To inspire the car designs of the future, Hyundai is creating the 'Heritage Series': reimagining its legacy models as vehicles for the electric car age. The first will be the Heritage Series Pony, a homage to the Original Pony. A Pony 3-door had to be brought to South Korea from Panama and was then taken apart. A wide range of new technologies and design features were added to the classic exterior. Then the car was put back together, creating a novel design with both the past and future living within it.

　The pointed rectangular appearance of the headlights and rear lamps of the Pony was kept. As a homage to the 8-bit pixel graphics of the 1970s and 1980s, parametric pixels were used. Since it was the most fundamental component of the car's image and a core design element of the digital era, it bridged the analog and digital eras. The Nixie Tube-style dashboard, widely used in 1970, was installed to further accentuate

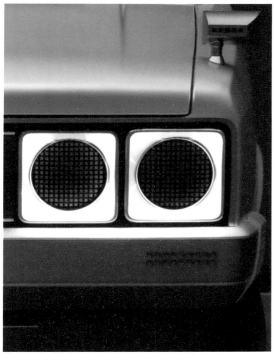

헤리티지 시리즈 포니의 리어 및 헤드램프
The Heritage Series Pony's rear and headlamp

지널 포니의 각진 차체 형상을 그대로 유지함으로써 고전적 감성을 살렸다.

첨단 사양 또한 과거의 형태에 미래 기술을 접목하는 방식으로 구현했다. 오리지널 포니의 3-스포크 스티어링 휠 형상을 유지하되 AI 음성 인식 기능을 적용했고, 기어봉이 있던 자리에는 기어 패널만 남겨두되 스마트폰에서 패턴을 입력하는 것처럼 터치스크린 방식으로 기어를 조작할 수 있도록 했다. 이 차에 깃든 스마트한 라이프스타일도 주목할 만하다. 트렁크에는 오리지널 포니에 있던 스페어타이어 대신 차내에서도 충전 가능한 '초소형 전동 스쿠터'를 탑재했다. 차량이 갈 수 없는 곳에서도 이동 경험을 제공하는 스마트 모빌리티 솔루션 디바이스로, 차에서 내려 최종 목적지에 이르는 짧은 거리의 이동 경험까지 섬세하게 배려하는 현대자동차의 인간 중심적 철학을 반영한 것이다.

the feel of that era, and the square chassis preserved that classic feel.

The technology of the future was integrated with the style of the past. The original 3-spoke steering wheel design was kept, but AI voice-recognition functionality added. A touchscreen gear selector panel that functions similarly to the pattern input on a smartphone has been integrated into the console where the traditional gear stick was located. The smart-lifestyle features of the car are also noteworthy. Instead of the spare tire found in the original Pony, a compact electric scooter that can be charged from the car has been installed in the trunk. This smart mobility solution device provides a seamless travel experience even in places where the car cannot go, reflecting Hyundai's human-centered philosophy that considers last mile mobility after getting off the car.

과거와 미래가 공존하는 헤리티지 시리즈 프로젝트의 첫 번째 모델, 포니
The first model in the Heritage Series, the Pony, which brings
together the past and future

아이오닉 5

아이오닉 5는 현대자동차 최초의 전기차 전용 라인업 '아이오닉'의 첫 번째 모델이다. '아이오닉(IONIQ)'은 전기적 힘의 결합과 분리로 새로운 에너지를 만드는 '이온(ion)'과 현대자동차의 독창성을 뜻하는 '유니크(unique)'를 조합한 말로, 전동화 모빌리티를 통해 고객에게 새로운 이동 경험을 제공하겠다는 의지가 내포되어 있다.

전기차 전용 라인업 아이오닉의 첫 번째 모델인 아이오닉 5의 디자인은 현대자동차 최초의 고유 모델 포니에서 영감을 받아 개발되었다. 이는 대중에게 더 나은 일상을 선사한 첫 국민차이자 대한민국 자동차 산업의 성장을 이끈 혁신의 아이콘인 포니를 오마주함으로써 전동화 시대에도 포니의 휴머니티와 혁신적 DNA를 변하지 않는 가치로 간직하고자 했기 때문이다.

이처럼 아이오닉 5는 과거에서 영감을 받아 만든 미래 자동차로, 특정 시대를 초월하는 영속성을 지닌 순수하고 정제된 디자인을 적용했다. 아이오닉은 아날로그와 디지털을

IONIQ 5

The IONIQ 5 is the first model of Hyundai's electric vehicle-exclusive lineup, IONIQ. The name IONIQ combines 'Ion' which makes electricity and 'unique', symbolizing the uniqueness of Hyundai. The name represents Hyundai's determination to give its customers a new travelling experience through electrified mobility.

The IONIQ 5's design was inspired by the Pony, which was Hyundai's first original model. The Pony was presented to the public as a car for the nation that would make people's lives better. It became the motor of growth for South Korea's car industry, and an icon of innovation. The IONIQ 5 is a homage to this, lovingly reinterpreting the humanity and unfailingly innovative DNA of the Pony for the electric era.

The IONIQ 5 was designed for the future yet drew inspiration from the past, transcending any particular era - a design with permanence, pureness and refinement. The IONIQ 5 fuses

오리지널 포니에서 영감을 받은 아이오닉 5 스케치
A sketch for IONIQ 5, inspired by the original Pony

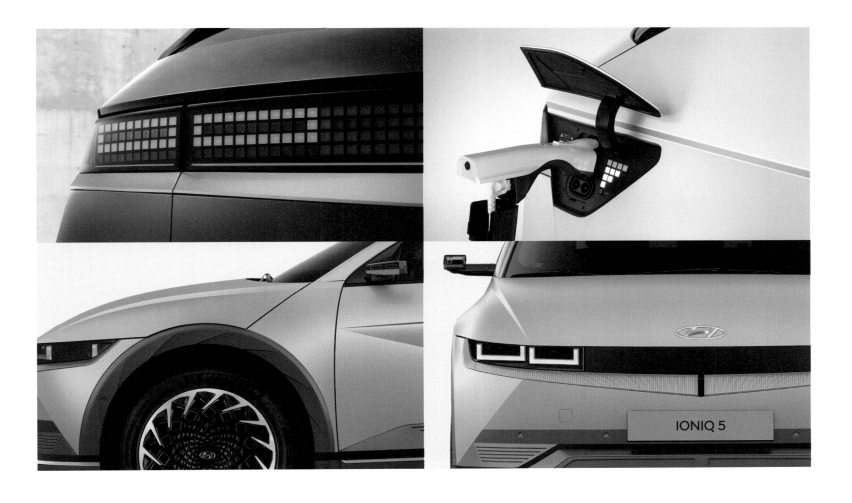

파라메트릭 픽셀을 적용한 아이오닉 5
Parametric pixels applied in the IONIQ 5

융합해 탄생한 파라메트릭 픽셀 형상을 헤드램프와 테일 램프, 그리고 휠과 충전구 등에 적용해 과거와 미래가 공존하는 창의적 타임리스 디자인의 전형을 담고 있다. 또 포니의 조형미와 기하학적 선을 계승해 간결하면서도 강인한 실루엣과 캐릭터 라인을 구현했다.

나아가 아이오닉 5는 현대자동차의 전기차 전용 플랫폼 E-GMP를 적용해 여유롭고 쾌적한 실내 공간을 확보했고, 차량 안팎에서 전자 기기를 사용할 수 있는 V2L 기능과 초급속 충전 시스템 같은 첨단 편의 사양을 적용, 그동안 이동 수단에 한정되어 있던 자동차의 개념을 일상의 생활 공간으로 확장했다. 이처럼 전기차로서 새로운 이동 경험을 제공한 아이오닉 5는 2022년 '세계 올해의 자동차'로 선정되는 등 글로벌 시장에서 호평받으며 다가올 전동화 시대에 현대자동차의 밝은 미래와 가능성을 제시했다.

the analogue and digital, with parametric pixels in the headlamps, tail lamps, steering and the recharging slot. This is the coexistence of past and future in the epitome of timeless creative design. The IONIQ 5 inherits the Pony's sculpted aesthetic and geometric lines to cast a crisp but strong silhouette imbued with character.

What is more, the IONIQ 5 creates a spacious and comfortable interior with E-GMP, Hyundai's EV-dedicated platform. The V2L function makes it easy to use electrical devices inside and outside the vehicle. And cutting-edge capabilities like the ultra-rapid recharging system expand the car's role in daily life beyond merely a means of getting around. The IONIQ 5, and the new travelling experience it provides, has received sterling reviews, being named the 'Global Car of the Year 2022'. It represents Hyundai's bright future and all the possibilities of the coming electric automotive era.

N 비전 74

고성능은 자동차 제조사가 표현할 수 있는 감성의 정점을 보여준다. 최첨단 기술과 매혹적인 디자인, 운전할 때의 짜릿한 즐거움은 자동차의 가장 감성적 영역이라고 할 수 있다. 고성능 자동차는 늘 동시대에 가장 앞선 기술을 선보여 왔으며, 이를 통해 사람들은 미래의 자동차에 대한 꿈을 꾼다. 그렇다면 전동화 시대의 고성능 자동차는 어떤 모습일까?

'N 비전 74'는 전동화 시대 고성능 자동차에 대한 비전을 보여주는 모델로 N브랜드 최초의 수소-전기 하이브리드 롤링 랩(Rolling Lab) *이다. 전동화 시대를 넘어 더 먼 미래에도 '운전의 재미'를 제공하려는 목적으로 개발되었다. 현대자동차는 2015년 고성능 N브랜드를 론칭할 당시 고성능 수소 콘셉트 카 '현대 N 2025 비전 그란투리스모'를 공개하면서 N브랜드의 지속 가능한 미래 방향성을 제시했다. 당시 상상 속 기술이던 고성능 수소 기술을 현실화하기 위해 현대자동차 연구진은 무려 7년 동안 고뇌했다. 고성능 수소 기술을 통해 운전의 재미를 지속 가능한 형태로 계승함으로써 소비

N Vision 74

Seductive design, cutting-edge technology, and exhilarating driving experiences define the characteristics of 'high performance', the highest form of emotional expression an automaker can make through an automobile. Representing cutting-edge technology of the time, high performance cars are often portrayed as objects of desire and elicit dreams about the future ahead. As the internal combustion era draws to a close, what else is out there that we can dream about in the future?

The N Vision 74 demonstrates Hyundai N's high-performance vision and to inspire a new generation of car enthusiasts. N Vision 74 is N brand's first hydrogen-electric hybrid rolling lab*, developed to expand our perception and anticipate a future beyond the EV era. It represents Hyundai N's determination to continue our passion for 'fun to drive' well into the future.

When Hyundai launched the high-per-

포니 쿠페에서 영감을 받은 N 비전 74
The N Vision 74, inspired by the Pony Coupe

*
롤링 랩(Rolling Lab): 모터스포츠를 위해 개발한 고성능 기술을 양산 모델에 적용하기에 앞서 연구 개발 및 검증하는 차량으로 '움직이는 연구소'라는 뜻이다.
Rolling Lab: A 'Rolling laboratory', i.e., a test car, used to research, develop and test high performance technologies from motorsport before these technologies are introduced into mass-production models.

N 비전 74의 측면
The N Vision 74's side profile

자, 팬들과의 약속을 지키고 꿈을 실현하려는 N브랜드의 정신을 보여준 것이다.

롤링 랩이라는 이름에 걸맞게 현대자동차의 미래 기술과 디자인 비전이 총망라된 N 비전 74는 내연기관 시대의 종말을 앞둔 시점에서 지속 가능한 모빌리티의 최고 성능을 엿볼 수 있는 모델이다. N 비전 74의 가장 주목할 만한 점은 이 차가 현대자동차 N브랜드 최초의 수소-전기 하이브리드 자동차라는 것이다. 이 차의 전면에는 85kW 수소 연료전지 스택이 자리하며, 운전자와 조수석 사이에는 62kWh 리튬이온 배터리, 후면에는 2.1kg 용량의 수소 탱크 2개가 장착되어 있다. 후륜에 장착된 좌우 독립형 듀얼 모터는 680마력의 출력으로 정지 상태에서 시속 100km까지 4초 이하의 가속 성능을 자랑하며, 주행거리는 600km에 육박한다.

현대자동차는 지속 가능한 고성능 차의 동력원으로 내연기관에서 완전히 벗어난 수소 연료전지 개념을 연구해 왔으며, N 비전 74는 수소-전기 하이브리드 기술을 통해 전기차의 기술적 한계를 극복했다. 전기차의 최대 출력은 주행 중

formance N brand in 2015, sharing the stage was the Hyundai N2025 Vision Gran Turismo, a high-performance hydrogen fuel cell concept car — representing the sustainable future direction of the brand a decade forward. Hyundai engineers sought to bring the high-performance hydrogen technology from pure imagination into reality. Nobody could have anticipated it would take 7 years, but Hyundai N was determined for it to become a fully functioning rolling lab and keep its promise made to its fans.

In keeping with the Rolling Lab, the N Vision 74 represents the pinnacle of Hyundai's future technologies and design vision. It represents the apex of sustainable mobility as we look toward the end of the internal combustion era. The N Vision 74 is most noteworthy for featuring a unique hydrogen-electric fuel cell hybrid technology. This advanced system features a hydrogen fuel cell with a capacity of 85kW in the front, and a 62kWh lithium-ion battery in-

배터리 충전량이 줄어들면서 일부 감소하는데, N 비전 74는 이러한 약점을 보완하고자 수소 스택과 전기 배터리를 직렬 배치했으며, 수소가 소진되지 않는 한 배터리는 상시 100% 충전 상태를 유지한다. 따라서 N 비전 74는 모터스포츠 상황에서 출력 680마력을 드라이버에게 안정적으로 전달할 수 있으며, 내연기관차의 주유 시간과 큰 차이가 없는 짧은 충전 시간을 자랑한다.

이렇듯 현대자동차가 보유한 최첨단 고성능 수소 기술과 N브랜드의 모터스포츠 감성을 모두 아우르는 롤링 랩은 어떤 모습이어야 할까? 현대자동차 디자이너들은 미래의 고성능 차 디자인에 대한 해답을 대담하고 진보적인 디자인 아이콘에서 찾았다. 'Envision 1974'라는 의미를 담은 이름에서도 엿볼 수 있듯이, N 비전 74의 디자인은 1974년 토리노 모터쇼에서 처음 공개한 포니 쿠페가 원형이다. N 비전 74는 과거 포니 쿠페가 이루지 못한 꿈에 대한 헌정인 셈이다.

N 비전 74의 전면부는 기존 포니 쿠페의 네모난 헤드램프를 현대자동차만의 전기차 전용 디자인인 파라메트릭 픽

stalled between the driver and passenger seat, while two 2.1kg hydrogen tanks are installed in the rear. The dual motor setup dedicates each motor to the left and right wheels generating a total of 500kW (680 PS). This enables an impressive acceleration from 0 to 100 kph in less than four seconds, and can cover almost 600 km.

The objective for N Vision 74's unique hydrogen-electric fuel cell hybrid technology is to overcome the technical limitations of electric cars. Despite the popularity of EVs, its key limitation is the drop in output power as the battery charge lowers. The N Vision 74 is designed to specifically overcome this limitation with power generated from the hydrogen fuel cells maintaining the battery's charge at 100% at all times. Thus, the N Vision 74 can consistently produce a stable 500 kW (680 PS) for the driver which is particularly critical in motorsport's high-pressure environment. It also boasts a hydrogen recharge time similar to a regular refuel of gasoline.

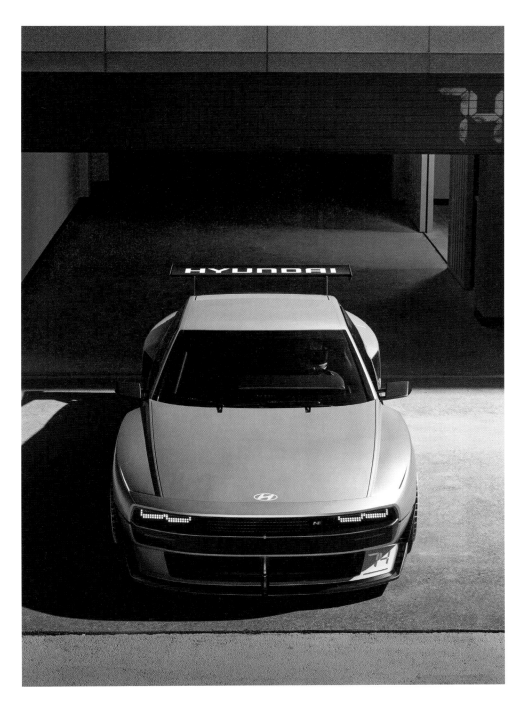

N 비전 74의 전면
The N Vision 74's front profile

셀로 재해석해 미래지향적으로 디자인했으며, 노란색 주간 주행등은 과거 포니를 연상시키는 동시에 모터스포츠에서 경쟁하는 GT 레이싱 머신들의 모습을 떠올리게 한다. 또한 길고 날렵한 N 비전 74의 몸체는 쐐기 모양의 길쭉한 앞머리에 뒤쪽으로 낮은 루프 라인을 지닌 포니 쿠페의 외관을 고스란히 물려받았다.

이처럼 N 비전 74는 포니 쿠페를 공개하던 당시 후발 주자였던 현대자동차가 새로운 길을 개척해 오면서 독자 기술을 개발하고, 그 결과 오늘날 수소 연료전지라는 선진적 기술을 보유한 회사가 되어 미래 비전과 기술을 이끌고 있음을

How should such a cutting-edge rolling lab with Hyundai's most advanced hydrogen fuel cell technology and the N brand's motorsports experience look like? Hyundai designers have found the answer in the most audacious and progressive design icon from Hyundai's heritage. The name N Vision 74 originates from 'Envision 1974', indicating its primary inspiration from the Pony Coupe, first unveiled at the 1974 Torino Motor Show. The N Vision 74 is a tribute to the unrealized dream of the iconic Pony Coupe.

The front of the N Vision 74 reimagines the Pony Coupe's square headlights with the parametric pixels used exclusively in electric-only Hyundai vehicle designs, recreating the original's futuristic design. The yellow-colored daytime running lights evoke the Pony and also references the GT class racing machines competing in motorsport. With a long and fast body line, the N Vision 74 features the distinctive, long wedge-shaped front with a backend that

보여주는 모델이다. 또 1974년 포니 쿠페에 담긴 대담한 꿈이 미래에도 지속되고, 현대자동차만의 독창적 방식으로 미래의 변화를 예견하고, 준비하며, 실행하고 있다는 것을 말해 준다. 2022년 공개하자마자 전 세계 자동차 매체와 전문가들에게 큰 주목을 받은 N 비전 74는 머지않아 이와 같은 자동차를 도로 위에서 만날 수도 있다는 기대감을 갖게 하는 진정한 미래 자동차로 평가되고 있다.

calls to mind the Pony Coupe's low roof line.

While the Pony Coupe was unveiled at a time when Hyundai was beginning as a startup, it inspired onlookers to imagine a future where Hyundai had advanced well ahead in the future. That legacy is still evident in Hyundai at present, developing the most advanced hydrogen fuel cell and pushing the technological frontier. The N Vision 74 is evidence that the progressive spirit of the original dreamers behind the Pony Coupe continues to inspire Hyundai's future direction. Anticipating and preparing for the future in the most uniquely Hyundai way possible. First revealed in 2022, the N Vision 74 was an immediate hit within the global automotive media, with many excited to imagine a future where one might be able to encounter one on the road.

고성능 N브랜드의 롤링 랩 RN22e와 N 비전 74의 주행 샷
Driving shot of the RN22e and N Vision 74,
the high-performance N brand Rolling Labs

대담하고 진보적인 디자인을 선보였던 포니 쿠페(왼쪽)와 이를
오마주한 N 비전 74(오른쪽)
The N Vision 74 (right), which was inspired by the Pony
Coupe (left) with audacious and progressive design

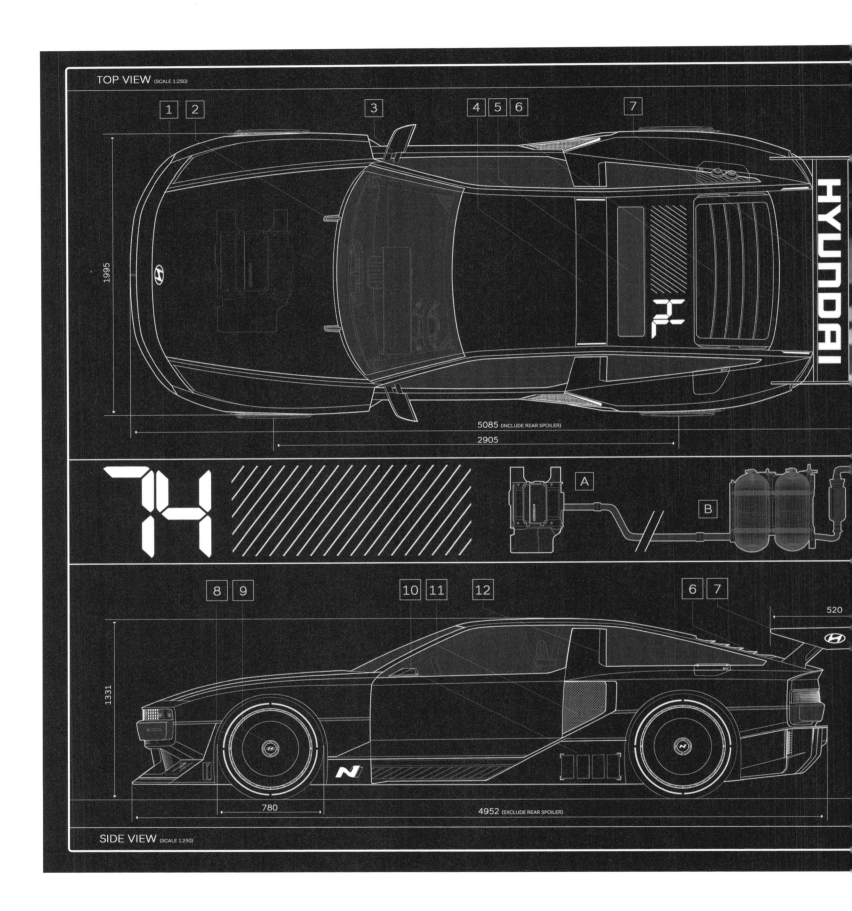

TOP VIEW (SCALE 1:250)

1 2   3   4 5 6   7

HYUNDAI

1995

5085 (INCLUDE REAR SPOILER)

2905

74

A

B

8 9   10 11 12   6 7

520

1331

780   4952 (EXCLUDE REAR SPOILER)

SIDE VIEW (SCALE 1:250)

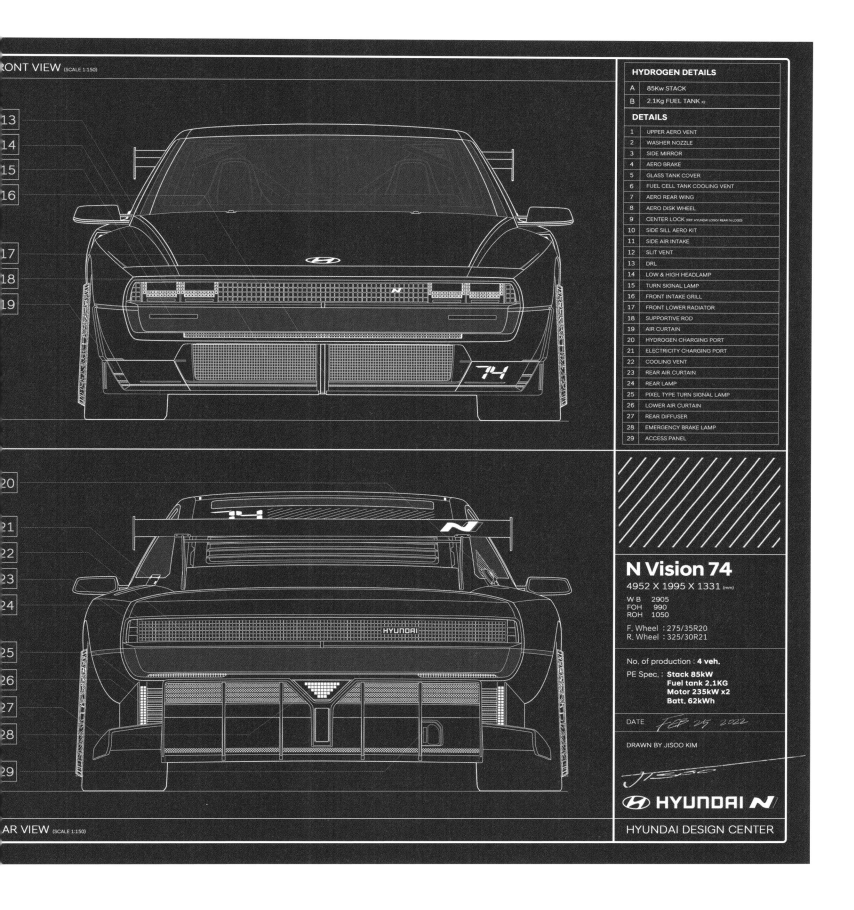

FRONT VIEW (SCALE 1:150)

REAR VIEW (SCALE 1:150)

HYDROGEN DETAILS

| A | 85Kw STACK |
| B | 2.1Kg FUEL TANK x2 |

DETAILS

1	UPPER AERO VENT
2	WASHER NOZZLE
3	SIDE MIRROR
4	AERO BRAKE
5	GLASS TANK COVER
6	FUEL CELL TANK COOLING VENT
7	AERO REAR WING
8	AERO DISK WHEEL
9	CENTER LOCK (FRT. HYUNDAI LOGO/ REAR. N LOGO)
10	SIDE SILL AERO KIT
11	SIDE AIR INTAKE
12	SLIT VENT
13	DRL
14	LOW & HIGH HEADLAMP
15	TURN SIGNAL LAMP
16	FRONT INTAKE GRILL
17	FRONT LOWER RADIATOR
18	SUPPORTIVE ROD
19	AIR CURTAIN
20	HYDROGEN CHARGING PORT
21	ELECTRICITY CHARGING PORT
22	COOLING VENT
23	REAR AIR CURTAIN
24	REAR LAMP
25	PIXEL TYPE TURN SIGNAL LAMP
26	LOWER AIR CURTAIN
27	REAR DIFFUSER
28	EMERGENCY BRAKE LAMP
29	ACCESS PANEL

N Vision 74

4952 X 1995 X 1331 (mm)

W B   2905
FOH   990
ROH   1050

F. Wheel : 275/35R20
R. Wheel : 325/30R21

No. of production : **4 veh.**

PE Spec. : **Stack 85kW**
           Fuel tank 2,1KG
           Motor 235kW x2
           Batt. 62kWh

DATE   FEB. 25. 2022

DRAWN BY JISOO KIM

HYUNDAI N

HYUNDAI DESIGN CENTER

길 너머를 향한 대항해

Beyond the road toward a great journey

길의 역사를 써온 현대자동차는 이제 '길'에 대한 관점을 획기적으로 바꾸고 '이동'에 대한 개념을 확장함으로써 미래의 삶과 풍경을 새롭게 그려나가는 대항해를 준비하고 있다. 과거 '포니'와 같은 독자 모델을 통해 더 잘사는 나라를 만들고 국민의 행복한 삶에 기여하겠다는 창업주의 사회적 책임감과 기업가적 포부가 이제는 '인류를 위한 진보'라는 다음 세대를 향한 현대자동차의 더 큰 비전으로 확대되고 있는 것이다.

현대자동차는 모든 사람에게 제한 없는 이동의 자유를 제공하기 위해 '스마트 모빌리티 솔루션' 기업으로 거듭나고자 한다. 자동차 회사로서 전동화, 자율주행 등 미래 핵심 역량을 확보하는 것을 넘어 미래 항공 모빌리티, 로보틱스 등 이동과 관련한 제품 포트폴리오를 확장하고, 여기에 지능형 모빌리티 서비스를 더해 고객에게 끊김 없는 이동의 자유와 맞춤형 서비스를 제공하는 것을 목표로 하고 있다.

이처럼 현대자동차는 스마트 모빌리티 분야로 외연을 넓힘으로써 지금까지 땅에 고착돼 있던 길과 자동차의 개념을 혁신하고, 도시 환경과 인간 사이의 긴밀한 상호작용을 통해 인류의 삶을 보다 편리하게 만들고자 한다. 끊김 없는 이동의 자유를 통해 인간 중심의 역동적 미래 도시를 실현하려는 것이다. 이와 더불어 현대자동차는 자동차 생산부터 운행과 폐기까지 전 단계에 걸쳐 탄소 순배출 제로(0)를 달성하기 위한 '2045 탄소중립 달성 비전'을 선포했다. 이러한 차세대 모빌리티와 탄소중립 비즈니스의 결합은 인류의 더 나은 미래를 위해 가장 올바른 선택을 하려는 현대자동차의 공고한 의지와 뜻을 같이한다.

1974년 아시아의 작은 나라에서 시작된 현대자동차의 도전은 더 나은 내일을 꿈꾸며 이전에는 상상으로만 가능했던 새로운 길을 현실에 구현해 가고 있다. "자동차 산업은 한 국가의 기술 수준을 알 수 있는 척도이자 그 나라의 산업 수준

The history of the road taken by Hyundai calls for a revolutionary transition from a perspective focused on the 'road' to one that expands how we think of 'movement', in order to be ready for a new journey of radical change in the lives and landscapes of the future. The social and corporate aspirations of the Founding Chairman to help his country prosper and contribute to the happiness of his people in developing the Pony, the first mass-produced model, have now expanded to a broader vision for Hyundai in seeking to contribute to progress for humanity for the next generation.

Hyundai is seeking to transform itself into to a 'Smart Mobility Solutions Provider', which provides limitless freedom of mobility to everyone. As a car company, Hyundai is going beyond core capacities of the future, like electrification and autonomous driving, to expand a portfolio of movement-related products including in Advanced Air Mobility and robotics. What is more, Hyundai is developing smart mobility services to provide seamless, tailored freedom of movement services.

Hyundai is expanding the boundaries of smart mobility. In so doing, it is attempting to innovate beyond the confines of roads on the ground and the existing concept of the car. The company aims to make people's lives even more convenient through the close interaction between the urban environment and its residents. Making a reality the vision of a dynamic, people-centered cityscape of the future through seamless freedom of movement. And Hyundai has announced its 'Vision for Carbon Neutrality 2045', which aims to make the entire lifecycle of

현대자동차의 미래 로보틱스 비전이 구체화된
MoT(Mobility of Things) 생태계. 사물에 이동성이
부여된 것이 특징이다.
The MoT (Mobility of Things) ecosystem, where
Hyundai's vision of future robotics has been
realized. As its name suggests, it is characterized
by mobility being imbued in things.

을 끌어올리는 견인차로, 자동차를 완벽하게 생산하면 그 나라의 기계공업은 항공기든 뭐든 다 완벽하게 만들 수 있다"라고 한 창업주의 선견지명대로 현대자동차는 문명 대전환 시대를 맞아 대한민국을 넘어 전 세계에서 그 창조성을 꽃피우고 있다. 특히 인간 편의적 기술 개발로 양적 성장에 치중해 앞만 보고 달려온 내연기관 시대의 끝에서 현대자동차는 인간과 자연이 공존하는 지속 가능한 기술의 진화를 꿈꾸고 있다. 그 꿈을 실현하기는 쉽지 않겠지만 인류의 열망이 깃든 담대하고 보람찬 도전이 될 것이며, 노력하기에 따라 새 문명의 풍경은 크게 바뀔 것이다. 20세기 자동차 산업 환경에서 후발주자로 시작한 현대자동차의 도전이 치열한 국가 경쟁과 중공업 중심 산업의 맥락에서 이루어진 것이라면, 21세기 현대자동차의 도전은 다양한 산업 간 협력과 데이터 기술, 다원적 문화 감수성이 결합된, 무엇보다도 지속 가능성을 고려한 공존의 기술이 좌우할 것이다.

이 길은 누구도 가보지 않았다는 점에서 다음 세대의 새로운 기원이 될 가능성이 높다. 현대자동차는 포니를 시작으로 창조적 도전의 역사를 써왔다. 포니는 기계적으로 뛰어난 자동차는 아니었으나 한국인의 가슴에 긍지를 불어넣었으며, 회색빛 도시 풍경을 다채롭게 바꾼 친근한 차였다. 포니가 남긴 유산은 이제 한 국가의 풍경과 국민의 삶을 넘어서 더 보편

the car, from production to use and disassembly, net carbon neutral. This combination of the next generation in mobility and carbon neutrality shows Hyundai's determination to make the best choices for a better future for humanity.

Back in 1974, the challenge for Hyundai began in a small Asian country. The challenge of forging a better tomorrow, and making a reality of the new path that lay ahead. This reflected the foresight of the founder who saw that the car industry was "the technological standard" by which a country is judged. And "if cars are produced properly, they can lift up the standards of the country's other industries making it possible to produce anything, even an aircraft." That foresight is now giving rise to creativity to meet this era of civilizational transformation not just in Korea, but across the world.

The end of the era of internal combustion engines represents a shift away from a time when convenient technologies were developed primarily for extensive growth. Hyundai's dream is sustainable technological progress that allows humanity to coexist with nature. The efforts needed to make this dream a reality will not be easy, but the fruits of such efforts will create the

"나는 자동차를 완벽히 생산하는 나라는 항공기든 뭐든 완벽한
생산이 가능한 나라라고 생각한다."

"A nation that can build cars can also build airplanes
or pretty much anything else."

정주영 선대회장 **Founding Chairman Ju-yung Chung**

현대자동차는 지상에서 하늘로 '길'에 대한 관점을 바꾸며
'이동'에 대한 개념을 확장해 나가고 있다.
Hyundai is expanding the idea of "movement" by
transforming the perspective on "roads" from the
ground to the skies.

적인 미래의 시간, 인류적 비전으로 발전해 나가고 있다. 그러므로 포니를 현대자동차와 대한민국 산업, 그리고 미래를 선도하는 특별한 헤리티지라고 말하지 못할 이유가 무엇이겠는가. 포니가 품었던 꿈은 포니가 처음으로 세상에 공개된 후부터 지금까지 현재진행형이다. 그때도, 지금도 그리고 앞으로도.

backdrop to a new civilization. This is a formidable but worthwhile challenge which holds the hopes of humanity.

Hyundai began as a second mover in the industrial automotive world of the 20th century. The challenges it faced back then were to be found amidst the context of stiff international competition and a heavy industry-centered industrial environment. The challenges of the 21st century require cooperation between a broad array of industries, and the combination of data technology and sensitivity for cultural diversity. Above all, this will result in technologies of coexistence that account for sustainability.

This path that lies ahead is likely to become the origin of the next generation. Hyundai already has a history of facing challenges with creative solutions, beginning with the Pony. The Pony was not a technologically advanced car, but it held the pride of the Korean people, and with its familiar colorfulness it transformed the monochrome cityscape. The legacy of the Pony now extends beyond the landscape of one country and the lives of its people. It is a heritage that is becoming a vision of a more universal future for humanity. Hence, we can proudly state that Pony is a special heritage leading Hyundai, the Korean industry, and the future. The dreams that the Pony represented when it was unveiled remain with us today. Back then as now, and hereafter too.

부록

Appendix

부록

참고 문헌
References

1   정주영, 「이 땅에 태어나서」, 솔, 2020, 35쪽.
     Ju-yung Chung, "Born of This Land." Sol, 2020, p35

2   「숫자로 보는 광복 60년」, 한국은행 경제통감, 2005, 65쪽.
     "The 60 Years of Liberation in Numbers", The Bank of Korea's Economic Perspective. 2005, p65.

3   세계은행 자료, https://data.worldbank.org/indicator/NY.GDP.MKTP.CD?view=chart&locations=JP-US
     World Bank, 'GDP (Current US$) - Japan, United States', 2023 https://data.worldbank.org/indicator/NY.GDP.MKTP.
     CD?view=chart&locations=JP-US

4   세계은행 자료, https://data.worldbank.org/indicator/NY.GDP.PCAP.CD?view=chart&locations=JP-US
     World Bank, 'GDP per capita (Current US$) - Japan, United States', 2023 https://data.worldbank.org/indicator/NY.GDP.
     PCAP.CD?view=chart&locations=JP-US

5   유다영·박병훈 외, 「경부고속도로 개통 50년의 사회경제적 직접효과 평가 연구」, 한국IT학회, 2021, 20권, 1호, 120쪽.
     Yoo Da-young, Park Byoung-hoon, et al. "An Evaluative Study on the Socio-Economic Direct Effect of 50-Year-Old
     Gyeongbu Expressway", "the Collection of the Journal of Korea Society of IT Services," Vol. 20, No.1, 2021, p120.

6   박정웅, 「이봐, 해봤어?」, 행복에너지, 2022, 69쪽.
     Park Jeong-woong, "Hey, Have You Tried it?", Happy Energy, 2022, p69.

7   국가통계포털, https://kosis.kr
     KOSIS, https://kosis.kr

8   국가통계포털, https://kosis.kr
     KOSIS, https://kosis.kr

9   국가통계포털, https://kosis.kr
     KOSIS, https://kosis.kr

10   정세영, 「포니정, 나의 삶, 나의 꿈」, 포니정재단, 2015, 261쪽.
     Se-yung Chung, "The Pony Chung, My Life, My Dream (The Pony Chung, Naui sam, naui kkum)",
     Seoul: The Pony Chung Foundation, 2015, pp. 261.

11   e-나라지표, 자동차 등록 현황, https://www.index.go.kr
     e-National Indicators, Vehicle registration figures, https://www.index.go.kr

12   강명한, 「응답하라 포니원」, 컬처앤미디어, 2022, 41쪽, 45쪽, 57쪽 참조.
     Kang Myung-han, "Respond, Pony One (Eungdaphara Poni-one)", Seoul: Culture and Media, 2022, p41, 45, and 57.

13   '개인택시 2,000대 또 증차', 동아일보, 1978년 8월 30일, 석간 6면.
     "2,000 more private taxis," Dong-A Ilbo, August 30, 1978, 6 pages of evening papers.

14   조선일보, 1977년 10월 28일.
     The Chosunilbo, October 28, 1977

15   e영상역사관(공공누리 제4유형 자료), LA 올림픽선수단 귀국 환영 카퍼레이드(1984 년 8월 16일)
     https://www.ehistory.go.kr/page/view/photo.jsp?photo_PhotoSrcGBN=PT&photo_PhotoID=6995&detl_photodtl=53851
     Los Angeles Olympic Team Homecoming Parade (August 16, 1984)

16   e-나라지표, 10대 수출입 품목, https://www.index.go.kr
     e-National Indicators, List of top 10 import and export items, https://www.index.go.kr

17   https://www.asiatoday.co.kr/view.php?key=20220928010016366

18   https://www.hankooki.com/news/articleView.html?idxno=64301

	1975	1976	1977	1978	1979	1980	1981	1982	1983	1984
포니(4DR) Pony(4DR)	1975.11 ——————————————————————— 1982.12									
포니 픽업 Pony Pickup		1976.5 ——————————————————— 1982.6								
포니 왜건 Pony Wagon			1977.4 ——————————————————————— 1983.1							
포니(1,400cc) Pony(1,400cc)					1979.8 ———————————————					
포니(3DR) Pony(3DR)						1980.3 ———————— 1982.4				
포니2(5DR) Pony2(5DR)								1982.2 ———————		
포니2 픽업 Pony2 Pickup								1982.6 ———————		
포니2 컨버터블 탑 Pony2 Convertable Top										
엑셀 Excel										
프레스토 Presto										
엑셀 스포티 Excel Sporty										
엑셀(4DR) Excel(4DR)										
엑셀(3/5DR) Excel(3/5DR)										
엑셀 밴 Excel Van										
엑센트(X-3, 4DR) Accent(X-3, 4DR)										
엑센트(X-3, 3/4DR) Accent(X-3, 3/4DR)										

1985
1986
1987
1988
1989
1990
1991
1992
1993
1994
1995
1996
1997
1985.12
1990.1
1989.12
4.9
1985.1
1985.2
1989.3
1985.7
1989.3
1986.9
1989.4
1989.4
1994.7
1990.1
1994.7
1991.8
1994.7
1994.4
1997.2
1994.8
1997.2

리트레이스 컬렉션 - 포니

2024년 6월 초판 발행

발행처   현대자동차
발행인   장재훈

기획·진행   현대자동차
편집·디자인   안그라픽스
제작   크레인

안그라픽스
경기도 파주시 회동길 125-15
www.agbook.co.kr

현대자동차
서울 서초구 헌릉로 12
www.hyundai.com

ISBN : 979-11-6823-072-9(03300)

RETRACE Collection - PONY

First published in June 2024

Published by Hyundai Motor Company
Publisher Jaehoon Chang

Planning and Directing Hyundai Motor Company
Edit and Design Ahn Graphics
Printing Crein

Ahn Graphics Co.,Ltd
125-15 Hoedong-gil, Paju-si, Gyeonggi-do, Republic of Korea
www.agbook.co.kr

Hyundai Motor Company
12 Heolleung-ro, Seocho-gu, Seoul, Republic of Korea
www.hyundai.com

ISBN : 979-11-6823-072-9(03300)